SUSAN MELD SHELL received her PH D from Harvard University. She has taught in the department of political science of Concordia University and is currently a research fellow at McMaster University.

Man, Kant claimed, is a 'being of needs' that are not met by nature as man's due but only through his own strenuous and imperfect efforts. This book is the first to examine Kant's understanding of the relation between man and nature as it bears on his theory of right. It sheds new and important light on Kant's politics and on his place in the history of liberal thought. Its sustained consideration of the theory of right also contributes to a newly integrated view of Kant's philosophy as a whole.

The Rights of Reason proceeds from a discussion of Kant's pre-critical understanding to a consideration of the critiques of pure and practical reason. The final chapter, a selective commentary on Kant's *Doctrine of Right*, explores in detail the implications of his theory of right for his politics and theory of knowledge.

Students of philosophy, political and social theorists, and those interested in the history of liberal thought in particular and intellectual history in general will welcome this thoughtful and significant examination of Kant's philosophy.

SUSAN MELD SHELL

The Rights of Reason:
A study of Kant's philosophy
and politics

UNIVERSITY OF TORONTO PRESS
Toronto Buffalo London

© University of Toronto Press 1980
Toronto Buffalo London
Printed in Canada
Reprinted in 2018
ISBN 978-1-4875-8220-3 (paper)

Library of Congress Cataloging in Publication Data

Shell, Susan Meld, 1948–
   The rights of reason.
   Bibliography: p.
   Includes index.
   1. Kant, Immanuel, 1724–1804. I. Title.
   B2798.S52   193   79-19801
   ISBN 0-8020-5462-5

TO MY PARENTS

Contents

ACKNOWLEDGMENTS ix
NOTE ON THE CITATIONS xi
INTRODUCTION 1

1
The pre-critical problem 9

1 / The problem of conditionality in Kant's early works 11
2 / The discovery of Rousseau and the ascendence of right 20

2
The critical context 33

1 / Critical philosophy and the Copernican hypothesis 35
2 / Dialectical illusion and the anthropology of reason 46
3 / Conclusion 60

3
The moral turn 63

1 / Criticism and moral experience 65
2 / Objectivity and the moral law 70
3 / The problem of happiness 74
4 / Typification of the moral law 81
5 / The incentives of reason 92
6 / The psychology of freedom 99

4
The Doctrine of Right: A selective commentary 107

1 / Right and opposition (*Doctrine of Right* introduction) 111
2 / Property and substance (*Doctrine of Right* part I) 127
3 / Public right and juridical community (*Doctrine of Right* part II) 152

CONCLUSION 181
BIBLIOGRAPHY 191
INDEX 199

Acknowledgments

Many people helped me in preparing this study. I owe special thanks to Allan Bloom, Harvey C. Mansfield, Jr., Judith N. Shklar, and Lewis White Beck for their invaluable criticism and encouragement. I should also like to thank Neil Hertz, William A. Galston, Horst Hutter, James Booth, and Robert Fishman for much helpful discussion and many useful suggestions over the years, and Marc Shell for his critical and much-enduring support.

I am also grateful to Harvard University for a fellowship that enabled me to begin this study and to McMaster University for a generous grant that enabled me to complete it. *The Rights of Reason* is published with the help of a grant from the Social Science Federation of Canada, using funds provided by the Social Sciences and Humanities Research Council of Canada, and a grant to the University of Toronto Press from the Andrew W. Mellon Foundation.

Note on the citations

In referring to Kant's works I generally include short titles, followed by volume and page numbers as they appear in *Kants Gesammelte Schriften*, edited by the Königliche Preussische Akademie der Wissenschaften (Berlin, Reimer 1902–) (indicated by the abbreviation GS). Also provided in parentheses are the page numbers of available English translations. A list of cited translations appears in the Bibliography below.

Exceptions to this procedure occur in the case of references to the *Critique of Pure Reason*, in which numbers preceded by A refer to the first edition (1781) and numbers preceded by B refer to the second (1787), and in the case of references to *Reflexionen*, in which I cite the number designated by the Akademie edition.

Translations provided in the text are occasionally my own.

Introduction

Plato and Aristotle claimed that nature is informed by an intelligible, eternal, and beneficial order to which man has natural and immediate access. In such a cosmos man could trust in the happy outcome of his natural pursuit of truth, as he could trust in the beneficence of nature generally. Modern scientists like Bacon rejected this spiritually reassuring but technologically unproductive understanding of nature. Their primary aim was not pursuit of truth in harmony with nature, but rather mastery of nature in order to better man's estate. In their efforts to master nature, the scientists discredited the claims of Plato and Aristotle, and taught that nature is indifferent to human ends. The discovery by Copernicus that the sun does not revolve around the earth was prototypical of this teaching.[1] According to modern science, the nature of things is at odds with common sense, as it is at odds with human inclination generally.[2]

Kant concurred in this scientific understanding of nature. For Kant, however, the material comforts which modern science provides could not compensate for its devastation of our sense of harmony with nature and our feeling of importance within it. Kant's philosophy begins with a recognition of man's fearful and humiliating helplessness. Human consciousness, according to Kant, begins with the perception of objects which, obstructing our desires, anger and vex us. By cultivating his reason, man can learn to overcome particular obstacles. Reason does nothing, however, to alleviate our anxiety and indignation over the human condition as such. On the contrary, it seems to represent this predicament with ever greater clarity.

Kant set himself the difficult task of recovering and reasserting the spiritual assurances which science seemed irrevocably to destroy. Human spiritedness is the vehicle of this spiritual recovery. Man reacts to nature with indignation. We perceive nature not only as hostile but also as unjust, and we claim a *right* to the satisfaction which nature denies us. By itself this claim cannot alleviate our troubles. In venting our anger at the world we rail against necessity. But our indignation can deliver us if we direct it inwards against ourselves. Such self-opposition makes possible self-overcoming or the transcendence of nature within us. Kant's final response to the human predicament is an assertion

1 See Immanuel Kant *The Critique of Pure Reason* B/xxii (hereafter cited as CR).
2 Kant made the following passage from the preface to Bacon's *Great Instauration* the epigraph of his *Critique of Pure Reason*: 'Of myself I say nothing; but in behalf of the business which is in hand I entreat men to believe that it is not an opinion to be held, but a work to be done, and to be well assured that I am labouring to lay the foundation, not of any sect or doctrine, but of human utility and power. Next, I ask them to deal fairly by their own interests ... and join in consultation for the common good ... Moreover, to be of good hope, nor to imagine that this Instauration of mine is a thing infinite and beyond the power of man, when it is in fact the true end and termination of infinite error ...'

4 The Rights of Reason

of the rights of man and of the power these rights confer to transcend in freedom and in dignity the natural world of which man is a conditioned and inconsequential part. Nature, Kant wrote, is a despot who does not care for man. Man, however, is 'for himself' both a creature of the natural world and a person, that is to say, 'a moral being, having rights.'[3] As a moral and juridical person, man finds the substantiality and permanence which as a natural being he lacks. With the redirection of anger, man becomes not only an asserter of claims but also a possessor of rights.

Rights, however, have their price. With his attainment of rational and moral personality, man gives up his formerly untroubled relation to desire. Hereafter desire is not to be trustingly obeyed but rather to be controlled and even suppressed. From such suppression even the desire for knowledge is not exempt. Desire, rational and material, tempts us wrongly to assume the possibility of satisfaction and so leads to error and vice. We can deliver ourselves from error only by recognizing that our powers are limited and that we ought not to expect a satisfaction we cannot ourselves secure. We can deliver ourselves from vice only by submitting our desires to the discipline of self-made law.

For Kant the rights of man do not include the right to satisfaction.[4] Kant's distinction between happiness, to which man has no right, and the pursuit of happiness, to which he has a right, suggests the fundamental liberalism of his thought, however illiberal some aspects of his thought appear. Kant is immoderate in the service of moderation. Drastic measures are necessary, he believed, if we are to learn to limit our demands and expectations. Later thinkers would adapt the extremity of his means to less moderate ends. The demand for satisfaction, a demand Kant hoped that by his drastic measures he would put to rest, re-emerged even more drastically in the thought of Marx and Hegel, for whom it was the central 'pivot' of history.[5]

To Kant the optimistic expectations of Hegel and Marx would have seemed even more dangerously mystical and misguided than those of Plato. Within what seemed to Kant to be the limits of the possible, however, he always counselled optimism and hope. His was not a resignation that glories in deprivation. Though man cannot secure happiness he has his rights and knows his worth. This, for Kant, was comfort and glory enough.

3 *Opus post.*, XXI 13–14; see also *Reflexion* #7093.
4 Even the virtuous who may be said to 'merit' happiness do not, strictly speaking, have a 'right' to happiness. In Kant's moral universe, one may hope for happiness proportional to one's merit; one may not, however, demand it as one's due. See, for example, Kant's 'On the Failure of All Attempted Philosophical Theodicies,' VIII 257n (285n); and below 94–5, 99.
5 See Hegel *The Philosophy of Right* 84. Cf. Kant *Reflexion* #1420: 'In history ... the idea of right conducts all.'

5 Introduction

This is a study of Kant's understanding of the relation between man and nature, as it bears on his philosophy of right. Serious attention to this subject, which has never before been the focus of a sustained study, can provide, as I hope to show, a more vital and fully integrated portrait of Kant's thought than otherwise available. It can illuminate passages that seem inexplicable and draw together arguments and works whose interrelation seems obscure. And it can shed new and useful light on Kant's place in the history of liberal thought.

In this study, I consider Kant's theory of right as it informs both his politics[6] and his philosophy as a whole. A study of Kantian right in the wider context of his thought is necessary to clarify the essential connection between his political philosophy and his philosophy as a whole, a connection which critics have sensed but never adequately explained.[7] *The Rights of Reason* draws on various critical, scientific, and occasional writings, as well as posthumously published notes. Chapter 1 considers Kant's pre-critical understanding of nature and right. Chapters 2 and 3 consider the critiques of pure and practical reason and the critical foundation of his theory of right. Chapter 4, a selective commentary on the *Doctrine of Right (Metaphysische Anfangsgründe der Rechtslehre)*, considers in greater detail the implications of Kant's theory of right for his politics and his theory of knowledge.

In order to make the study more widely accessible, general summaries of Kant's thought have been included at a number of points. My attention to

6 On the general place of right in Kant's politics see Georges Vlachos *La Pensée politique de Kant: Métaphysique de l'ordre et dialectique du progrès*; Christian Ritter *Der Rechtsgedanke Kants nach den frühen Quellen*; Pierre Hassner 'Immanuel Kant'; Eric Weil 'Kant et le problème de la politique.' Vlachos' otherwise painstaking treatment of Kant's politics suffers from his inattention to Kant's 'analyses and deductions,' over which, Vlachos asserts, 'it isn't necessary to pause long' (103). Ritter claims to uncover the true Kantian doctrine of right ('die *kant*ische Rechtslehre') by faithfully tracing its development from early sources, and especially from 1763 onwards. His insistence, however, that the continuity of this development 'excludes' the possibility of a 'critical' theory of right fails to come to terms with Kant's own critical insistence to the contrary. See also Jeffrie G. Murphy *Kant: The Philosophy of Right*; William A. Galston *Kant and the Problem of History*; and Patrick Riley 'Kant on Will, "Moral Causality," and the Social Contract.'
7 See, for example, Karl Jaspers' cryptic remark in *Die Grossen Philosophen* I (Munich, Piper 1957) 563: 'Kant's philosophy is *political* philosophy, in that he wanted it to be an element of politics; and it is political *philosophy*, in that it is bound to a path of free, rational self-knowledge ...' Hans Saner (*Kant's Political Thought*) presses a similar line of thought. Saner reduces Kant's politics and metaphysics to fundamental 'thought forms' of conflict and resolution. Saner makes a number of illuminating comparisons between Kant's early mechanics and later doctrine of right. However, his overall argument is flawed by overattention to Kant's 'polemics' and insufficient attention to his critical arguments.

6 The Rights of Reason

Kant's *Anthropology* (an elaboration of his academic lectures on knowledge of man and the world, *Menschen- und Weltkenntniss*, conducted over the course of many years), and to his anthropological doctrines generally, requires an additional note of explanation. Scholars have long puzzled over the philosophic status of Kant's anthropology.[8] He does not present his anthropology as transcendental; much of it, however (for example, his doctrine of human desire), seems to be more than merely 'empirical' in the sense of being susceptible to ordinary experiential disproof. Kant seems neither to have felt compelled to justify these anthropological doctrines transcendentally, nor to have been particularly worried about the possibility of future empirical researches disproving them.[9] We might therefore expect these doctrines, whatever their ultimate critical status, to be especially revealing of Kant's fundamental assumptions and concerns; and so in a number of cases do I read them.

While I have attempted to interpret Kant's thought systematically, I am not fully in agreement with his understanding of the relation between man and nature, nor am I uncritical of many of the arguments drawn from that understanding. I indicate these criticisms along the way, as well as suggesting alternative conceptions of nature and justice and their interrelation.

The word *right* in the title of this study is drawn from the German *Recht*, which for Kant means both 'right' in the sense of '*a* right' (or 'rights') and

---

8 The prevailing consensus among English-speaking scholars seems to peg that status rather low. In Europe, where 'rational anthropology' has a long academic history, scholars have tended to rate it somewhat higher. Sometimes Kant does indeed seem to insist on an absolute separation of the anthropological from the *a priori* and transcendental, e.g., in his introduction to the *Metaphysics of Morals*, where he says: 'Just as, in the metaphysics of nature, there must be principles for the application of those supreme universal principles of nature in general to objects of experience, so likewise a metaphysics of morals cannot dispense with similar principles of application ... But this will not detract from the purity of such laws or cast any doubt on their a priori origin; that is to say, a metaphysics of morals cannot be founded on anthropology, although it can be applied to it' (*Doctrine of Right*, VI 216–17 (16–17); hereafter cited as DR). Yet in this same passage, he also insists on certain 'principles of application' to mediate between the two. Obviously much hinges on the status of these 'principles of application.' Cf. Kant's subsumption, in the introduction to his *Logic*, of the three critical questions – What can I know? What ought I to do? What may I hope? – under a fourth 'anthropological' question – What is man? In Kant's restatement of this passage at A/805 = B/833 of the *Critique of Pure Reason*, the fourth question is dropped.

9 Thus, despite his intention in the *Critique of Practical Reason* to treat morality 'without particular reference to human nature,' Kant feels at ease in 'borrow[ing] from psychology' a human and presumably *a posteriori* conception of pleasure and desire. See *Critique of Practical Reason*, V 9 (9) (hereafter cited as *Crit. Prac.*)

7 Introduction

justice generally. Kantian justice, at least in its mature form, is a system of rights. It differs from several modern rights-centred theories of justice (inspired by Kant) in that Kant attempts, as these modern authors do not, to provide his theory with a metaphysical basis supported by and supportive of his understanding of human experience generally. Many modern authors try to keep their moral and juridical claims free from both 'epistemology' and dependence on natural facts, as if the realms of nature and freedom were, as Kant implies, entirely separable. But, as Kant also states, these two realms are joined, however mysteriously, by a common inhabitant – man. To the nature of this problematic juncture, Kant's understanding of rights, man's quintessential 'property,' provides unique access.

1
The pre-critical problem

1 / THE PROBLEM OF CONDITIONALITY IN KANT'S EARLY WORKS

Concerning the humiliating and discrediting effect of astronomy Kant has left us a remarkable confession: 'It annihilates my importance.' Nietzsche *Genealogy of Morals* III 25

The predominating concern of Kant's thought is the reconciliation of nature, scientifically understood, with the requirements of moral life. This is not to say that Kant's understanding of nature, science, and the requirements of morality did not change during the long course of his philosophically productive life. They did, and in those changes one may chart Kant's progress from his earlier dogmatic stand to his later critical one. Yet one problem which precipitated these formulations and reformulations did not change. It is significant that from the standpoint of his critical solution Kant repudiated his earlier efforts but not the aim which prompted them, the aim of reconciling human conditionality and human worth.

Kant began his academic career as a philosopher of nature. Schooled in the Leibnizian rationalism popularized by Wolff which dominated the Prussian universities of his youth, Kant also took a keen and early interest in the competing system of Sir Isaac Newton, which by the 1750s had won the academic field in Germany and throughout Europe.[1] In his earliest years as a lecturer and a scholar, Kant strode the path of mediation, hoping to resolve, through the accommodation of one system to the other, the difficulties which each system alone could not resolve. In 1755, which saw the publication of his *Universal Natural History and Theory of the Heavens*, a cosmology 'according to Newtonian principles,' his adherence to Newton's system seemed complete.[2] Yet in this ingenious work, which foretells the mechanical evolutionism of a later century, Kant displays a certain uneasiness with the implications of Newton's mechanistic teaching.[3]

---

1 See Herman-J. De Vleeschauwer *The Development of Kantian Thought* 8–11.
2 *Universal Natural History and Theory of the Heavens*; the full title of Kant's essay is *Allgemeine Naturgeschichte und Theorie des Himmels oder Versuch von der Verfassung und dem mechanischem Ursprunge des ganzen Weltgebäudes, nach Newtonischen Grundsätzen abgehandelt*' (hereafter cited as *Natural History*).
3 On Kant's moral pessimism see Paul Menzer 'Der Entwicklungsgang der Kantischen Ethik in den Jahren 1760–1785'; cf. Paul Arthur Schilpp *Kant's Pre-Critical Ethics* 15–21; Victor Delbos *La Philosophie pratique de Kant* 69–76; and Théodore Ruyssen 'Kant est-il pessimiste?' *Revue de metaphysique et de morale* 12 (1904): 535–50.

12 The Rights of Reason

Kant's disquietude makes itself felt in a number of ways. In his *Natural History* he explicitly attempts to reconcile Newtonian science with religion, by attributing the fundamental mechanical properties of matter to an original creative act of God.[4] However, this step (one with which some Newtonians might have agreed) does little to establish a place for reverence within the mechanical universe itself, or to assure us that God is a creator who cares for man. Kant's apparently easy answer to the religious question engenders the more difficult question of theodicy and of the justice which man may expect to encounter in the universe.

Kant's mechanical cosmology attempts to explain not only static order, but also the orderly development of the universe according to the properties of matter, which express the susceptibility of matter to the fundamental laws of attraction and repulsion. In accounting for the orderly direction of the universe in terms of mechanical causes, Kant's cosmology is un- and even anti-teleological, however much he tries to accommodate his theory of mechanical development to the perfectionism of the Wolffian school. Matter brings order out of chaos, in obedience to the laws of attraction and repulsion.[5] The universe, Kant hypothesizes, is most dense at the centre, where the principle of attraction first established order. New systems, which form at ever greater distances from the centre, in turn run down and condense, dispersing matter for 'new productions by the same mechanical laws, whereby the waste space will again be animated with worlds and systems.'[6] The development and extension of heavenly systems throughout the universe is explained in terms of a single mechanical process, endlessly repeated.

The laws of attraction and repulsion establish a kind of 'economy of nature,'[7] in which whole worlds and world systems are created and destroyed. For this cavalcade of creation and destruction Kant shows a certain melancholy fascination. The perishing of a world, he writes, is no 'loss to Nature.' 'She proves her riches by a sort of prodigality.' In one place innumerable

---

4 In his preface Kant attempts to answer the pious critic of science who finds in the mechanistic explanation of nature no need and hence no place for God: 'If the structure of the world with all its order and beauty ... is only an effect of matter left to its own universal laws of motion ... then the proof of the Divine Author which is drawn from the spectacle of the beauty of the universe wholly loses its force. Nature is thus sufficient for itself ... Epicurus lives again in the midst of Christendom ...' (*Natural History*, I 222(18)). Kant admits his kinship with Epicurus but draws different religious conclusions, finding a place for God as the source of the lawfulness of nature. Nature, Kant already believed, cannot be the source of its own laws.
5 Ibid. 262–9 (72–82)
6 Ibid. 321 (154)
7 *History of the 1755 Earthquake*, I 458

13 The pre-critical problem

creatures perish; in another 'this loss is again compensated for to superabundance ... Nature proves that she is quite as rich and quite as inexhaustible in the production of what is most excellent ... as of what is most trivial, and that ... destruction is a necessary shading amid the multiplicity of her suns, because ... production costs her nothing.'[8] 'Worlds and systems perish and are swallowed up in the abyss of eternity, but at the same time creation is always busy constructing new formations in the heavens, and advantageously making up for the loss.' 'Considerable portions of the earth which we inhabit are being buried again in the sea' while elsewhere nature 'repairs the loss and brings forth other regions which were hidden in the depths of being in order to spread over them the new wealth of her fertility.' 'Innumerable animals and plants are daily destroyed and disappear as the victims of time; but not the less does nature by her unexhausted power of reproduction bring forth others in other places to fill up the void.'[9] Nor is man, 'who seems to be the masterpiece of creation ... excepted from this law.' Pestilence, earthquakes, and inundations 'sweep whole peoples from the earth; but it does not appear that nature has thereby suffered any damage.'[1] The economy of nature is indifferent to human costs. The exchanges of matter which ensure a balance between creation and destruction assign no special weight to human interests.

Out of the exchange of matter arises an almost limitless productivity and power. The reciprocal laws of attraction and repulsion set in motion a progressive dynamic in which, proceeding from the centre of the universe outwards, chaos will give way to order and the decay of old worlds will be compensated for by the appearance of new ones.[2] In his *Critique of Judgment*, written forty years later, we hear the echoes of Kant's early meditations on the impotence of man before the potency of nature: the violence of volcanoes, hurricanes, and the boundless sea 'shows our power of resistance to be insignificantly small in comparison with their might.'[3] However, that theory of knowledge which, in the *Critique of Judgment*, enables the mind to transcend its dependency on nature is unavailable to Kant in his *Natural History*, in which he declares man virtually helpless against the overwhelming power of nature.

In the face of a nature at once so potent and so indifferent to human aims and interests Kant counsels resignation. 'Let us then accustom our eyes,' he

---

8 *Natural History*, 1 318 (150)
9 Ibid. 317 (149)
1 Ibid. 318 (150)
2 Ibid. Cf. Lucretius *De rerum natura* v ll. 235–349.
3 *Critique of Judgement*, v 261 (part 1, 110) hereafter cited as CJ (my translation)

urges, 'to these terrible catastrophes as being the common ways of providence, and regard them even with a sort of complacency.'[4] Kant finds some solace in the wilful abandoning of the human perspective, to which nature pays no special regard, for a divine one. This divine perspective is contemplative and not active. Having created the cosmic mechanism, God is now content to watch without tinkering. Kant here cites Alexander Pope, whose God observes 'with equal eye' the death of hero or sparrow, bubble or world.[5]

Men can approximate this divine complacency, born of divine omnipotence, by attempting to assume the perspective of the Creator. They can find a certain comfort in the contemplation of the cosmic system as a coherent and beautiful whole. As in the *Critique of Judgment*, the experience of beauty is contemplative, and goes together with a disinterestedness, or indifference, towards one's personal fate. In the *Natural History*, however, contemplation is not a mere aesthetic experience, but a religious and philosophic one. The contemplative frame of mind, whereby men may escape the fearful awareness of their own helplessness, requires above all that their reason enable them to comprehend the cosmic system. Reason, which awakened men to the vulnerability of their own condition, also gives them solace.[6]

Rational solace has its price, however. Having abandoned the merely human perspective one must also relinquish its comforting delusions concerning one's own importance. Having recognized that nature brings forth all of its riches with 'like necessity,' one may no longer be so 'arrogant ... as to flatter oneself' concerning one's paramount importance, nor take pride in the 'necessity of one's existence.' No being could be absent 'without destroying the beauty of the whole, which lies in its coherence.'[7]

Solace, moreover, does not mean peace. Even in its fullest elaboration, nature is a transitory system which 'cannot adequately satisfy the soul.'[8] The soul requires a sense of permanence to enable it to fend off nature's physical assault on its security and spiritual assault on its dignity. 'Happy [would] be the soul, if, amid the tumult of the elements and the crash of nature she [were] always elevated to a height from whence she [could] see the devastations which their own perishableness brings upon the things of the world as they thunder past beneath her feet.' This security against the indiscriminate flux of nature constitutes happiness. To such happiness, however, 'Reason ... could not be bold enough even to aspire.' God is omnipotent and infinite. Reason,

---

4 *Natural History*, I 318–19 (151)
5 Ibid.
6 Ibid. 321–2 (155)
7 Ibid. 353–4
8 Ibid. 321 (154)

15 The pre-critical problem

then, cannot aspire to the happiness which would attend a divinely disinterested contemplation of the universe. 'True felicity' would require the liberation of man 'from dependence on finite things.'⁹ But to be part of nature is to depend on finite things. True felicity would require the liberation of man from nature.

Far from supporting human aims and interests, nature frustrates them. Man, as Kant later observes, is by nature 'a being of needs.'¹ Even reason, which provides his sole means of relief from the insecurity and indignity of his natural state, is naturally limited in its power. This limitation on human reason is felt as a 'humiliation' or 'degradation' (*Erniedrigung*) brought about by the obstruction of reason by matter. 'If one seeks the cause of the obstacle which holds human nature in humiliation one finds it in the grossness of matter, in which its spiritual part is sunk.'² The acquisition of knowledge always entails a toilsome struggle against matter, whose opposition may be blamed for both man's trouble and his proneness to error.³

Kant's portrayal of the combat between spirit and matter goes well beyond the fundamentally Newtonian boundaries of his cosmology proper. In his efforts to account for the finitude of human reason he appends to his mechanical cosmology a rationalistic continuum of matter and spirit which suggests the doctrines of Wolff far more than those of Newton.⁴ Kant locates mankind at the centre of this continuum, midway between spirit and matter, 'Wisdom and Unreason.' Kant regards this station as one of 'misfortune.'⁵ Men, who are too rational not to aspire, are not rational enough to succeed.⁶

---

9 Ibid. 322 (155)
1 *Crit. Prac.*, v 25 (24)
2 *Natural History*, I 356: 'The grossness of the stuff and fabric in the construction of human nature is the cause of that inertia which maintains the capacities of the soul in stagnation and powerlessness [*Kraftloskeit*].' The activity of reflection and representation clarified by reason is 'a troublesome condition, in which the soul cannot remain unopposed, and from which the soul, through the natural inclination of the bodily machine, at once falls back ... The exertion [*Bemühung*] of reason to heave up against itself and expel this confusion is like the sunshine, when thick clouds darken its ... serenity.'
3 Ibid. 354–7
4 Kant's emphasis on 'clear and distinct' ideas also suggests the lingering influence of the Wolffian school (ibid. 355).
5 Ibid. 365
6 Like many of his contemporaries, the young Kant was concerned to show the compatibility of modern science and belief in God. Impressed by the lawful order and regularity in nature revealed by modern science, he imputed to that order a divine origin. The graded perfection and finality of nature, which Kant sometimes draws from, sometimes uses to support the premise of its divine origin, differs significantly, as he indicates, from the teleological doctrines of Aristotelean and Scholastic science. Contrary to the teachings of that older science,

For relief from this misfortune men must turn from science and nature to Revelation and the 'sweet hope' of a Hereafter, where the soul might enter into 'a new relation with all of nature.' Here, no longer distracted by 'outer objects,' the soul might 'find the source of its happiness in itself.'[7]

The indifference of nature to human ends is also the subject of an essay occasioned by the Lisbon earthquake of 1755. Concluding his examination of the relation of natural catastrophes to human ends, Kant derides men's efforts to lodge a claim to comfort and support in the face of nature's scientifically established indifference. We refuse to acknowledge the laws of natural economy, to 'purchase advantages by paying the cost.'[8] Instead 'we lodge an illegitimate claim on all the amenities of life.' We cannot bear to die, or to lose the goods which nature inevitably takes away. But we are in fact 'strangers on earth, possessing no property.' Against nature we have no rights. Man must therefore adapt to nature and not demand that nature should adapt herself to him.[9]

Man naively believes that the goods which he desires are naturally his due. To support this belief, he assumes that the relations between nature and humanity are governed by a kind of justice. When in the face of natural adversity man does not get what he thinks he deserves, he blames himself and prefers to think himself punished for some unknown fault, rather than relinquish altogether his belief in the justice of nature. Hence he interprets natural disaster as an act of divine vengeance. But this second tendency is as much the folly of human arrogance as is the first. 'Whatever in the world serves our convenience and pleasure we take to be for our own sake,' just as 'whatever changes nature undertakes which might cause human hardship we take to be vengeance.'[1] Man claims to be but is not the measure. Nature's indifference

---

the 'ends' of nature, according to Kant, bear no essential relation to human interests and concerns. Whatever purposiveness in nature mechanical science will admit, it is not a purposiveness directed towards man. If the end of nature is its contemplation by rational beings, as Kant at one point in the essay on *Natural History* suggests, it is not an end that man, who is 'of all creatures the least able to achieve his purpose,' can fulfil. When Kant reports the effects of nature on men it is not the cooling breezes of Jamaica but cataclysms and catastrophes that seize his imagination. Man's middling station in the universe is one of 'misfortune' (*Unglück*), and if he can feel superior to inhabitants of lesser planets he must envy the creatures infinitely greater than himself. On Kant's troubled correlation of the perfection of nature and the interests of rational beings generally, see Pierre Laberge *La Théologie Kantienne précritique* (Ottawa, Université d'Ottawa 1973) 40–7.

7 *Natural History*, I 367.
8 *History of the 1755 Earthquake*, I 455
9 Ibid. 456
1 Ibid. 460

17 The pre-critical problem

not only to man's desires, but also to that sense of justice by means of which he asserts those desires, renders futile all of his claims to the contrary.

Man can better secure his interests by adapting to the indifference of nature than by defying it. Through the study of nature as it is, rather than as we wish it to be, we may prevent some calamities and mitigate others. But reason, which must accept the limitations which its finite and dependent nature imposes upon it, should not expect too much. 'From the Prometheus of recent times, Mr. Franklin, who wanted to disarm thunder, down to the man who wants to extinguish the fire in the workshop of Vulcanus, all these endeavours ... result in the humiliating reminder ... that man can never be anything more than a man.'[2]

Science devastates human self-esteem. This devastation might be offset by adopting the more-than-human perspective to which human reason gives partial access, did not reason itself also succumb to the opposition of matter. The necessity of such submission constitutes, according to Kant, the essence of man's 'humiliation.' The indifference of nature to human adversity is from the human perspective an injury. Man's only route of escape from the assaults of nature upon the security and integrity of his person – complete indifference to his own material condition – is blocked by that natural finitude which lies in his dependence on material beings. Nature poses for man a problem whose adequate solution it precludes. The turn to Revelation and uncertain hopes of a Hereafter which will set things right suggests that nature has somehow wronged us.

The problem of theodicy arises with some frequency in Kant's early writings, particularly those in which he remains faithful to the teachings of Leibniz, who himself coined the word *theodicy*, meaning 'the justice, or justification, of God.' This project Leibniz believed he had accomplished in his demonstration that God, who possesses every perfection, can create nothing other than the best of all possible worlds. This demonstration may

---

2 Ibid. 472. In his continuing efforts at theodicy, Kant relies less and less on 'physico-theology,' or the extrapolation of divine wisdom from the apparent adaptation of nature to man. The 'useful effects' of the Lisbon earthquake (i.e., the appearance of new thermal springs) seem altogether out of proportion with the fifty thousand lives lost; and while he observes these effects, he also states that 'man must adapt himself to nature' for 'nature will not adapt herself to him.' In his essay *On Optimism* (1759) Kant argues *a priori* and without recourse to man's experience of nature that God is all-sufficient and that his creation is therefore good. In his *Only Conceivable Proof of the Existence of God* (1763), Kant explicitly admits the philosophic inadequacy, not only of physico-theology, but also of the cosmological theology (based on the alleged finality of nature as such) which he put forward in his early essay on natural history. Without repudiating that essay directly, he dismisses as 'hazardous hypotheses' much of its theology.

itself have been a more or less popular concession, designed to ease over some of the moral difficulties inherent in his monadology.³ It was, however, taken with utmost seriousness by many of his contemporaries, and it received from Kant himself, in one short essay, a seemingly orthodox defence.⁴

In his Newtonian *Natural History*, however, Kant cites not the optimism of Leibniz but that of Pope, who in his 'Essay on Man' combines elements of the theories of Newton, Leibniz, and the Neo-Platonists. It is the early, more 'Newtonian' portion of Pope's poem which Kant draws on in his own cosmology. Pope's announced intention in his 'Essay on Man' to 'vindicate the ways of God to man' culminates in the proclamation that 'whatever is, is right!'⁵ The tension which men generally feel between what is and what is right results from folly, born of pride, which nature, and presumably God, do not support. Kant, who in the later chapters of his work quotes extensively from Pope's 'Essay,' adopts Pope's formulation of the problem of theodicy in the face of an inscrutably indifferent nature, without assuming his tone of cheerful complacency. So adopted, the problem of theodicy is adapted. In blaming on pride man's dissatisfaction with God's universe, Pope echoes Milton, who also sought to 'justify the ways of God to men.' Yet Milton, who in his piety remained a Christian, could seriously attempt to make us feel the weight of pride as sin, whereas Pope, with his easy-going stoicism, cannot make us feel guilty or remorseful for our pride, but only foolish. He can do so, however, only by reiterating the original complaint: humanity demands from nature a respect which nature does not pay. Pride is not sinful but foolish; and it is foolish because futile. But this is merely to restate the problem with which Pope begins and not to answer it.

The question is not whether man's complaint against nature and God will be answered but whether it is justified. Kant, who understands the character of man's grievance more profoundly than does Pope, doubts that it can be

---

3 See Bertrand Russell *A History of Western Philosophy* (New York, Simon & Schuster 1945) 590–6.
4 On Kant's essay *On Optimism*, cf. Pierre Fontan 'Histoire et philosophie: la théodicée de Kant' *Revue Thomiste* 76 (1976): 381–93. Hannah Arendt notes the essay's equivocal tone: 'Kant repeats the old consoling thought, "that the whole is the best, and that everything is good for the sake of the whole," but seems himself not quite convinced ... for he suddenly injects: ... "I call out to every creature ... Hail to us that we are!"' (*Thinking* 148). Kant's own discomfort with the essay is suggested by the vehemence with which he repudiated it in later years. Borowski reports that when he asked Kant late in his life for a copy of the work Kant refused, adding that should a copy come into Borowski's hands he must immediately destroy it. Cf. Olivier Reboul *Kant et le problème du mal* (Montreal, Les Presses de l'Université de Montréal 1971) 48–9.
5 Alexander Pope 'Essay on Man' part 4, l. 394

19 The pre-critical problem

assuaged merely through familiarity with the very indifference of nature which engenders it. For Kant the force of nature as an obstacle to human happiness is not to be denied, nor is man required to like it. Kant does not leave us with the smug conviction that whatever is, is right, but rather with an almost wistful hope that what may be will set things right. Our very ignorance of the Hereafter, of what men may become, permits Kant to engage in reassuring speculation. If the purely rational in man could be liberated from its dependence on the material, he could view nature from the point of view of God. Nature, as seen from this centre would show on all sides 'utter security, complete adaptation.' From such a vantage point 'the changeful scenes of the natural world' could no longer 'disturb the restful happiness of [the] spirit.'[6] Kant is not guilty of the confused audacity of Pope, who expects that man can, by 'see[ing] through nature,' attain the vantage point of God.[7] Instead, he cautiously describes that in which human happiness, were it possible, would consist. This understanding of the supernatural requirements of human happiness expresses most clearly Kant's dissatisfaction with nature scientifically understood. Nature is imposing and transitory, happiness independent and secure. Kant's later doctrine of moral freedom as a liberation from dependence upon nature has seeds in his earliest scientific works.

As yet, however, Kant is unconcerned in his writings with moral action. His speculations about the spirit world are intended for private solace, not as a guide to action in the world. They are aids and comforts for the individual trying to reconcile the scientific understanding of man with personal requirements of security and self-esteem:

When one has filled one's mind with such considerations, the sight of a starry heaven on a serene night gives a kind of pleasure which only a noble soul can feel. In the general silence of nature and calm of the senses, the hidden knowledge-power of the immortal spirit speaks an ineffable language, and yields undeveloped concepts which we can experience but not express.[8]

---

6 *Natural History*, I 322 (155–6)
7 'Essay on Man' part 4, l. 332. Later notes suggest Kant's discomfort with his defence of Pope in 1756. In 1762, around the time of his first serious reading of Rousseau, he writes 'after Newton *and Rousseau* the ways of God are justified – and Pope's thesis is henceforth true' (emphasis added; GS XX 59). In the same notes he also writes that man need not 'envy the angels,' and that he may find his sole pride 'in the fact that he is a man' (GS XX 47). In notes composed during his critical period, Kant observes that 'if we had to consider the earth as the sole field in which divine wisdom manifests itself, we would be prey to grave doubts' *Reflexion* #6091). Prior to the influence of Rousseau, Kant is able to justify nature and God only by belittling man.
8 *Natural History*, I 367

Thus it is possible for a few 'noble souls' in contemplating nature to find a certain mute pleasure and transitory calm.

The conclusion of the *Critique of Practical Reason*, written thirty years later, speaks directly to these early meditations:

Two things fill the mind with ever new and increasing admiration and awe, the oftener and more steadily we reflect on them: the starry heavens above me and the moral law within me ... The former begins at the place I occupy in the external world of sense, and it broadens the connection in which I stand into an unbounded magnitude of worlds ... The latter begins at my invisible self, my personality, and exhibits me in a world which has true infinity but which is comprehensible only to the understanding – a world with which I recognize myself as existing in a universal and necessary (and not only, as in the first case, contingent) connection ... The former view of a countless multitude of worlds *annihilates* [*vernichtet*], as it were, *my importance* as an animal creature, which must *give back to the planet* (a mere speck in the universe) *the matter from which it came*, the matter which is for a little time provided with vital force, we know not how. The latter, on the contrary, *infinitely raises my worth* as that of an intelligence by my personality, in which the moral law reveals a life independent ... of the whole world of sense.[9]

In the radical dualism of his mature philosophy Kant secures a ground for human worth, a ground which, in his early writings, he stubbornly sought. The distinguishing mark of his critical philosophy is his conviction that the moral law within us is a subject of far greater awe than nature can inspire. It is the recognition of this inner law as an objective guide to moral action which decisively establishes the priority of practical reason, of morality, over contemplation.

2 / THE DISCOVERY OF ROUSSEAU AND THE ASCENDENCE OF RIGHT

From Rousseau Kant learned to regard morality with a new seriousness. Prior to 1762, when he first obtained the *Social Contract* and *Emile*, Kant's published works do not explicitly consider moral issues. After 1762 he released a rash of works of moral concern, all influenced in some degree or other by

---

9 *Crit. Prac.*, v 162 (166) (emphasis added)

the British moralists, some still bearing the lingering signs of Wolffian rationalism,[1] but all marked most distinctively by the impress of Rousseau.

This influence was observed by many of Kant's contemporaries. Herder claimed that Kant was the first and steadiest of Rousseau's German admirers.[2] Kant, as Borowski noted, interrupted his usually unswerving schedule to finish reading *Emile* (as he did twenty-seven years later to read news of the French revolution).[3] Kant himself left a remarkable record of the impact which his discovery of Rousseau made upon him. A series of loose-leaf notes (the *Bemerkungen*) appended to his own copy of his *Observations on the Feeling of the Beautiful and Sublime* expresses the shock and fascination of that first acquaintance.

A much quoted but too little understood confession from these notes reveals a decisive turning point in his intellectual career:

I am by inclination an investigator [*Forscher*]. I feel the thirst for knowledge and ... the deep satisfaction after every step forward. There was a time when I believed all this could be the honour of mankind and I despised the people, who know nothing. Rousseau has set me right ... I learned to honour mankind and I would be less worthy than the average worker if I did not believe that [philosophy] could contribute to what really matters, restoring the rights of mankind.[4]

This passage charts the beginning of the priority of morality in Kant's thought. Before Rousseau, Kant had defined the purpose of philosophy as the attaining of knowledge. After Rousseau 'what really matters' is the rights of man. No longer does Kant believe that the honour of mankind lies in intelligence and learning, the province of a few 'noble souls.' Rather that honour lies in the rights of mankind, the property of all. Heretofore knowledge absorbed itself in the self-sufficient pleasures of contemplation; hereafter it must justify itself; it must 'contribute' and 'restore.'

Rousseau had a powerful effect on Kant's estimation of the value of science and knowledge in general. Before reading Rousseau, Kant, in keeping with

---

1 For a more detailed discussion of these early influences see Victor Delbos 'Rousseau et Kant'; Dieter Henrich 'Hutcheson und Kant'; Keith Ward *The Development of Kant's View of Ethics* 3–33; Christian Ritter *Der Rechtsgedanke Kants nach den frühen Quellen*; Schilpp *Kant's Pre-Critical Ethics* 22–40.
2 J.G. Herder *Briefe zur Beförderung der Humanität, Sämmtliche Werke* (Berlin 1789) XVIII 324–5
3 L.E. Borowski *Darstellung des Lebens und Charakters Immanuel Kant's* 170
4 *Bemerkungen*, XX 44

the rationalist school, regarded reason as the measure of the perfection of man and all the other orders of the universe. After Rousseau he finds 'the greatest perfection' to lie in 'the subordination of everything to freedom' (*freie Willkür*).[5] 'Truth,' he writes, 'has no worth in itself,' whatever the inhabitants of other planets may think.[6] Truth can have only a conditioned worth, and can have it only in the service of the practical. Science must advance the rights of man. To be sure, Kant never doubts as radically as does Rousseau in his *First Discourse* that science can serve human rights. Kant is always far more confident than Rousseau of the potential beneficence of science.[7] One does not find even in the early Kant the powerful longing expressed by Rousseau for a pre-enlightened era. Kant laboured to blur this difference, however,[8] and credited directly to the teaching of Rousseau his own subordination of science to right.

Corollary to the primacy of right, for Kant, is the fact of human equality, and this, he reports, a philosopher could learn only from Rousseau. The learned man thinks himself superior to others, for he fails to recognize that inequality is a matter of opinion: 'The opinion according to which we are unequal also makes us unequal. Only the doctrine of Herr Rousseau can convince even the most learned philosopher that he should not consider himself better than the common man, and this without the help of religion, but solely by means of his own honest wit.'[9]

It is a moral need, shared equally by all, which justifies science. If there is any science necessary to man, writes Kant, it is that which teaches him to fill befittingly the place assigned to him by Creation; then he can learn what he must do to be a man. He should learn 'to recognize illusive seductions [*täuschende Anlockungen*] above and below him which have, in his ignorance, propelled him from his proper place.' Such knowledge 'will lead him back to the estate of man, and then, as small and imperfect as he still finds

---

5 Ibid. 144
6 Ibid. 175
7 See Delbos *La Philosophie pratique de Kant* 124.
8 See, for example, *Anthropology*, VII 326 (187): 'Rousseau at bottom did not hold that man should return to the state of nature, but rather that he should cast a backward glance at the level he there achieved.' See also 'Conjectural Beginning of Human History,' VIII 116 (60) (hereafter cited as 'Conjectural Beginning'); *Anthropology*, VII 324 (185); *Reflexion* #1454.
9 *Bemerkungen*, XX 176; see also ibid. 23-4: Mankind mistakenly thinks that its worth lies in its great artists and scholars alone, and considers the peasant and labourer as means of support: 'The injustice of this judgment already shows that it is false.' According to Kant, economic and social superiority is to be had only at the expense of others: 'Man cannot change nature's law. He must work himself or have another work for him, work which will rob the other of his happiness as he himself ascends above the average' (ibid. 39).

himself, he will be upright and good in terms of the place to which he is assigned, for he will be precisely what he ought to be.'[1] The only needful science serves morality. It teaches man what he is so that he may learn what he ought to be. It does so, however, in a negative way, by destroying that false knowledge which has seduced man away from his rightful place. It protects him from these false seductions by exposing them as such, that is, by teaching man his limits. This science of man points towards the path which critical philosophy will take, establishing the limits of reason and thereby removing the illusive seductions which deflect man from that which is, morally speaking, his proper course. Already Kant conceives the science of man as a twofold undertaking: man must learn first his limits, and then what he ought to be. The moral function of philosophy is not, however, to set virtue forth, but to strip away the false doctrines which eclipse its natural pre-eminence. One is again reminded of Rousseau's *First Discourse*, in which 'true philosophy' means disposing of all learned doctrines which obstruct the moral conscience.[2] Kant's understanding of the moral role of philosophy is here closer to Rousseau than it will later be. Kant does not yet (Rousseau never did) believe that virtue requires its own doctrine and metaphysic. The essential role of speculative philosophy, however, will remain for Kant a negative one. 'Where error,' Kant later writes, 'is entangling and at the same time dangerous, negative knowledge and criticism are more important than positive knowledge ... Socrates had with regard to speculation a negative philosophy, by which I mean a philosophy of the non-value of many so-called sciences, a science of the limits of our knowledge. The negative part of education is the most important. Rousseau (marked the limits with precision).'[3] Already in the *Bemerkungen* Kant defines 'metaphysics' as 'a science of the limits of human reason.'[4]

Man asserts his dignity and his honour as a race, a species, a humankind, for which the dignity of each is that of all, and all that of each. The pre-eminence of equality in Kant's discussion of right, undertaken in the 1760s, dispels any suspicion that the democratic element in Kant's thought was primarily the result of his enthusiasm for French events of 1789.[5] But what is even more interesting than this democratic turn of mind, twenty years before

1 Ibid. 45–6
2 J.J. Rousseau *The First and Second Discourses* trans. Roger D. Masters (New York, St Martin's Press 1964) 64
3 *Reflexion* #193
4 *Bemerkungen*, xx 181
5 See, for example, ibid. 55, 165, 35–6: 'Out of the feeling of equality springs the idea of justice ...'

the French revolution, is Kant's change of heart from a longing after truth to a respect for the rights of man, a respect which Rousseau awakens even against Kant's own inclination. Kant does not thereby cease to be a *Forscher*, a seeker, but he does cease to regard that seeking as his primary task. There is already in this general confession an element of self-denial and self-overcoming. The assertion and establishment of human right requires the submission and subjugation of the inclination towards truth. The desire to know and the satisfaction which knowledge affords were in any case never strong enough to stave off entirely that desire's demoralizing consequences. The problems which scientific knowledge posed for human dignity can be conclusively solved by making truth serve right. The dialectic of desire and frustration which characterized Kant's earlier works is now superseded by an attitude of confident self-reliance. In Kant's eyes man no longer depends on nature for those things which matter most.

Kant's reading of Rousseau causes him to revise his understanding of 'the honour of mankind.' Previously he believed that that honour lies in knowledge, which, by placing man on a higher rung of nature, draws him closer to the perspective of a contemplative God. But that solution was a tenuous one, a reassuring fantasy tacked on to a scientific theory which did not well support it.[6] Previously Kant looked to nature to honour knowledge, by giving reason a pre-eminent place within the scheme of things. But in fact Newtonian science had banished rank and preference from the natural order. A world of interchangeable matter, to which all laws are equally applicable, brooks no hierarchies. Knowledge of such a nature could well terrify men with visions of their dependence and insignificance.

Rousseau taught Kant how much man might make good the stint of nature by doing for himself rather than by turning to God, as Kant did in his early scientific writings.[7] As the equation of honour and knowledge led to a sterile dependence upon nature, so the equation of honour and right leads to fruitful co-operation among men. Right pertains to the sphere of humanity, not to the relations of man to nature, but to the relations of men to men. Once man recognizes the pre-eminence of his rights, which are in his power to assert and in the power of others to respect, nature's stint will not seem so painful. Honour is not bestowed on man, either by nature or by God, but rather lies in his doing 'what he ought to do to be a man.'[8]

This notion of right makes possible a new solution to the problem of theodicy. Kant brings to the surface and rejects the feeling of natural injustice

---

6 See Vlachos *La Pensée politique de Kant* 13ff.
7 Cf. *Bemerkungen*, XX 172: 'Man is needy, but also has power over his needs.'
8 Ibid. 41

which his earlier thought could not satisfactorily dispel. The feeling is recognized for what it is: a misplaced assertion of human right, misplaced because it is directed not against the wilful opposition of other men, who can pay it heed, but against the necessary opposition of nature, which can pay it none. The struggle for respect and dignity is properly conducted not upon the natural but upon the social field. This is so not because nature treats us well – we are still and always natural beings of need – but because this good which 'matters most' is one we can supply ourselves. For this good at least, man does not depend on the material economy of nature. 'The motion of matter is maintained by a certain determined rule, but the wilfulness of man is without rule.'[9] The wilfulness of man is understood as made possible by a kind of lapse of nature. Out of this lapse or lack of a natural law arises that human wilfulness which constitutes the basis of his freedom. But one man's wilfulness meets the opposition of another, and it is at this juncture that rights are properly asserted.

In a section of the *Bemerkungen* entitled 'On Freedom' Kant distinguishes between dependence on the necessity of nature and dependence on the wil(fulness) of another human being. 'Man depends on outer things,' through his need for them and through his wantoness [*Lüsternheit*]; in this respect he is 'the administrator of nature but not its master ... he must yield himself to the compulsion of nature, because he will not find that it always yields to his wishes. But what is harder and more unnatural is for a man to submit to the will of another.'[1] To submit to the will of another is not only difficult; it is 'more unnatural.' One discerns in Kant's distinction between natural necessity and human wilfulness the influence of Rousseau, who in his *Emile* makes a similar distinction the cornerstone of his pedagogy. According to Rousseau, 'there are two kinds of dependence, dependence on things, which is the work of nature, and dependence on men, which is the work of society.' Dependence on things is 'non-moral' and 'begets no vices.' Dependence on men, on the other hand, is 'out of order' and 'gives rise to every kind of vice.'[2] Rousseau traces this distinction to a fact of experience observable in any young child: we only feel wronged by pain which we regard as intentional. Thus the infant takes the heavy blows of chance in his stride, while lighter blows, which he recognizes as intentional, cause not only greater pain but even rage. This example evinces, according to Rousseau, man's 'innate sense of justice and injustice.'[3] Pain may meet with tears but ill will arouses anger. We feel anger

---

9 Ibid. 93
1 Ibid. 91; cf. 164, 94: 'Even the slightest degree of dependency is a very great evil ...'
2 J.J. Rousseau *Emile* trans. Barbara Foxley (London, Everyman's Library 1966) 49
3 Ibid. 33

only when we feel wronged. Our capacity for anger is essential to our sense of justice and injustice.[4]

According to Rousseau nature cannot injure man because his very sense of injury presupposes his recognition of an intentionality which cannot properly be attributed to nature. Prior to his recognition of the intentionality of others, the history of man is non-moral. With this recognition comes the possibility of vice, which lies in the 'mutual depravity of master and slave.' In this relation of mutual depravity each is aware of his dependence on the other. The slave depends on the master for his very life; the master depends on the slave for the satisfaction of new needs and is thereby as surely ensnared. Moral and civic virtue become means whereby men strive to win back in some form the independence which they enjoyed in the state of nature. 'If the law of nations, like the law of nature, could never be broken by any human power, dependence on men would become dependence on things.' Civil law, or the general will armed with strength beyond that of any individual will, becomes a substitute for the necessity of nature.[5]

Rousseau presents human liberty and natural necessity as perfectly compatible. Man, he argues, does not mind those compulsions which he regards as necessary. Only those restrictions which appear to place him at the mercy of another will call his own freedom into question. In the *Bemerkungen* Kant seems to agree. Nature is no longer presented as the greatest threat to man's security and dignity. The obstruction of matter is far more easily borne than is compulsion from another will. From the *Bemerkungen* emerges a concept of liberty approaching that which Kant later calls external freedom, asserted wholly against other men.

Like Rousseau Kant distinguishes man from animal on the basis of man's self-awareness. 'An animal,' Kant writes, 'is not yet a complete being because it is not conscious of itself.'[6] Man, however, knows of his own existence and, until another will obtrudes upon that existence, is whole and free. This wholeness and this freedom characterize natural man, who is distinguished from the beasts only by his self-consciousness, or what Kant will later call his

---

4 Thus Rousseau urges the educator to 'keep the child dependent on things only' by which course one will 'follow the order of nature.' Let the child's unreasonable wishes be met only by 'physical obstacles.' The tutor must in his encounters with the child disguise his own wilfulness. Let the child 'early find upon his proud neck, the heavy yoke which nature has imposed on us, the heavy yoke of necessity, under which every finite being must bow.' But 'let him find this necessity in things, not in the caprices of man ... Thus you will make him patient, equable, calm and resigned, even when he does not get all he wants; man naturally bears patiently the nature of things, but not the ill-will of another' (ibid. 49–55).
5 Ibid. 49
6 *Bemerkungen*, XX 93

ability to reflect. But this self-consciousness also entails an ability to recognize a similar self-consciousness in others. Thus man becomes aware of others like himself, conscious of themselves, and of their power to lift an arm, a rock, a tool for their own use. As he first distinguished between himself and outer things, so now he distinguishes between things and other men, and gradually it dawns on him that he too can be a tool, a mere thing to other men. To allow oneself to be used as a tool, to become a thing in the eyes of another, that is the meaning of submission (*Unterwürfigkeit*). To yield to the will of another is to cancel one's own essence, and is as such a 'contradiction' which indicates the injustice (*Unrechtmässigkeit*) of the deed. 'That man should need no soul of his own and have no will of his own, and that another soul should move his limbs, this is absurd [*ungereimt*, 'unrhymed,' 'blank'] and inverted [*verkehrt*, 'exchanged,' 'turned the wrong way']. Such a man is the mere tool of another.' To stand in dependence on another is to lose one's standing and to be 'only a possession.' The man who submits to another is 'no longer a man.'[7] Man is distinguished from the beasts, not only by his self-consciousness, but also by his capacity for self-contradiction. Nature makes man sound and man destroys himself. 'God makes all things good, man meddles with them and they become evil.'[8] Here, as in Kant's later works, self-consistency is the standard of both metaphysical and moral legitimacy. Self-consistency is here understood as freedom from dependence on the will of another. Such freedom is the basis of right. Like man's ability to distinguish himself from outer things, and outer things from other wills, this right is an essential constituent of his humanity; without it he would cease to be a man.

To Rousseau, Kant attributes both his new appreciation of right and his new understanding of man. Kant calls him 'the Newton of the moral world.' Like Newton, Rousseau discovered order where those before him encountered confusion. 'Rousseau was the first to discover beneath the varying forms human nature assumes the deeply concealed essence of man and the hidden law in accordance with which Providence is justified by his observations.' Before Newton and Rousseau 'the objections of King Alfonso and the Manichaeans were still valid. After Newton and Rousseau, the ways of God are justified – and Pope's thesis is henceforth true.'[9]

The problem of theodicy, with which Kant struggled in his earlier works, he

---

7 Ibid.; cf. 66: 'Submission of a human will to a foreign will is contradictory; for man possesses *spontaneitatem*.' At this early stage Kant does not yet distinguish between inner and outer freedom.

8 J.J. Rousseau *Emile* 5; cf. Kant *Reflexion* #1427: 'All the evils on earth are caused to man by man.'

9 *Bemerkungen*, XX 58–9

now considers solved. We have seen how in those early works Newtonian science gave rise to the problem in a special form. The flux of nature opposed by our natural desire for permanence, the indifference of nature to our ends and the opaqueness of its own, all this aroused the suspicion that nature does not do justice by us. Rousseau sets Kant right by showing him that the fundamental fact about man is his awareness of his freedom to use his own power as he will. Nature does not challenge this awareness. The onslaught of things merely provides the necessary arena upon which man may consciously exercise his powers. Things may pose a hardship to man; it is, however, natural and consistent to strive consciously to overcome these hardships. To yield to the necessity of things does not harm human freedom.[1] But to submit to the will of another is to contradict and so subvert one's very essence.

Such subversion is itself a wilful act. The will cannot be cancelled by nature but only by the will itself. Kant's new theodicy redeems nature by implicating man. Injustice is our creation, a kind of self-mutilation. Our rights are a part of us; and it is we who must restore them. If human life is not all that it could be, it is because we have done ourselves injury. This, then, is Kant's early solution to the problem of theodicy, a solution begun by Newton and completed with the aid of Rousseau. One must accept the solution as tentative: in Kant's philosophical maturity he will dismiss the entire problem of theodicy as incapable of theoretical solution.[2] Nevertheless one discerns in these earlier convictions the signs of a drastic reorientation in Kant's thought. This is not to say that Kant's studies of Wolff, Newton, and the British moralists did not in an important sense constitute a preparation for this reorientation. Those nagging difficulties, of a sort Kant would later call practical, which science raised but could not solve, supplied the questions to which Rousseau suggested an answer.

Rousseau's distinction between dependence on things and dependence on other wills had both an immediate and a lasting effect on Kant. In works as late as his *Anthropology*, the last complete book Kant saw published, and his *Pädagogik*, published posthumously, the distinction plays a significant role. Kant in large part rests his discipline on a simulation of natural necessity, an artifice similar to that which the tutor employs in *Emile*. Both Kant and Rousseau recognize the discovery of other wills as having morally crucial consequences. Between Kant and Rousseau there is, however, an important

---

1 In his critical period Kant will decisively modify this Rousseauian teaching.
2 See, for example, Kant's essay 'On the Failure of All Attempted Philosophical Theodicies' (1791).

difference: Kant emphasizes the indignity and self-abnegation implied in submission to another will, whereas Rousseau dwells on the damage that discovery can do to the natural balance in man between desire and power.[3] Kant is more concerned with dignity, less with happiness. For Rousseau it is the possibility of tyranny, the use of others for the limitless expansion of one's own powers, that constitutes the gravest danger of the discovery.[4] The tutor expends great effort in preventing this tyranny by stopping or retarding in the child the development of new desires.[5]

As Kant sees it, the appearance of new and dangerous desires unavoidably accompanies the development of reason, a development that is unquestionably desirable. For Kant the central problem is not tyranny and enslavement through an expansion of desire but rather submission and self-contradiction. Kant is less concerned with forestalling the development of new desires than with instilling in the young child strength to 'renounce' desires already present, when as 'passions' they threaten to overwhelm him. The discipline of education should accustom the child to opposition, less to stimulate self-sufficiency (as with Rousseau) than to encourage self-control.[6]

The despotism of infancy which occupied Rousseau is for Kant merely one occasion for aggrievement. In his *Anthropology*, Kant describes anger as the first human passion, experienced by the infant even before it has learned to distinguish between things and men:[7]

When an infant is forced to approach certain objects, or merely to change his general state, he feels that he is checked. This impulsion to have his own will and to take offence at that which obstructs him is ... signalled by the tone which he takes ... The same thing happens when he falls by his own fault. Animal young play; children quarrel very early; it is as if a certain concept of right (which relates to external freedom) develops at the same time as animality, instead of being progressively learned.[8]

Unlike Rousseau, who traces the awakening of the sense of right to the discovery of other wills, Kant locates the first inkling of right in the child's experience of things. The opposition of matter itself occasions a child's first

---

3 See, for example, *Emile* 126–8.
4 Ibid. 33
5 Ibid. 54–7, 60–3
6 *Pädagogik*, IX 458–61, 463. On some textual difficulties see Lewis White Beck *Essays on Kant and Hume* 193–7.
7 Anger is 'a good kind of passion in the innocence of nature' but bad in society (*Bemerkungen*, XX 63).
8 *Anthropology*, VII 269 (136) (my translation)

sense of injury and injustice, even as it calls to life the child's sense of his own liberty.

From his earliest scientific writings to his latest critical ones, Kant presents matter as an obstacle against which man tests his liberty. It is the nature of matter to obstruct the fulfilment of human desire. Happiness is not the destiny of a being whose desires are naturally insatiable. The destiny of man lies not in satisfaction but in work,[9] in struggle to overcome the limitations imposed by matter and man's material nature. Man should regard as his destiny not happiness but the struggle for freedom.

One finds in Kant an impatience with the moral possibilities of the natural world never so openly expressed by Rousseau. Kant is not so easily reconciled to the necessary limitations which the natural world imposes on our moral lives. In his generally ironic *Dreams of a Spirit-Seer*, published in 1766, Kant gives straightforward reasons for his moral discontent:

The moral quality of our actions can, according to the order of nature, never be fully worked out in the bodily life of men ... The true purposes, the secret motives of many endeavours, fruitless by impotency, the victory over self, or the occasional hidden treachery in apparently good actions, are mostly lost as to their physical effect in the bodily state.[1]

By failing to express fully the moral quality of our actions, the material world denies us full moral satisfaction. The moral quality of our actions lies in our motives; for it is the motives of our acts, and not their material results, which are wholly within our power and for which we may be held accountable. However, good motives often lead to bad results, while good results often derive from bad motives. There is, then, a fundamental incongruity between the moral quality of our actions and their effects within the material world. This physical realm, moreover, hides from us the moral quality of our own acts. The material world denies us moral satisfaction by beclouding our accountability.

The inadequacy of the physical world as a stage for morality induces Kant to posit a spirit world, in which the moral quality of our actions can be 'worked out.' In such a world, hidden intentions could be regarded as 'fruitful causes'

---

9 Work (*Arbeit*) is 'occupation not pleasant in itself, but undertaken for the end in view' (*Pädagogik*, IX 470). Man is the only creature who must work (ibid. 471); hence it is 'of utmost importance that the child learn to work.' Cf. *Emile* 162–171 and Judith N. Shklar *Men and Citizens* 24, 45–6. For both Rousseau and Kant work is naturally unpleasant. Only for Kant is it also morally imperative.

1 Immanuel Kant *Dreams of a Spirit-Seer* II, 336 (65)

31 The pre-critical problem

and 'would mutually produce and receive effects appropriate to the moral quality of free will.'[2] These moral promptings are still understood by Kant as matters of sentiment. Morality has not yet attained the status of a 'fact of reason' which it enjoys in his critical thought. Nevertheless they are the occasion for the playful positing of a new dualism which (unlike the old spirit/matter continuum of Kant's *Natural History*) incorporates Rousseau's moral teachings. For this is a world of spirits defined not by their intelligence as such, but by their moral unity. They are not partakers in divine wisdom but participants in 'a community of all thinking beings' organized into a 'spiritual constitution according to purely spiritual laws.' Our access to this spirit world is not through knowledge but through moral sentiments. These impulses of duty and benevolence conflict with our selfish inclinations and so make us realize that 'in our most secret motives, we are dependent on the rule of the will of all.' Kant teasingly elevates the general will to the heavens, making of it an effective but invisible force with the power to move our very wills. Inner conflict is explained by the presence of a higher will within us. In *Dreams* moral awareness arises from our recognition of an inner conflict between the sentiments of selfishness and those of duty and benevolence.[3] In *Dreams* inner conflict is the fact which 'awakens' us to the moral world, and so to recognition of physical/moral dualism.

In the *Critique of Pure Reason* the conflict between morality and nature scientifically understood will be a problem not only for morality, but also for reason. Kant there makes it clear that, should scientific reason and morality prove to be in necessary conflict, morality would have to give way. But in fact the case for morality (or moral responsibility, which implies freedom to act upon the material world) proves to be the case of reason itself. In judging between what are, rationally speaking, equally compelling arguments for moral freedom and for natural necessity, reason puts itself on trial.

Kant made no secret of the importance of moral considerations in the development of his thought. But that particular moral problem which he claimed most deeply influenced his theoretical inquiries was one which seemed to challenge the integrity of reason itself. 'The origin of critical philosophy,' said Kant, 'lies in moral theory,' and specifically 'in reference to [the problem of] moral responsibility for actions.'[4] The problem of moral responsibility in a determined universe, the problem broached in *Dreams* and playfully solved through the positing of an invisible world of morally united

2 Ibid.
3 *Dreams of a Spirit-Seer*, II 334–5 (63–4)
4 *L. Blät.*, GS XX 335

spirits, returns in Kant's *Critique of Pure Reason* as an 'antinomy' which reason must solve if it is not to lose its guiding principle of self-consistency. It was not the investigation of general metaphysical questions, Kant wrote to Christian Garve and repeated in the *Prolegomena to Any Future Metaphysics*, but rather the antinomy of reason which first awakened him from his 'dogmatic slumber' and drove him to undertake a critique of reason 'in order to resolve the scandal of ostensible contradiction of reason with itself.'[5] Yet if the source of critical philosophy lies in the antinomies of reason, the source of the antinomies lies in the 'desire' [*Begierde*] of reason for what Kant calls the unconditioned [*Unbedingt*], which lies beyond the conditionality of empirical experience. 'All antinomies occur because we seek the unconditioned in the sensual world.'[6] Critical philosophy will attempt to free reason from the seductions of the unconditioned and from the philosophically and morally damaging contradictions which those seductions generate. Like Kant's infant, reason can achieve coherence only by suppressing desire.

---

5 Letter to Christian Garve, 21 September 1798 (GS XII 256–8 (250–52); *Prolegomena to Any Future Metaphysics*, IV 338–9 (86–7). Kant also attributes his awakening to his reading of David Hume (*Prolegomena*, IV 260 (8)).

6 *Reflexion* #6418

2
The critical context

1 / CRITICAL PHILOSOPHY AND THE COPERNICAN HYPOTHESIS

Objective knowledge and its relationship to the dependency of reason are thematic in many of Kant's early works. We have seen how in his *Natural History* he presents knowledge as a liberation of the rational soul from material obstructions. In 1766 he still spoke of the soul as 'present in the world, both in material and non-material things,' but he also introduced a distinction between the active and receptive capacities of the soul, a distinction fundamental to his later theory of knowledge. Already in 1766 he considered his most important problem to be 'how the soul is present in the world.' 'We need to discover,' he wrote to Mendelssohn, 'the nature of that power of external agency, and the nature of that receptivity or capacity of being affected by an external agency, of which the union of a soul with a human body is only a special case.' Remarking, however, on the impossibility of ever encountering in experience data sufficient to support this distinction, Kant questioned whether it is possible to gain from experience such knowledge of the nature of the soul – a knowledge 'sufficient to inform us of the manner in which the soul is present in the universe.' 'Here,' he concluded, 'we must decide whether there really are not limits established by the bounds of our reason, or rather, the bounds of experience that contain the data for our reason.'[1]

Increasingly, Kant linked his metaphysical inquiries with his consideration of the problem of objectivity. In 1765 he told Lambert that he was working on a book 'on the proper method of metaphysics.'[2] Kant's Inaugural Dissertation of 1770 gives evidence of the progress of his thought. In attempting to explain objective knowledge, he put forward new theories concerning the 'active' and 'passive' faculties of the mind and drew a distinction – crucial to his later critical thought – between appearances and things-in-themselves. According to the Dissertation, all sensible knowledge, 'which depends upon the special nature of the subject, insofar as it is capable of being modified in diverse ways by the presence of objects ... is knowledge only of things as they appear.' For such modifications 'may differ in different subjects in accordance with the nature of these subjects,' while 'whatever is exempt from this subjective condition regards only the objects.'[3] Our capacity to be (sensibly) affected by

1 Letter to Moses Mendelssohn, 8 April 1766 GS X 69–73 (54–7)
2 Letter to J.H. Lambert, 31 December 1765, GS X 54–7 (47–9)
3 *Dissertation on the Form and Principles of the Sensible and Intelligible World* (Inaugural Dissertation) II 392–3 (44)

the object prevents us from knowing it directly, as it is. Only a knowledge that is purely intellectual and 'conceptual,' unrelated to receptive intuition, gives access to things as they are.

In his Inaugural Dissertation Kant identifies certain 'subreptions' of reason, which result from the contamination of intelligible or noumenal knowledge by the sensible or empirical. (In the *Critique of Pure Reason*, he will, on the contrary, protest contamination of the empirical by the noumenal.) These subreptions involve a conflict between the 'demand' of reason for absolute totality or wholeness (Kant here taking the demand as proof of its object's reality) and the mind's inability to intuit such a totality, intuition being subject to forms of space and time which allow for unlimited extension but not completeness.[4] The gap between what the mind can intuitively achieve and what it can conceptually demand is the necessary counterpart of Kant's dichotomy between the world of appearances and the world of things-in-themselves, the wholeness of the former conferred by the informing power of the mind, that of the latter independently and objectively real.

Kant's treatment of sensible knowledge anticipates much of the Aesthetic of his later *Critique*. He failed, however, in the Dissertation to present a parallel account of non-sensible, intelligible knowledge, which, as he confessed to Marcus Herz two years later, he was unable to explain. In his letter to Herz he discussed the problem of objectivity, describing it as the 'key to the whole hitherto still obscure metaphysics.' What, asks Kant, is the ground of the relation to an object of that in us which we call representation? 'If a representation is only a way in which the subject is affected by the object, then it is easy to see how the representation is in conformity with this object.' If, on the other hand, the representation actively produces its object, it is also easy to understand the conformity of representation and object. Thus, 'the possibility of both an *intellectus archetypi* (on whose intuition the things themselves would be grounded) and an *intellectus ectypi* (which would derive the data for its logical procedure from the sensuous intuition of things) is at least intelligible.' Our mind is not, however, the cause of its object, nor is the object the cause of intellectual representations in the mind. Such pure concepts of the understanding, which must have their origin in the nature of the soul, neither are caused by the object nor bring the object into being. How then, Kant wondered, is it possible that a representation can refer to an object without in any way being affected by it? Kant remained unable to explain the possibility of intelligible knowledge, involving as it must a relation between object and intelligence in which the object is not affected by intelligence nor

---

4 Ibid. 389 (38)

intelligence by the object. Rejecting as absurd traditional solutions such as neo-Platonic 'influx' and Leibnizian 'pre-established harmony,' solutions he had formerly in part assumed, Kant recognized a grave difficulty in his previous teaching. The relation between our representations and their objects, he concluded, is neither wholly active nor wholly passive. In the case of human, as contrasted with either a wholly receptive or wholly creative understanding, the important and difficult problem is to explain the conformity of representations and their objects, to explain, that is to say, the possibility of objective knowledge.[5]

Nine years later the *Critique of Pure Reason* provided this explanation, along with a new understanding of objective knowledge. Published in 1781 and revised in 1787, the *Critique of Pure Reason* is the first and most fundamental of Kant's works to present his mature philosophic teaching. Whereas his previous works were searching and exploratory, the *Critique of Pure Reason* and the 'critical' works which follow it elaborate a single, philosophically definitive system of thought.

Critical philosophy is an inquiry into the power of reason as a faculty of knowledge. As philosophy it is concerned with knowledge of as certain a character as possible.[6] As *critical* philosophy, however, it begins by assuming that reason's powers may be limited.[7] The *Critique of Pure Reason* concludes that reason's powers are indeed limited. For its knowledge reason depends in part on something other than itself.[8] If it is to know anything, reason requires an object which it cannot itself produce but instead must reproduce from something that is 'given.'

Kant's new understanding of objectivity required rejection of the possibility of theoretical knowledge of the thing-in-itself, knowledge he had never been able adequately to explain, and with it a rejection of his previous two-world theory. His new understanding instead entailed a new host of complex and interrelated dualisms, including that of (unknowable) noumenon and (knowable) phenomenon, intuition and understanding, understanding and reason, knowledge and belief, constitutive and regulative principles, theory and practice.

---

5 Letter to Marcus Herz, 21 February 1772, GS X 129–35 (70–6)
6 See CR A/xv.
7 On the relation for Kant between criticism and delimitation, see Martin Heidegger *What is a Thing?* 119–21.
8 CR A/76–A/79 = B/102–B/105, B/69, B/164–5. See also S. Körner *Kant* (London, Penguin 1955) 63: 'The human understanding does not produce the manifold.' The notion of an understanding productive of its object became, as Körner points out, the cornerstone of the philosophy of Fichte.

In the preface to the *Critique* Kant describes his new understanding of objectivity. That knowledge and its object must agree he takes as beyond controversy. What he disputes is the source of this agreement. Previously men assumed that knowledge must conform to objects. Instead Kant supposes that objects conform to knowledge. The possibility, heretofore shrouded in mystery, of agreement between knowledge and object is explained by the fact that the mind gives the object its form.[9]

Kant describes this hypothesis as 'Copernican,'[1] likening it on several levels to the suppositions and discoveries of the founders of modern science. These judicious investigators attacked nature with suspicion, addressing it as 'an intransigent witness,' and compelled it to answer questions of their own devising. Scientists examined nature on their own terms, not passively waiting for nature to yield up its secrets, but forcing it to do so, by means of experiments themselves guided by the principles and laws of human understanding. Kant draws from the success of the new scientific method a lesson for metaphysics: 'Reason has insight only into that which it produces after a plan of its own.' Reason must detach itself from 'nature's leading strings'; instead it must 'itself show the way' by compelling nature to answer questions based upon fixed laws to which reason has access because they are reason's own.[2] Reason learns from nature only when guided by what it puts into nature. The success of science suggests that reason indeed puts something into nature, that nature is somehow informed by reason.

This conclusion is as shocking to common sense as the original Copernican teaching that the earth revolves around the sun.[3] We experience nature, and the objects which compose it, as entities outside and apart from us. Objects (*Gegenstände*) 'stand against' and resist us. How then make persuasive the supposition that we are in part the 'makers' of those objects? Kant's tentative answer is 'success.' Kant's Copernican solution makes it possible to explain the failures of all previous efforts towards a scientific metaphysics. Heretofore, according to Kant, philosophers sought to ground and certify their knowledge in a necessity which they attributed to objects. Philosophers perceived nature as possessing a necessity apart from and independent of the reason which seeks to discover it. But according to Kant such necessity is in principle unavailable to reason, which has insight only into that which it produces according to a plan of its own. Thus if reason is to have any certain

9 CR B/xvi
1 CR B/xxii
2 CR B/xi–B/xiv: the Copernican hypothesis, like other turning points in the history of science, makes possible a 'revolution' in thought. See also CR A/853 = B/881.
3 CR B/xxii

39 The critical context

knowledge at all, it must be *a priori* knowledge, available through reason's own resources.[4]

At stake is the very possibility of a metaphysics which pertains to objects. Metaphysics, as an inventory of all *a priori* knowledge, has to do, not with the objects of reason, 'but only with [reason] itself and the problems which arise entirely from within [it],' problems, in other words, 'which are imposed upon (reason) by its own nature, not by the nature of things which are distinct from it.'[5] If knowledge conformed to objects, rather than the reverse, if our knowledge of objects arose entirely out of things which are distinct from reason, we should have to give up all efforts to attain *a priori* knowledge which pertains to objects. If, however, objects take their form from reason, metaphysical knowledge pertaining to objects is in principle possible, and the success of science is at least in part explained.

Like Copernicus, who ascribed the apparent motion of the heavenly bodies to the motion of the earth, Kant ascribes our awareness of an objective world to our own active contribution to the formulation of that world. Reason is not a passive contemplator but an active worker and producer,[6] which constructs, through rules of its own devising, the world of objects which we experience as things apart. But the labours of reason are not entirely *sui generis* and self-determined. In order for reason to form its concept of an object, it must receive through sensibility some material on which to work. The fundamental activity of reason, in its capacity as understanding, is combination or synthesis. To set to work, however, understanding must first receive from intuition some 'manifold' of data to combine.

Sensibility receives raw data, which intuition represents according to the *a priori* forms of space and time. Understanding, in turn, combines, according to its own *a priori* categories, that which is given to it in intuition. In thus bringing the manifold of representations under what Kant calls the unity of apperception, understanding makes possible both self-awareness and awareness of objects. The mind is both spontaneous, in its capacity to act according to the rules it gives itself, and responsive, in its relation to the source of that which it combines.[7]

---

4 CR B/xvi–B/xix
5 CR B/23
6 CR B/129–B/136, B/137, B/145
7 On mental 'production' and 'reproduction' see CR A/97–A/110; cf. A/118, B/151. On production as 'Erzeugung' see B/115, A/143 = B/183, A/163 = B/204, A/170 = B/211, A/141 = B/181, A/471 = B/499, A/626 = B/654. P.F. Strawson attempts to expunge from the *Critique* portrayals of reason as spontaneous, receptive, productive, etc., which he finds 'psychologistic.' Whatever the intrinsic philosophic merit of his reconstructed arguments, Strawson's approach tends to

Because every sensation brought to our awareness is subject to the same *a priori* categories, and because all our experience of objects ultimately requires sensation, we can be sure of the systematic interrelation of all our concepts and their objects; the unity of consciousness and consciousness of objects go hand in hand. Understanding does not merely effect the concept of an object, but also an orderly and objective world corresponding to the unity of consciousness.[8] Guided by its own principles, both constitutive and regulative, the mind constructs the systematic and dynamic whole which science calls nature. The fundamental laws of nature (for example, the law that every event has a cause) correspond to the fundamental categories and principles of the understanding. In this sense, understanding is nature's legislator.[9]

However, understanding only supplies formal rules, which have no part in objective knowledge unless they are brought to bear upon the given.[1] Knowledge of objects requires both combination and receptivity, the reception of the given by sensibility as well as its synthesis by understanding. As Kant expresses it in a famous but enigmatic phrase, 'Thoughts without content are empty, intuitions without concepts are blind.'[2]

The spontaneity of understanding is limited by its dependence on the given. Unlike Fichte and Hegel, who portray the mind as fully constitutive of its object, Kant presents it as productive of the object's form alone. According to Kant, one aspect of objective knowledge must remain fundamentally mysterious.[3] The given, upon which objective knowledge depends, is available to reason only in so far as it is affected and transformed by the synthesis of understanding. Perceptions represent this given, the true nature of which always remains hidden from us. Understanding knows the given only by working upon it and so transforming it. The given is available to understanding to work over, but not to know; for understanding knows only what it has already transformed. And yet it is upon this original given, altogether independent of the mind, that it depends for the objective knowledge which it

---

obscure fundamental problems which concerned Kant and which concern us here. For a systematic and avowedly 'psychologistic' reading of the Analytic of the first *Critique*, see Robert Paul Wolff *Kant's Theory of Mental Activity*; see also idem *The Autonomy of Reason* 13–14; and Arendt *Thinking* 45.

8 CR A/148–A/158 = B/188–B/197, B/129, B/137, B/145. On Kant's 'deduction' of the categories and its relation to the 'transcendental unity of apperception,' see below, 133.
9 CR A/126
1 CR A/126; for a discussion of the rule-governed activity of understanding, see Wolff *Kant's Theory of Mental Activity*.
2 CR A/51 = B/75
3 Cf. Edward Caird *A Critical Account of the Philosophy of Kant* 666.

enjoys. In this paradox lies a mystery, which gives the objects of our knowledge their peculiar status as 'appearances' (phenomena), rather than things as they are in themselves.[4] The critical distinction between appearance and thing-in-itself, or alternatively, that between phenomenon and noumenon,[5] is the central tenet of the doctrine which Kant calls Transcendental Idealism, which asserts that appearances are to be regarded as being, one and all, representations only, not things in themselves.'[6]

Kant's early fable of reason struggling against matter, along with his later dreams of noumenal knowledge, have been superseded by a new, more resigned hypothesis. Dependence on sensation is no longer to be fought but rather to be recognized as a condition of objective knowledge. But what is in one sense an empowering condition is in another a binding check. Kant's Copernican model of reason, a model which combines spontaneity with receptivity and responsiveness, accounts for both the possibility of knowledge and the necessity of its limits.

By establishing the boundaries of objective knowledge as co-extensive with those of sensible experience, Kant places beyond the reach of human knowledge those beings and properties, such as God, Freedom, and the Immortality of the Soul, which transcend sensible experience. Objects which transcend the limits of sensible experience cease to be possible objects of knowledge. At the same time, by establishing the dependence of objective knowledge on something 'given' to sensation, Kant reduces the claims of objectivity to knowledge of appearances only. There is a reality outside the range of human knowledge on which that knowledge nevertheless depends. This reality consists of things as they are in themselves, independent of reason.[7] Sometimes Kant suggests that these things-in-themselves are the condition of the given or manifold out of which understanding constructs the objective world that constitutes the realm of our experience.[8] Strictly speak-

---

4 See CR A/104–A/110, A/118, B/72, B/130–B/131, B/135, B/138–9.
5 *Prolegomena*, IV 360–1 (109); see also T.D. Weldon *Kant's Critique of Pure Reason* (Oxford, Clarendon Press 1958) 193.
6 CR A/369
7 See CR A/250 and Wolff *Kant's Theory of Mental Activity* 137. Many critics, including Bennett, Cohen, Kemp Smith, and Strawson, find a 'reality' of things unknowable to reason unintelligible, and hence would prefer to dispense in one way or another with Kant's Transcendental Idealism altogether. For Kant, however, the thing-in-itself has a delimiting function essential both to knowledge in general and to morality. For Kant, our thought beats against impenetrable limits (Gottfried Martin *Kant's Metaphysics and Theory of Science* 205, cf. 134–5, 170).
8 CR A/494 = B/522; cf. Jonathan Bennett *Kant's Analytic* (Cambridge, Cambridge University Press 1966) 25.

ing, we can know of the thing-in-itself and of the source of the given only that they exist and not that they coincide. Nevertheless, the possibility suggests itself of a quasi-causal relation between things-in-themselves and the realm of appearance (the realm of ordinary and scientific experience). Theoretically speaking, the thing-in-itself is a mere chimera of reason, a cipher which marks the outer limits of experience. Morally speaking, however, it must and can exist.

Kant's denial of the possibility of knowledge beyond the confines of sensible experience undermines metaphysics as traditionally understood and practised. At the same time it sustains those morally necessary beliefs to which that metaphysics was thought to lend indispensable support.[9] Traditionally metaphysics sought knowledge of that which exists independent of reason, or, as Kant puts it, the unconditioned. While it was recognized that the outcome of this inquiry would have important moral consequences, particularly with regard to such manifestations of the unconditioned as the ideas of God, Freedom, and the Immortality of the Soul,[1] that inquiry itself was perceived as theoretical (or 'speculative'). Kant regarded as a major positive achievement of the first *Critique* the radical separation of theoretical from practical inquiry. In effecting this separation Kant takes advantage of the fact that morality does not require knowledge of the ideas of God, Freedom, and the Immortality of the Soul, but merely a use of them unopposed by reason. Morality, in other words, need not know that freedom exists, or even that it is possible, but merely that reason has nothing valid to say to the contrary. Thus the moral use of the metaphysical ideas, a use which traditional metaphysics also desired, is preserved, precisely by destroying the traditional claim that such use can be grounded in knowledge.[2]

Transcendental Idealism enabled Kant to resolve a crucial conflict between the principle of mechanical causality and moral notions of accountability and free will. This conflict between science and morality had long troubled him.

---

9 CR B/xxix–B/xxx; for a discussion of critical philosophy as moral and theological substitute for a metaphysics discredited by modern science, see Gerhard Krüger *Philosophie und Moral in der Kantischen Kritik*.

1 Kant's treatment of God, Freedom, and the Immortality of the Soul calls to mind the Confessions of Rousseau's Savoyard Vicar (see George Armstrong Kelly *Idealism, Politics, and History: Sources of Hegelian Thought* 89).

2 This destruction constitutes the 'negative achievement' of the *Critique*, a destruction so successful that it is often treated as the whole. Most contemporary Anglo-American criticism has devoted itself almost exclusively to the 'destructive' aspects of the *Critique*. But cf. Martin *Kant's Metaphysics* and 41, note 7, above. For a discussion of Anglo-American criticism and its revisionary contribution to Kant scholarship, see J.N. Findlay 'Kant and Anglo-Saxon Criticism' *Proceedings of the Third International Kant Congress* (Dordrecht, Reidel Publishing Co. 1970) 128–48.

43 The critical context

To his concern with it he ascribed the origin of critical philosophy;[3] its resolution he described as the greatest positive achievement of the first *Critique*.[4]

The preface of the *Critique of Pure Reason* sets forth the conflict which the work as a whole resolves: morality requires the freedom of our will; scientific reason seems to deny its possibility. Morality 'necessarily presupposes freedom (in the strictest sense) as a property of our will,' for morality yields 'practical principles – original principles, proper to our reason – as *a priori* data of reason' and this requires freedom.[5] Reason, however, discovers laws of nature which raise doubts concerning the possibility of freedom. If these doubts were conclusive, freedom would have to give way, and morality 'would have to yield to the mechanism of nature.'[6] But these doubts are not conclusive. Reason cannot definitely exclude the possibility of freedom; on the contrary, it finds itself disturbingly capable of arguing either side of the question. As to either the impossibility or the necessity of freedom, reason seems able to make equally compelling arguments.[7]

On the one hand, the laws of reason prescribe that every event, without exception, has a cause. Hence every act is conditioned and cannot be free. On the other hand, the laws of reason prescribe that every event has a sufficient cause. Every event, then, presupposes all the causes which condition it, that is to say, its sufficient cause. But a conditioned cause cannot be a sufficient cause. Every event, then, presupposes all the causes that condition it, up to and including an unconditioned cause, that is, an event which has no cause. Hence not every event has a cause, and the concept of 'free act' is not self-contradictory.

In considering the question of freedom, and other questions involving a serial regress, reason succumbs to an 'antinomy,' a condition in which reason's own laws seem to oppose each other. Thus the conflict between morality and science, a conflict which morality would have to lose, is transformed into a conflict within reason itself, a conflict which reason could not win without implicitly discrediting itself.[8]

---

3 *L. Blät.*, GS XX 335: 'The origin of the critical philosophy is moral, in reference to moral responsibility for actions.' De Vleeschauwer emphasizes the importance of the problem of space over that of the antinomies for the development of Kant's critical philosophy (47–51); but cf. Vlachos *La Pensée politique de Kant* 19–26. As I argue below, both problems are important.
4 CR B/xxiv–B/xxxv
5 CR B/xxviii–B/xxix
6 CR B/xxix; for 'it is only on the assumption of freedom that the negation of morality contains any contradiction.'
7 CR A/444–A/451 = B/472–B/479
8 CR A/407 = B/434, B/xxi n, A/xiii

In destroying the traditional pretensions of metaphysics, Kant meant to save morality from the onslaughts of science, and reason from the abyss of antinomy and self-contradiction. Resolution of the antinomies is not only a morally happy consequence of criticism, but also an independent proof of its validity.[9] The critical distinction between appearance and thing-in-itself is necessary if reason is to avoid self-contradiction.[1] Even one instance of self-contradiction is intolerable, because it robs reason of its fundamental principle, self-consistency. Even a single break would render this lifeline useless and leave reason without a rule or method of proceeding. At stake is the validity of reason's trust in itself, the alternative a scepticism verging on nihilism that might have made even Hume shudder.[2] To be sure, reason, in Kant's view, is never wholly at peace with itself. A certain tension between reason's desire for knowledge of the unconditioned and the impossibility of its achieving it proves inevitable. This tension reason can and must tolerate; self-contradiction, however, is self-annihilation.[3] Thus the mere existence of a conflict between the laws of science, for example, and the requirements of morality is not in itself a threat to the integrity of reason. When, however, reason finds itself supporting both the case of science and that of morality, reason is brought to trial against itself.

The antinomies of reason concern reason's ability to complete series whose extension it necessarily pursues, its ability, that is to say, to finish tasks at which it is compelled to labour. Each thesis asserts the finitude of its series, each antithesis its infinity. Both thesis and antithesis assume that if the conditioned is given, so too are all of its conditions.[4] Thus if one begins a series with a given condition, it should be possible to complete the series by arriving at the unconditioned. Each thesis, which reflects the stand of dogmatic rationalism, leaps upon this logical relation and proclaims it real. Each antithesis, which reflects the stand of empiricism, points up the impossibility, given the infinity of space and time and the universality of causality, of

---

9 CR B/xix–B/xxi
1 CR A/462–A/465 = B/490–B/493; A/424 = B/452: 'The antinomy which discloses itself in the application of laws is for our limited wisdom the best criterion of the legislation that has given rise to them.'
2 If the antinomies were truly insoluble the fundamental law of non-contradiction would be breached and even 'analytic' knowledge thereby undermined; cf. CR A/407 = B/434, A/xiv
3 See below, 121, note 5. Cf. Harvey C. Mansfield, Jr. 'Hobbes and the Science of Indirect Government,' *American Political Science Review* 165 (1971) 97–110.
4 CR A/409 = B/436. The first antinomy sets the thesis of an absolute beginning against the antithesis of an infinite temporal regress; the second sets the thesis of an absolutely simple atom against the antithesis of an infinite spatial regress; the third sets the thesis of an undetermined cause against the antithesis of determinism; the fourth sets the thesis of an absolutely necessary being against the antithesis of contingency.

experiencing the unconditioned and so rejects it as an empty concept. To this dilemma, Transcendental Idealism and the Copernican hypothesis supply a solution. So long as reason posits the absolute totality of its series – that is, assumes that this totality is real – it falls into inevitable self-conflict. Once reason properly distinguishes between appearances and things-in-themselves, however, it recognizes the conditioned as a mere appearance. This conditioned-as-appearance gives us its conditions as a series to pursue, without thereby implying our power to complete it.[5] This series is recognized as a mere function of the systematic interrelatedness of our own rules and categories. We may therefore conclude nothing about the real existence of the totality to which the completion of the series, were this possible, would attain.

The critical distinction between appearances and things-in-themselves enables reason to acknowledge the unconditioned as a necessary idea without postulating it as a knowable reality.[6] Both the thesis and the antithesis err because they confuse appearances with things-in-themselves. If the conditioned were a thing-in-itself, its conditions would be fully given and the totality of its conditions real. But the conditioned is merely an appearance. Its conditionality refers only to the fact that we must be able to connect it, according to the *a priori* forms of intuition and categories of understanding, connect it, that is to say, temporally, spatially, and causally, with any other actual or potential appearance, as a requirement of the unity of our experience. The unconditioned, then, is not given as real. Instead we set regress to the unconditioned before ourselves as a task. What is more, we set before ourselves an endless task. It is always possible for us to carry the regress back another step: every body we encounter can be divided and redivided, every cause attributed to a prior cause.

Thus we can conclude neither that the world we experience is temporally, spatially, or causally limited, nor that the unconditioned can be real for us. For the world we experience is merely a realm of appearance; we give the world its form. The endless series we seem to find in it refer to nothing in itself but only to our own modes of combining the data given to us we know not how. We have discovered that so long as we suppose that our empirical knowledge conforms to objects as things-in-themselves, 'the unconditioned cannot be thought without contradiction.' Once we suppose, however, that these objects are mere appearances which conform to our mode of representation, 'the contradiction vanishes.'[7] The Copernican hypothesis cuts through the knot of the antitheses and, by releasing reason from its dilemmas, confirms itself.

---

5 Cf. CR A/491–A/497 = B/519–B/525; and Weldon *Kant's Critique of Pure Reason* 206–7.
6 CR A/482–A/484 = B/510–B/512
7 CR B/xx

46 The Rights of Reason

If moral accountability and the antinomies are the 'source of critical philosophy,' Kant's Copernican hypothesis and the Transcendental Idealism which it installs serve as his 'key to the entire system of the world.'[8]

2 / DIALECTICAL ILLUSION AND THE ANTHROPOLOGY OF REASON

The antinomies have now been resolved from a strictly logical point of view, through recognition of the error which engenders them. Yet the illusion of a problem persists. Even when reason is firm with itself, it is likely to slip back into the mistaken position that puts it at apparent odds with itself. In reason there is, it seems, some natural tendency to err, a tendency which also must be recognized and properly dealt with if reason is to remain free, effectively as well as theoretically, from its dialectical illusion. It is not sufficient merely to locate the source of reason's conflict in its error; it is also necessary to locate the source of that error in the nature of reason.[9] While the solution of the cosmological problems was an exercise in metaphysics proper, examination of their source is sub- or pre-metaphysical, an example of what Kant elsewhere calls the anthropology of reason.[1]

An examination of the source of dialectical illusion demands an inquiry into the nature of reason. We have already had occasion to observe something of that nature – how reason, through its faculty of understanding, combines the manifold of intuition in a process which yields the knowledge of objects essential to our experience. Understanding is only capable of combining that which is given in sensible intuition. All of its knowledge is ultimately dependent for its content or 'matter' on intuition. The objects which inhabit its world are all, in one way or another, empirical. Understanding by itself is incapable of setting before itself an object which oversteps the limits of possible experience.

Were this the extent of our mental faculties, we would never fall prey to dialectical illusion. A creature possessing only the faculties of intuition and understanding is perhaps conceivable. Such a creature, however, would never overstep the limits of experience by claiming knowledge of that which is

8 *Opus post.* XXI 38
9 CR A/293–A/298 = B/349–B/355, A/642 = B/670, A/704 = B/732
1 CR A/849 = B/877; CJ V 178n, (part 1, 16n). Both Martin Heidegger (in his early *Kant and the Problem of Metaphysics*) and Gerhard Krüger argue that Kant's anthropology is the unifying stratum of his thought.

47 The critical context

independent of the given, that which is unconditioned.[2] Such a creature would never try to grasp the unconditioned, which understanding does not require and the manifold does not elicit.

The human mind, however, does claim possession of the unconditioned. This capacity Kant attributes to another fundamental faculty which he calls reason. Like understanding, reason (in this special sense) is a synthesizing or combining faculty, and like understanding it requires something to combine. Yet whereas understanding combines the manifold of intuition according to its *a priori* concepts or categories, reason combines the products of understanding according to its pure ideas. On a sliding scale between receptivity and spontaneity, reason is one step farther from sensibility, one step closer to absolute freedom.

Ideas are generated when reason 'demands' for a given conditioned that is available to it through understanding, the absolute totality of all of its conditions. It 'makes this demand in accordance with the principle that if *the conditioned is given, the entire sum of conditions, and consequently the absolutely unconditioned* (through which alone the conditioned has been possible) *is also given.*'[3]

Reason is, as we have seen, absolutely unwarranted in adopting this principle. The Copernican hypothesis enabled us to detect the error in which reason here engages itself, an error which is the source of all subsequent dialectic. Reason may not assume that 'if the conditioned is given, the entire series of all its conditions is likewise given.' It may and must assume, however, that 'if the conditioned is given, a regress in the series of all its conditions is *set* us *as a task.*' This principle is an analytic proposition, true because its predicate is contained in the very concept of its subject. For it is, according to Kant, 'involved in the very concept of the conditioned that something is referred to a condition, and if this condition is again itself conditioned, to a more remote

---

2 CR A/326 = B/383
3 CR A/409 = B/435–B/436. Kemp Smith and others have noted in the *Critique* two separate theories concerning the origin of the ideas, one linking them directly with the categories of understanding, the other with the syllogistic forms of reason. At issue is the degree to which the ideas may be regarded as spontaneous products of reason. The answer to this question touches on the all-important transition from theory to practice. The very looseness with which Kant employs the term *reason*, which designates both the mind in general and a special faculty in its own right, suggests the difficulty of this transition. The 'demand' of reason for the unconditioned is important to both theories and serves as a bridge between the 'earlier' account of reason as little more than an extension of understanding and the 'later,' more 'practically oriented' account of reason as an independent and spontaneous faculty. Cf. Norman Kemp Smith *A Commentary to Kant's 'Critique of Pure Reason'* 478–80; Lewis White Beck *A Commentary on Kant's Critique of Practical Reason* 264–5.

48 The Rights of Reason

condition, and so through all the members of the series.'⁴ The performance of this regress constitutes the whole of reason's legitimate theoretical activity.⁵

And yet reason is impelled to overstep these warranted limits and to venture 'by means of ideas alone, to the utmost limits of all knowledge, and not to be satisfied save through the completion of its course in [the apprehension of] a self-subsistent systematic whole.'⁶ What then is the source of that illogical leap by which reason comes illegitimately to demand to achieve that which it legitimately sets as a task?

The source lies partly in 'a quite natural illusion of our common reason,' deriving from the 'logical requirement that we should have adequate premises for any given conclusion.'⁷ The source lies also in the 'interested' character of reason itself.⁸ 'Interest' (*Interesse*) Kant defines as 'the delight which we connect with the representation of the real existence of an object.'⁹ Reason, as we recall, can relate to an object in one of two ways – either as merely determining it and its concept, or as also making it actual. In the former case the relation is theoretical, in the latter practical.¹ Reason taken in the narrow sense (that is, as distinguished from understanding) contributes nothing by way of knowledge. Its unique product, the ideas, are empty shells, lacking the intuitive content that knowledge requires. In the realm of practice, however, reason comes into its own. Reason as a producer of ideas *is* practical reason in its *a priori* mode. But practice is concerned with nothing other than the actualization of objects, an actualization Kant calls pure desire. In this way Kant links reason with desire. In general, knowledge and desire, the two ways in which reason may be related to an object, are strictly separate. Reason's pursuit of the unconditioned, however, an activity which is both theoretical and 'interested,' presents a special case.

The anthropology of reason is concerned with reconciling reason to its finitude – that is, with bringing reason to accept the 'legitimacy' of what are in any case necessary limitations.² The introduction of legal language here is warranted by the extensive use that Kant makes of juridical terms and forms.

4 CR A/497–A/498 = B/525–B/526
5 CR A/500–A/501 = B/529
6 CR A/797 = B/825
7 CR A/500 = B/528
8 CR A/703–A/704 = B/732: 'Because of the interest which we take in these judgements, [dialectical illusion] has a certain natural attraction which it will always continue to possess.' Cf. *Anthropology*, VII 136 (17).
9 CJ V 204 (part 1, 42)
1 CR B/ix–B/x
2 CJ, V 178n (part 1, 16n): 'Why our nature should be furnished with a propensity to consciously vain desires is a teleological problem of anthropology.'

49 The critical context

Reason appears in the *Critique* both as a judge and as a defendant, pressing 'claims' to knowledge upon whose 'rightfulness' only reason can decide.[3] The most difficult and most logically crucial arguments in the *Critique* Kant calls deductions, a term he intends not in the geometric but rather in the juridical sense, as signifying the presentation of a legal claim. Our 'right' to employ *a priori* concepts always [requires] a deduction or explanation of its legitimacy.[4] The antinomies too assume the form of a legal struggle, though one which is ultimately thrown out of court.[5] Rhetorically, the *Critique of Pure Reason* presents itself as an extended legal brief supporting reason's rightful claims before the bar of self-consistency.[6] Without this criticism, reason can never be sure 'of its claims or of its possessions,' but must be prepared for 'humiliating disillusionment.'[7] To avoid humiliation reason must submit its unauthorized and dogmatic claims to the 'law of renunciation.'[8] Criticism consists in distinguishing the well-grounded claims of understanding from the dogmatic pretentions of reason:[9]

In the absence of this critique reason is, as it were, in the state of nature, and can establish and secure its assertions and claims only through *war*. The critique, on the other hand, arriving at all its decisions in the light of fundamental principles of its own insitution, the authority of which no one can question, secures to us the peace of a legal order, in which our disputes have to be conducted solely by the recognised methods of *legal action*.[1]

Reason, according to Kant, takes a 'speculative interest' in the unconditioned, because it sets regress to the unconditioned before itself as a task.[2] In its speculative employment, reason sets before itself a phantom object, neither known nor actualized. Reason compels itself to proceed from condition to condition 'without ever gaining unconditioned footing and support in any self-subsistent thing.'[3] How much easier it would be for reason to com-

---

3 See, for example, CR A/236 = B/295, A/238 = B/297, B/424, A/669 = B/697, A/739 = B/767, A/777 = B/805, A/764 = B/792, A/767 = B/795, A/781 = B/809.
4 CR A/84–A/92 = B/116–B/124. See also *Reflexion* #5636; cf. DR, VI 345.
5 CR A/462–A/463 = B/490–B/491; A/501 = B/529
6 CR A/xi
7 CR A/238 = B/297
8 CR B/424
9 CR A/462 = B/490, A/768 = B/796
1 CR A/751 = B/779
2 CR A/466–A/468 = B/494–B/496
3 CR A/467 = B/495: 'In the restless ascent from the conditioned to the condition, always with one foot in the air, there can be no satisfaction.'

plete its task once and for all. It is part of the architectonic character of reason to be 'satisfied' in nothing save 'the completion of its course in a "self-subsistent, systematic whole."'[4] It is, says Kant, an essential principle of all use of reason to push its knowledge to a consciousness of its necessity, for otherwise it would not be rational knowledge. But it is also an equally essential restriction on this very same reason that it cannot discern the necessity of what is unless a condition under which it is is presupposed. The satisfaction of reason is thus only further and further postponed by the constant inquiry after the condition. Reason 'restlessly seeks the unconditionally necessary' and sees itself compelled to assume it, although it has no means by which to make it comprehensible.[5] For Kant the stance of reason towards the unconditioned is 'longing' (*Sehnsucht*) as distinguished from 'desire' (*Begierde*) in the strict sense. 'Desire' for Kant is the actualization of an object, 'longing' the mere attempt.[6] Longing is abortive desire. Unlike its practical counterpart, speculative reason cannot actualize the object it seeks.[7] Nor is the speculative interest of reason elicited (like the Platonic desire for wisdom) by the object sought. Rather it is self-engendered and self-imposed.[8] Kantian reason posits an idea which experience neither prepares for nor requires, an idea which, because it is beyond the limits of experience, is also beyond the limits of knowledge. What reason seeks in extending itself beyond experience is a kind of knowledge it can never have. The ideas of reason are empty, bereft of that sensible, intuitable content which human knowledge requires. The ideas, so many forms of the unconditioned, are for reason perpetual but unreachable goals. The finitude of reason reveals itself in reason's inability to know things which it can think.

The 'discipline of reason' culminates in a discussion of the 'rights of reason,' which Kant distinguishes from its unwarranted demands:

The critique of pure reason can be regarded as the true tribunal for all disputes of pure reason; for it is ... directed to the determining and estimating of the rights of reason in general, in accordance with the principles of their first institution.[9]

It is in the form of an unwarranted demand (*Forderung*) that reason's desire

---

4 CR A/797 = B/825
5 Immanuel Kant *Groundwork of the Metaphysic of Morals*, IV 128 (131) (hereafter cited as *Groundwork*)
6 CJ, V 178n (part 1, 16n). Kant also refers to reason's relation towards the unconditioned as one of 'inextinguishable desire' (*nicht zu dämpfende Begierde*) (CR A/796 = B/824).
7 CR A/482 = B/510
8 CR A/763 = B/791
9 CR A/751 = B/779

51 The critical context

(*Begierde*) for the unconditioned typically expresses itself.[1] Reason's dialectical stance towards the unconditioned is, so to speak, less plaintive than assertive. The demands of reason are also to be distinguished from its legitimate requirements (*Verlangen*). So long as reason addresses itself to things-in-themselves, it 'requires the unconditioned' by 'necessity and by right.'[2] Knowledge of the unconditioned, however, is no legitimate requirement of reason, but rather an unneedful and unrightful assertion.

Out of such assertions and demands stems the conflict which Kant compares to Hobbes' state of nature. Out of the renunciation of these demands stems the 'legal order' which Kant likens to Hobbes' civil society:

As Hobbes maintains, the state of nature is a state of injustice and violence, and we have no option save to abandon it and submit ourselves to the constraint of law, which limits our freedom solely in order that it may be consistent with the freedom of others and with the common good of all.[3]

Like man's renunciation of the unrightful claims which he asserts in the state of nature, reason's renunciation of its proud pretentions is a combination of necessity and choice; it is, in short, a necessary choice.

We can be reasonably sure that Kant, who took the trouble to elaborate with consistency and precision the comparison between philosophy and jurisprudence, meant that comparison to be instructive. Just how he meant it to instruct he indicated in what might be called his teleological anthropology of reason.[4] That predicament to which Kant compares the state of nature, he also describes as a fated fall. 'Human reason has in a field of its knowledge,' the first *Critique* begins, 'this special fate: that it is troubled [*belästigt*] by questions, which, being set as a task by the nature of reason itself, it cannot dismiss, but which, as exceeding all the powers of human reason, it cannot answer.' Reason 'falls into this predicament' but 'without fault.' It begins with principles which in the course of experience are unavoidable and which experience justifies it in using. With these it rises to ever higher, more remote conditions. But reason becomes aware that 'in this way – its questions never ceasing – its work must always remain incomplete; so it finds itself compelled to take refuge in principles which overstep all possible empirical employment, and yet seem so unsuspectable that even ordinary consciousness stands in

[1] See, for example, CR A/332 = B/389, A/338 = B/396, A/407 = B/433, A/485 = B/513, A/603 = B/631.
[2] CR B/xx
[3] CR A/752 = B/780
[4] CJ, V 177n (part 1, 16n); *Prolegomena*, IV 362 (111)

agreement with them.' Through this procedure 'human reason precipitates itself into darkness and contradictions from which issue all the battles of metaphysics.'[5] It is in order that reason may escape from this wayward condition that Kant suggests his method, or 'way,'[6] which consists in relying on what reason can know *a priori*. We should note that this method already presupposes a distinction between the *a priori* and the *a posteriori*, between that which reason discovers within itself and that which it encounters from without. Kant would have reason extricate itself from its difficulties by relying only on itself.[7] In reacting to a problem forced upon it reason comes to know a kind of independence.[8]

Like the infant, reason is born, through no fault of its own, into a world of trouble from which only it can extricate itself. The method of escape which Kant proposes is that of self-reliance. Reason's trouble derives from its natural tendency to demand what it cannot have. Its mode of deliverance therefore entails a recognition of and a reconciliation with its own necessary limits. Plato, who failed to acknowledge such limits, 'made no real advance.' Like 'the light dove, [who,] cleaving the air in her free flight, and feeling its resistance, might imagine that her flight might be still easier in empty space,' Plato 'left the world of the senses ... and ventured out beyond it on the wings of the ideas, in the empty space of the pure understanding.' But Plato made no real progress because he met with no resistance that might 'serve as support upon which he could take a stand, to which he could apply his powers, and so set his understanding in motion.'[9] Kant resorts to a mechanical image in order to suggest that knowledge, like all work, requires opposition. What Kant means by reason's limits is precisely its encounter with resistance. On this resistance, reason can depend. The fact of resistance (unlike the everchanging things that resist us) is permanent and constant, a touchstone from which reason can take its bearings and its stand. In the fact of limitation reason finds necessity and universality. Knowledge of reason's limits is not knowledge of the unconditioned;[1] for knowledge of our limits presupposes our existence,

---

5 CR A/vii–A/viii (my translation)
6 CR B/vii. 'Way' or *Weg* translates the Greek *hodos*, etymological root of 'method' (*meta* + *hodos*). Cf. CR B/723, B/506.
7 Lucien Goldmann calls reason's pursuit of the unconditioned its 'authentic destiny' (*Introduction à la philosophie de Kant* (Paris, Presses Universitaires de France 1948) 142). Goldmann's analysis is, however, undermined by his inclusion of satisfaction in this destiny (176), and by his general confusion of destiny (*Bestimmung*) and fate (*Schicksal*). For Goldmann, Kant's view of man is 'tragic,' not because man is fated to pursue that which he cannot have, but because he is unable to fulfil his destiny.
8 CR B/8–B/9
9 CR B/9
1 CR A/592–A/593 = B/620–B/621

which is itself conditional. We cannot escape the conditionality of our own existence.[2] Yet so long as reason, by assuming self-consciousness, posits its own existence, the limits of reason (as the 'Transcendental Deduction' demonstrates) surely follow. In the fact of limitation reason finds a relative necessity.

In Kant's earliest studies of cosmology, reason was limited by matter. In the *Critique of Pure Reason*, the relation between matter and reason is more complex: matter is not only experienced by reason as an obstacle but is also (in part) constituted by reason (which, in its capacity as understanding, supplies the categories without which there could be no experience of matter). In the *Critique* reason is not limited by matter, but rather by something which both resists reason and remains profoundly inaccessible to it; it encounters not material but rather transcendental impenetrability. Reason's earlier effort to work its way free of matter[3] is replaced by its recognition of its own nature in and through the resistance which it encounters. Philosophy begins with the concept of an object, of something which stands against us and from which we can take our stand.[4]

Kant does not, however, define reason entirely in terms of an oppositional relation (as do Fichte and Hegel). For Kant, what is unavailable to theoretical reason is accessible to it in its practical capacity. The thing-in-itself is both the far side of a boundary and an empty field which practical reason is free to employ for its own guidance and support. While reason is theoretically limited, it is morally free. The oppositional relation for Kant does not become dialectical in the Fichtean or Hegelian sense. For both Fichte and Hegel, the oppositional relation already contains its own transcendence and so gives rise to a dynamic logic. For Kant, on the contrary, the limits of pure reason are static and final, not to be transcended through the logic of the mind, but only through our deeds in the world.

Kant begins his *Critique* by noting certain problems pertaining to the unconditioned, problems which reason has never been able satisfactorily to solve. He proceeds to demonstrate that such problems, which arise from reason's mistaken opinion (what Kant calls dialectical illusion) that the unconditioned can be real for it, are both illusory and avoidable. In absolving reason of self-contradiction, however, criticism challenges reason on another level. The attribution of dialectical illusion to the idea-making faculty of reason seems to call into question the teleological integrity of reason.[5]

2 CR A/380, B/422–B/424, B/152–B/153; see also Wolff *Kant's Theory of Mental Activity* 143.
3 See above, 15.
4 Immanuel Kant *The Doctrine of Virtue*, VI 217n (16n)
5 *Prolegomena*, IV 361 (109–10)

By showing reason to be the source of error, Kant gives methodological assurance that reason may also dispel that error. If the source of error were elsewhere, that is, if reason were unconditionally forced to err, reason could hardly hope to correct its mistake. Paradoxically, then, reason's responsibility for its own confusion is a precondition of its ultimate clarity. This argument can, however, be carried too far. Reason, if it is to be sure of eventual clarity, must be the source of its confusion;[6] yet it must retain the capacity to mend itself.

Belief in this capacity for self-correction is aided by belief in reason's teleological consistency. Error is thereby attributed not to the nature of reason's faculties but only to their misuse. Even that faculty responsible for dialectical illusion has its proper use. Dialectical illusion lies, not in the ideas themselves, which arise 'from the very nature of our reason,' but rather from their 'misemployment.' For 'it is impossible that this highest tribunal of all the rights and claims of speculation should itself be the source of deceptions and illusions. Presumably, therefore, the ideas have their own good and appropriate vocation as determined by the natural disposition of our reason.'[7]

The ideas have as their good purpose facilitation of the systematic extension of empirical knowledge. The ideas have a *regulative* as distinguished from a *constitutive* use. They do not constitute empirical knowledge, but they do serve as guides to its acquisition. The ideas, so many variations on the notion of the unconditioned, serve as 'schemata' constructed in accordance with the conditions of the greatest possible unity of reason and so secure maximum systematic unity to reason's empirical researches.[8] Empirical psychology, for example, is aided by the idea of a simple soul or ego, physics by the idea of an ultimate cause. Without its demand for the unconditioned, reason would get no farther than the synthesis of the understanding, which combines some manifold according to its concept. What reason adds to understanding is the systematization of objective knowledge into an endlessly expandable and coherent whole. Reason understood in this narrow and specific sense makes a truly systematic science possible. The concepts of understanding constitute 'the intellectual form of all experience' and so 'it must be always possible to show their application in experience.' The ideas of reason, however, contain the unconditioned and so do not allow themselves to be contained within experience.[9] This capacity to conceive of the unconditioned in any of its many forms enables reason to extend itself beyond the

---

6 The 'blame' (*Schuld*) lies with ourselves; cf CR A/482 = B/510.
7 CR A/669 = B/697
8 CR A/670–A/674 = B/698–B/702
9 CR A/310 = B/366–B/367

limits of the sensible. A creature who only possessed understanding would never try to grasp the unconditioned, which the understanding does not require and the manifold does not elicit. Reason, however, directs itself towards 'absolute totality in the synthesis of conditions and never terminates save in what is absolutely ... unconditioned.' Reason is thus able to 'prescribe to the understanding its direction toward a certain unity of which [understanding] has ... no concept,' so as to attempt to 'unite all the acts of the understanding, in respect of every object, into an *absolute* whole.'[1] A creature who merely possessed understanding could experience objective knowledge; but it would not be able systematically to connect the objects of its knowledge. It could combine the manifold, but not concepts of objects. It would lack that drive for maximum necessity, universality, and unity which renders human reason 'architectonic.'

The unity of reason is the unity of system, that is, the unity of combination according to a principle. This principle calls forth a maximum unity of reason, which is neither given by nor exemplified in experience. The capacity to overstep the limits of experience, to err dialectically, is partly justified in the regulative service which it performs for science. Reason's susceptibility to dialectical illusion arises from reason's independence of sensation. Pure reason is 'occupied with nothing but itself. It can have no other vocation. For what is given to it does not consist in objects that have to be brought to the unity of the empirical concept, but in those modes of knowledge supplied by the understanding ...'[2]

To employ the idea of systematic unity, however, reason must somehow objectify it. 'Reason cannot think this systematic unity otherwise than by giving to the idea of this unity an object.'[3] Out of this necessity arises the phantom object or schema of the unconditioned, which tempts reason to err. Reason errs because it posits this object as real, as having an existence separable from the reason which invents it. Reason's insistence on the reality of the unconditioned springs from its failure to recognize its own independence. The capacity of reason to overstep the limits of experience is thus at once the source of its error and the badge of its freedom.

The independence of reason, however, is also coeval with its dissatisfaction. For the purpose of extending empirical knowledge reason's idea of the unconditioned has an essential regulative use. But this proper regulative use requires that reason resign itself to the futility of its primary aim – knowledge of the unconditioned. Reason takes in the empirical territory which it helps to

1 CR A/326–A/327 = B/382–B/383
2 CR A/680 = B/708
3 CR A/681 = B/709

56 The Rights of Reason

conquer by, as it were, a sidelong glance which does not entirely deflect it from its original goal.⁴

The fact remains that speculative reason cannot obtain that which it naturally seeks. To maintain its own coherence reason must renounce its demand for the unconditioned. It must pursue that which it desires, reconciled to the inevitability of frustration.⁵ Reason's labours are never complete, and philosophy (which can never be effortless or playful as Plato imagined) always entails work.⁶

That reason 'achieves nothing in its pure employment' and even 'stands in need of discipline to check its extravagances' constitutes a 'humiliation' for it. Reason, to be sure, is 'reassured and gains self-confidence, on finding that it itself can and must apply this discipline, and that it is not called upon to submit to any outside censorship.' Still, one must conclude that speculative philosophy has a merely negative use which limits rather than extends pure reason, and 'instead of discovering truth, has only the modest merit of guarding against error.'⁷ There must, then,

> be some source of positive modes of knowledge which belong to the domain of pure reason, and which ... give occasion to error solely owing to misunderstanding ... How else can we account for our inextinguishable desire to find firm footing somewhere beyond the limits of experience? Reason has a presentiment of objects which possess a great interest for it. But when it follows the path of pure speculation, in order to approach them, they fly before it. Presumably it may look for better fortune in the only other path which still remains open to it, that of its *practical* employment.⁸

Practical reason emerges in the first *Critique* as the 'ultimate end of the pure employment of our reason' and so as the ultimate source of dialectical illusion.

---

4 'It would seem that were we not to be determined to the exertion of our power before we had assured ourselves of the efficiency of our faculty for producing an Object, our power would remain to a large extent unused' (CJ, V 177n (part 1, 16n)). On vain desire as a prod of human labour and cultivation, see also below, 121, note 7. Science is the laboured by-product of reason's vain pursuit of the unconditioned.
5 Cf. Kant's statement in his later pre-critical period that it was his 'fate to fall in love with metaphysics,' of whose 'lotus land' and 'bottomless abyss' he also speaks (GS II 367, 356, 65; and the opening of the *Critique of Pure Reason* (A/vii)). See Arendt *Thinking* 9; and CR A/850 = B/878: metaphysics is like an 'old mistress' to whom one may return so long as one does not demand too much.
6 See below, 179, note 2.
7 CR A/795 = B/823; discipline is the 'liberation of the will from the despotism of desires' (CJ, V 432 (part 2, 95)).
8 CR A/795 = B/824

Morality emerges as an explanation for the sufferings of reason, whose insatiable longings are excused as 'presentiments' of an ultimate interest which lies not in knowledge, but in morality.[9]

The *Critique of Pure Reason* has about it a narrative quality which Hegel noted.[1] The inquiry which it pursues, that of the *origins* of knowledge, itself takes the form of a narration: first sensation, then understanding, finally reason. To be sure, this narration bears a peculiar relation to time, which also comes under critical scrutiny. It is not a chronology in the ordinary sense; for ordinary chronologies describe empirical events while the *Critique* describes the mental faculties which construct these events. Nevertheless, Kant is tempted or compelled continually to resort to a narrative mode, the stages of his argument recapitulating the steps which reason must take to arrive at objective knowledge.

This narrative quality also informs the anthropological level of Kant's argument: reason is burdened, strives for relief, and in the course of that vain striving discovers its true practical vocation. In the *Critique of Practical Reason*, Kant summarizes the basic argument: reason has its dialectic, based on an illusion, which would not be discovered as deceptive were it not betrayed by the antinomies which compel reason to investigate and so discover both its speculative limits and its practical possibilities. The antinomy of reason 'finally compels us to seek the key to escape from this labyrinth,' a key which 'once found, discovers that which we did not seek and yet need,' namely, a view into a higher, moral order in which we already are, and in accordance with which we may now direct ourselves by definite precepts.[2]

Reason progresses by indirection.[3] Following its natural desires, it lands in perplexity. Extricating itself, it relinquishes the vain objects of its desires but gains awareness of its own freedom. The 'step-motherly'[4] character of nature, who furnishes us with a propensity to (consciously) vain desires, is thus vindicated and transformed.

The anthropological argument is a kind of history of the discovery by speculative reason of its own freedom. Another narrative account of the emergence of freedom (in a brief essay Kant entitled 'Conjectural Beginning of Human History') sheds light on the nature of that discovery. In this essay Kant attempts to give a quasi-historical account of the 'first development of

---

9 CR A/795–A/796 = B/824–B/825
1 See G.F.W. Hegel *Lectures on the History of Philosophy* III, trans. E.S. Haldane and Frances H. Simson (London, Routledge and Kegan Paul 1896) 432–3.
2 *Crit. Prac.*, V 107 (111)
3 Ibid. 5 (5)
4 Ibid 146 (152)

freedom from its original predisposition in human nature.'[5] The aim of the exercise is to uncover a bridge between these two realms, a bridge necessary to man as a being who is both natural and free. An explicit, if playful, reinterpretation of Genesis, it also bears an often-noted likeness to the *Second Discourse* of Rousseau,[6] to which Kant refers in his essay.

Like the *Second Discourse*, Kant's essay seeks to uncover the origin of man's moral faculty, and like Rousseau Kant concludes that the moral faculty arises both out of and against nature. It arises out of nature because man is a natural being. And it arises against nature because morality requires a freedom which deterministic nature does not allow. Both works ask how man as a being of nature could acquire such freedom, or, to put it otherwise, how nature could compel man to be free. Kant and Rousseau answer this question in different ways, and for different ends. For Rousseau natural man enjoys a different sort of freedom not obviously inferior, despite Kant's protests, to moral liberty. Rousseau's account is therefore heavy with the recognition of a free and blissful innocence, irrevocably lost. For Kant, who dismisses or corrects Rousseau's pessimism in the light of Rousseau's more optimistic works,[7] freedom is unique, the capstone of metaphysics, and the only true basis of human dignity and self-respect.

Nevertheless, in Kant's 'Conjectural Beginning' a certain ambiguity surrounds the idea of freedom. The problem of accounting for the emergence of freedom out of a state of nature or non-freedom leads Kant to posit a transitional stage of non-moral freedom, midway between natural instinct and full-blown moral freedom, a stage in apparent defiance of the critical severance of the realms of nature and freedom.[8] This transitional freedom entails the awakening of limitless desire, of reason, and of awareness of choice. Nature gave man instincts, but also a capacity to forgo them. Reason, instituting comparisons, 'sought to enlarge its knowledge of foodstuffs beyond the bounds of instinctual knowledge.' In addition reason enjoyed a capacity to 'create artificial desires' which were not only unsupported by natural instinct but even contrary to it. Kant locates in some initial desertion by reason of natural instinct, occasioned perhaps by curiosity, perhaps by another 'created desire,' man's 'first attempt to become conscious of his reason as a power which can extend itself beyond the limits to which all animals are confined,' his 'first attempt at free choice.' At this moment man stands 'at the brink of an

---

5 Kant 'Conjectural Beginning' VIII 109 (53)
6 See, for example, Emil L. Fackenheim 'Kant's Concept of History'; Kelly *Idealism, Politics, and History* 100; William A. Galston *Kant and the Problem of History* 75.
7 'Conjectural Beginning,' VIII 116 (60–1)
8 Fackenheim 'Kant's Concept' 396

abyss.' Heretofore instinct had directed his desire toward specific objects. Now there opened up before him an infinity of objects, between which he did not yet know how to choose. Nor could man return to the restful life of pure instinct, for new desires already incited and plagued him.[9]

Desirous reason plays an essential if ambiguous role in the emergence of freedom as Kant conjecturally and tersely recounts it. Like its anthropological counterpart, Kant's conjectural history ascribes to reason an interim freedom, a spontaneity which is not yet fully free.[1] And, like its counterpart, it associates that interim spontaneity with a capacity for insatiable and pathological desire which both precedes and is the precondition of full moral awareness. One is in a sense free to go wrong before one is free to do right. Nature permits us, nay even encourages us, to defy her. It is she, after all, who implanted in us that capacity for insatiable desire which, once aroused, both raises our sights and plunges us into misery. The anthropology of reason recapitulates the prehistory of man. For the same reasons that the source of dialectical illusion was difficult to locate, culpability for the fall of man is hard to assign. In each case the fault is ours, and it is not ours. The scrutiny of man's original state teaches on the one hand that 'because he could not be satisfied with it, man could not remain in this state, much less be inclined ever to return to it'; and on the other that he 'must, after all, ascribe his present troublesome condition to himself and his own choice.'[2] In each case Kant presents reason in such a manner as to collapse his usually rigorous distinction between nature and freedom. This should not entirely surprise us. Reason is, after all, a dual citizen, which inhabits both the realm of nature and the realm of freedom. The great gulf which separates nature and freedom also divides reason from itself, but without disrupting its essential unity. Theoretical or practical, reason is ultimately one and the same. This unity is, however, as we shall see, a moral rather than a logical necessity. Theoretically, the unity of theory and practice, like the morally necessary juncture of nature and freedom, is incomprehensible. Nevertheless, Kant's conjectural account of this unity will prove useful to an examination of the political juncture of theory and practice.

The transition from theory to practice in the first *Critique*, like the transition from nature to freedom in the 'Conjectural Beginning,' is accomplished through resort to a conjectural theodicy, an effort to justify our condition as beings of need. Kant's 'Conjectural Beginning' is the first chapter of his

---

9 'Conjectural Beginning,' VIII 111–12 (55–6)

1 For a parallel account of interim freedom, see Kant's discussion of transcendental freedom in CR A/534 = B/562; see also Beck *Kant's Critique of Practical Reason* 190n.

2 'Conjectural Beginning,' VIII 123 (68) (cf. Plato *Republic* 620 a–e).

incipient but unfinished philosophy of history, while his anthropology of reason is the first chapter of his incipient but disjointed pragmatic anthropology. Both the 'Conjectural Beginning' and the anthropology of reason are kinds of histories of freedom. Neither has the rigour of pure philosophy, yet each supports it. The anthropology of reason teaches the necessity of discipline, and so prepares us for Kant's practical philosophy. The 'Conjectural Beginning' helps us to live with its severity.

3 / CONCLUSION

We have seen how certain fundamental concerns of the critical philosophy emerged both out of and against Kant's pre-critical thought. In his early scientific writings, he presented the natural world as a threat to human security and dignity. He tentatively suggested contemplation as the vehicle of deliverance. But this possibility was foreclosed by the obstructing corporeality of man. Kant's discovery of Rousseau precipitated a revolution in his thought. Hereafter, he locates the dignity of man in his moral rather than his contemplative capacities. Hereafter what really matters is the securing of the rights of man. This enhancing of practice goes together with a constriction of the ambitions of theory. In his early notes on Rousseau Kant writes for the first time of metaphysics as a science of the limits of knowledge.

At the same time Kant was struggling with the problem of objective knowledge. In an early letter he wondered about the relation of our representations to their object, a problem the solution to which was, according to Kant, inspired by his understanding of science. According to Kant's 'Copernican hypothesis' metaphysics, like science, must first attend to rules of reason's own making. Just as the scientist forces nature to answer questions devised according to the scientist's own plan, so may reason, Kant hypothesized, force nature to conform to rules of its devising. According to this hypothesis, experience conforms to our concepts, and knowledge of nature is demonstrably possible because we constitute its laws. Absolute knowledge of nature, on the other hand, is impossible, because we depend on something given to our faculty of sensible intuition for the content of our knowledge. The Copernican hypothesis both explains science and protects faith. This means, however, that the objects of our knowledge are mere appearances and not things-in-themselves. Thus science is in no position either to affirm or to deny the existence – essential to morality – of Freedom, God, and the Immortal Soul as things-in-themselves. Yet the price of this solution is resignation to the impossibility of objective metaphysical knowledge.

The gap between the mind's conceptual demands and its intuitive achievements – a gap externalized in the two-world ontology of the Dissertation – is internalized as dialectic in the *Critique*.

In its final form, Kant's anthropology of reason has an unmistakably Rousseauian cast. Reason is by nature vexed with problems that are occasioned by its desire for the unconditioned. Previous philosophers placed themselves in the service of this desire. Kant, however, insists that reason submit this desire to the discipline of self-consistency. Reason cannot trust its desire; its error has been supposing that it can have what it wants.

The first step of critical philosophy lies in doubting nature's beneficence: reason is by nature burdened. The second step lies in recognizing that burden as inevitable: what is not reason's fault is not in reason's power to change. The third step lies in distinguishing the burden, which is inevitable, from the error, which is not. It is not the burden of metaphysical problems which makes men err, but rather trust in their solubility, trust which reason has the power to give up.

But why does reason cleave so obstinately to its trust? Reason expects (as an infant expects) its desires to be satisfied. It asserts a *right* to satisfaction, a right to the knowledge for which it longs. This claim is, however, opposed by a necessity established by reason's own principle of self-consistency. Reason's claim to know the unconditioned leads to contradictions which undermine reason's claim to know anything at all. Reason finds legitimation only when it ceases to expect that which it cannot itself secure. Reason, which includes both desire and judgment, must learn to discipline its desire according to its judgment. In the first *Critique*, Kant repeatedly compares reason both to a judge and to a defendant, a conceit which makes more sense once we realize that it is reason as judgment which sits in judgment, reason as desire which stands before the bar.

Through self-scrutiny, reason comes to recognize that by its very nature it sets itself a task which it cannot complete. Yet does not this planned futility in itself constitute a kind of inconsistency? If so, it disappears once we cease to regard the task as the vehicle of satisfaction or happiness, and see it as the vehicle of freedom. It disappears when reason chooses as its end, not happiness, but freedom. In making the choice, reason ceases to be theoretical and becomes practical. The mode in which it makes this choice, in accordance with the categorical imperative, is the subject of the following chapter.

3
The moral turn

1 / CRITICISM AND MORAL EXPERIENCE

Freedom, leaving our actions, as it does, quite undetermined, is a terrible thing. Kant
Lectures on Ethics

Virtue will avow nothing but what is done by and for itself alone. Montaigne
Essays I 37

The fundamental intention of critical philosophy is to facilitate the redirection of rational interest from happiness to freedom. This philosophically and morally decisive turn of mind was initiated in the *Critique of Pure Reason* (1781). It was carried forward in several short essays on enlightenment and history and in the popular *Groundwork of the Metaphysics of Morals* (1785). These moral works are not, however, critical in the precise sense of establishing and justifying the extent of reason's activity, nor do they explicitly establish their connection with the critical enterprise as a whole. In the spring of 1787, while he was preparing a second edition of the *Critique of Pure Reason*, Kant began the *Critique of Practical Reason*, which he completed nine months later.[1] The *Critique of Practical Reason* is both critical and moral. To its elaboration and clarification of the turn to freedom this chapter is devoted. Reason, in Kant's view, must assert its rights against itself. In choosing freedom, reason transcends external opposition only to discover opposition within.

Practical criticism, like its theoretical counterpart, is self-criticism; but it is self-criticism of a different sort. The first *Critique* argued its case from the single premise of critical or reflective self-consciousness. The second *Critique* must take as its point of departure a special kind of experience which cannot be deduced from the nature of self-consciousness. This special kind of experience, which already contains the essence of the practical, is the moral experience familiar in one way or another to every human being.

Moral philosophy begins with 'ordinary rational knowledge of morality,'[2] that is, with the considered moral understanding of ordinary men. As theoretical criticism asked 'How is experience possible?' so practical criticism asks 'How is moral experience possible?' If we do not already recognize ourselves as sharing in this experience, there is no way Kant can make us comprehend it, let alone accede to its existence. In order to understand morality we must ourselves exhibit a practical turn of mind.

1 Lewis White Beck *A Commentary on Kant's Critique of Practical Reason* 17
2 *Groundwork*, IV 393 (61)

The *Groundwork* of the Metaphysic of Morals presents the ordinary moral experience which a critique of practical reason must presuppose.[3] This experience begins with an undemonstrable and irrefutable assessment of good will as unconditionally good. It is impossible, states the first sentence of the *Groundwork*, for us to think of anything as good without qualification besides a good will.[4] The *Groundwork* starts with a discussion of unqualified or unconditioned goodness. Relative goods, such as health, wealth, and moderate temperament, derive their value from the ends they serve.[5] They are good *for* something else, not in themselves.[6] The reader's assessment of good will as unconditionally good carries him beyond the first *Critique*, in which the unconditioned remained a taunting cipher. Already something unconditioned is not only thinkable but practically real.

Moral value attaches only to that which a person can do or omit – that is to say, only to willing itself. If nature is niggardly and the will wholly lacking in power to carry out *its* intentions, if by the will's 'utmost efforts it still accomplishes nothing, and only good will is left ... even then it would still

---

3 *Crit. Prac.*, V 4 (3). The forming of a definite concept of morality and freedom (just what the first *Critique* seemed to say could not be done) is thus the first task of practical criticism. To the *Groundwork* belongs the first stage in the performance of this task; for upon the *Groundwork* the second *Critique* depends 'to give preliminary acquaintance with the concept of duty' and 'to justify a definite formula of it.'

In the *Critique of Practical Reason* Kant himself makes clear the function which the *Groundwork* serves within the scheme of practical criticism in general. It might be thought that a critique of pure reason, which denied knowledge and made room for faith, left little or nothing by way of criticism to be done. In the preface to his second *Critique*, however, he acknowledges 'objections' to the *Critique of Pure Reason*, the 'most considerable' of which turn on two points: '... first, the reality of the categories as applied to noumena, which is denied in theoretical knowledge but affirmed in practical; and, second, the paradoxical demand to regard one's self, as subject to freedom, as noumenon, and yet from the point of view of nature to think of one's self as a phenomenon in one's own empirical consciousness. So long as one had no definite concept of morality and freedom, no conjecture could be made concerning what the noumenon was which should be posited as the ground of the alleged appearance, and even whether it was possible to form a concept of it, since all the concepts of the pure understanding in their theoretical employment had already been assigned exclusively to mere appearances. Only a detailed *Critique of Practical Reason* can set aside all these misconceptions and put in a clear light the consistency which constitutes its chief merit' (V 6–7 (6–7)).
4 *Groundwork*, IV 393 (61); the will also proves to be itself the unconditioned cause vainly sought as an object of knowledge.
5 Ibid. 396 (64)
6 Ibid. 394–6, 428, 434–5 (62–4, 96, 102)

shine like a jewel for its own sake as something that has full value in itself.'⁷ Virtue must be measured by motives rather than by success. Our success depends on nature, our intentions on ourselves alone.

The moral quality of our actions is, to this extent, divorced from the effects at which our actions aim. To ease his reader over the perplexities of moral common sense, which confutes our natural interest in success, Kant resorts to a conjectural and by now familiar teleology. If success or happiness were the final aim of man, nature would have left us under the tutelage of instinct, providing us with ends and means alike. Reason, if we still possessed it, would not guide our actions – already well-directed – but rather enable us to contemplate 'the happy disposition of [our] nature,' to admire, enjoy, and be grateful for it.⁸ Reason would, in short, fall easily into that role which Kant's early works set forth as a self-abnegating ideal. If happiness were naturally ours, reason could contemplate nature gratefully, without the hard-won and unnatural indifference to its own fate which Kant's earlier ideal demanded. Men are not made for happiness but for freedom. We are distinguished from the beasts by our capacity to choose our own ends. Human reason is not made for contemplation but for action. Men plan their own lives and select themselves the means towards their self-chosen ends.⁹ Because nature does not guide it, moral experience is inevitably jarring and disjointed. Morality draws us up against nature, and most especially against our own nature.

Moral experience, according to the *Groundwork*, implies inner conflict. Our concept of a will 'estimable in itself and good apart from any further end'¹ emerges from our concept of duty, which 'includes that of a good will, exposed, however, to certain subjective limitations and obstacles.'² The hostility of our nature to morality (a hostility which is, theoretically speaking, merely a possibility) proves in practice to be the vehicle of morality's accessibility. Only when opposing inclinations throw duty into relief is it fully visible. The inclinations must be sacrificed in order for the moral character of our acts to stand revealed to us. Only in 'paying the highest price' in natural goods do we experience the possibility of inestimable worth. Such sacrifice is not the precondition of moral worth; duty need not hurt. It is, however, a precondition for our sensing of an act as worthy. The sacrifice of natural inclination, the highest price that we can pay, renders palpable an otherwise subjectively

7 Ibid. 394 (62)
8 Ibid. 395 (63)
9 Ibid.
1 Ibid. 397 (64)
2 Ibid. 397 (65)

obscure distinction between the immoral and the moral. Conflict between desire and duty, want and ought, is not a proof of moral worth but a route to its initial apprehension.[3]

Duty calls upon the regard of reason for its own self-legislating power, a power which is the only conceivable source of virtue. Kant ascribes the moral quality of our actions to the *a priori* legislative form of willing rather than to its object or material content. As understanding makes formal laws which govern nature, so reason makes *a priori* laws to rule itself. Kant combines the finding of the first *Critique*, that reason is a spontaneous law-maker, with the conviction of ordinary moral understanding, that worth lies only in what we freely do. Through the moral law we command ourselves to act only on maxims which we could at the same time will to become universal laws.[4] Duty conflates necessity and freedom; it is, in short, a 'necessitating' freedom, obliging us to act 'out of esteem [*Achtung*] for the law.'[5]

Esteem is the positive complement of the negative capacity for sacrifice which awakens the will to its moral power. Esteem is our regard for that which 'has no price,' that which 'outweighs' and so compels us to give up all that we naturally hold dear. Esteem subjectively marks the escape of reason from what Kant in his early writings called the 'economy of nature.' By sacrificing all, reason leaves measured worth behind and gains a sublime access to infinity.[6] In his early writings Kant expressed dissatisfaction with a natural economy which little valued man. The first *Critique* revealed nature herself to be in part reason's creature. This discovery, which cost philosophy so many pains, is to some extent already present in common moral understanding. Popular morality implicitly acknowledges that the value of all things in nature is strictly relative to the moral worth of man. Man, however, is nature's creature, too, and experiences his own worth only by denying nature in himself, this self-enhancing self-denial the very model of what Kant elsewhere calls sublimity.[7]

Practical criticism begins with our subjective impressions of morality. These impressions do not, however, in themselves supply us with concepts adequate to our sense of duty. Experience does not give proof of any moral virtue in the world.[8] And as our knowledge is restricted to this world, our

---

3 Ibid. 398 (66)
4 Ibid. 402, 421 (70, 88)
5 Ibid. 400 (68) (my translation)
6 Ibid. 426, 442 (93, 110). For a more detailed discussion of the relation of sublimity to morality see below, 116, note 6.
7 See CJ, part 1, book 2
8 *Groundwork*, IV 407 (74)

deserts lie finally beyond our ken. The moral quality of one's own acts cannot be known with certainty.

It might seem, then, that morality requires no philosophy after all. This Kant emphatically denies. Knowledge is not altogether foreign to good willing: to will well we must know what to will; and while this knowledge is in principle available to ordinary reason, it is also easily corrupted.[9] As suggested in Kant's earlier works, the role of moral philosophy is not so much to inform common belief as to reform it according to its own first principles. Such reformation requires knowledge, but knowledge for the sake of practice. Practical philosophy is both theoretically and morally imperative.

Morality is, according to the *Groundwork*, an enterprise of reason. And the concept of absolute worth indicates what sort of rational enterprise it must be. Since we cannot derive our notion of absolute worth from an empirical realm in which all value is relative, our moral concepts must 'have their seat and origin in reason completely *a priori*.' By 'completely *a priori*' Kant means to distinguish the absolute purity of practical philosophy from the relative purity of speculative philosophy, which was subject to the special nature of human reason. The concept of absolute worth indicates the absolutely *a priori* character of morality; for by no 'right can we bring what is perhaps valid only under the contingent conditions of humanity into unlimited esteem.'[1] In their notion of absolute worth men discover a potential link between their own finite rationality and unlimited rationality as such, the first intimation of their citizenship in a community of fully rational beings.

Philosophy cannot, however, lose touch entirely with the merely human. The purely rational will remains ideal for us. 'The relation of objective laws to a will not good through and through is conceived as one in which the will of a rational being, although it is determined by principles of reason, does not necessarily follow these principles in virtue of its own nature.'[2] Our relation to the unconditioned law is somehow conditioned by us. The moral law, which a purely rational or holy will would invariably follow, is laid on us as a categorical command or imperative. The moral imperative, according to the *Groundwork*, expresses 'the relation of objective laws of willing' to 'the subjective imperfection of the human will.'[3] Morality implies an inner revolution, which, in this life at least, is never complete.

---

9 Ibid. 404–5 (72–3)
1 Ibid. 408 (76) (my translation)
2 Ibid. 413 (80)
3 Ibid. 414 (81)

2 / OBJECTIVITY AND THE MORAL LAW

The categorical imperative commands us to '*act only on that maxim through which [we] can at the same time will that it should become a universal law.*' This moral imperative is a 'fact of reason' requiring no further proof or deduction. The fundamental problem of practical criticism is not to demonstrate the binding character of the law, but rather to explain its possibility. The central task of book 1 (the Analytic) of the *Critique of Practical Reason* is to explain how such unconditional moral necessity is possible. Kant assumes from the beginning that unconditional necessity must have its source in reason, and hence 'in us.' The necessities of theoretical reason were derived in part from without, or more precisely from an 'outside' which both defined and was defined by reason's limits. But to ground practical necessity in reason's limits would imply a conditionality and dependency which the pure unconditionality of the moral law does not allow. A moral law conditioned by the frailty of humanity could not impart to the obedient an unconditioned moral worth. A moral law whose necessity derived from the peculiarities of 'human nature' could not claim superiority over the necessary but hardly unconditioned truths of theory. The problem for practical criticism becomes to explain how a law can have its source in us without thereby being merely 'subjective,' to explain, in short, the possibility of practical objectivity.

According to the first theorem of practical reason, 'all practical principles which presuppose an object [material] of the faculty of desire as the determining ground of will are without exception empirical and can furnish no [objective] practical laws.'[4] Theoretical objectivity implied and depended on the possibility and existence of things external to reason. Practical objectivity cannot be so derived. Practical reason does not grasp the existence of objects as facts, but instead sets them forth as goals of action. For practical reason in the strictest sense, objects are not facts but merely possibilities, the actualization of which depends on the activity of reason itself. Reason in its practical employment lacks the external, objective correlate in which all of its theoretical necessities were ultimately grounded. There is a further reason why practical objectivity cannot derive from the objects to which reason addresses itself. If it is to have morally imputable causality, rational desire cannot be reactive. If the power to determine action lay in the content or object of will, the 'form' of willing would serve only as a kind of structuring machine, awaiting animation from without. Kant rejects Plato's belief that objects can

[4] *Crit. Prac.*, V 21 (19)

rationally elicit desire. How then is Kant's notion of the relation between practical reason and its object to be understood? The object of practical reason is the reality of an idea whose actualization is a thing in the world which reason sets before itself as a goal. The relation between reason and its object is dynamic, reason moving towards an actualization which, securing the object as a thing of nature, obliterates it as an object of desire.[5]

Practical objectivity does, however, have an external dimension. Because practical necessity is grounded in reason alone, it can be defined as a necessity shared by other rational beings. The *Critique of Practical Reason* begins with such a definition:

Practical principles are propositions which contain a general determination [*Bestimmung*] of the will, having under it several practical rules. They are subjective, or maxims, when the condition is regarded by the subject as valid only for his own will. They are objective, or practical laws, when the condition [*Bedingung*] is recognized as objective, i.e., as valid for the will of every rational being.[6]

Theoretical reason determined objects through its dependence on what is given in sensation; practical reason, on the other hand, is a kind of 'self-determination' – not, to be sure, a determination of self as an object of knowledge, but rather a determination of self as will bent on action. The moral law adds to the negative concept of freedom (elucidated in the first *Critique*) a positive definition of reason as determining the will directly 'through the condition of the universal lawful form of the maxims of the will.' The moral law gives 'objective reality' to this concept of causality. In this way, reason, 'which with its ideas always became transcendent when proceeding in a speculative manner,' can also for the first time be given 'objective reality.' Reason attains objectivity as 'an efficient cause through ideas.'[7]

Practical objectivity has two aspects, one stemming from the corroborating universality of a community of rational beings,[8] the other stemming from a

---

5 See ibid. 9n (9n) and CJ, V 186–7, 177–8n (part 1, 27 16n). Kant's definition in the *Critique of Judgment* of desire as a faculty which by means of its representations is the cause of the actuality of the objects of those representations blurs the distinction between anticipating the completion of a goal and its actual completion.
6 *Crit. Prac.*, V 19 (17)
7 Ibid. 48 (49). Cf. *Reflexionen* #2519, #2537, where Kant notes that moral freedom is a kind of non-reciprocal causality.
8 Kantian universalization differs from the principles of universalization recently put forward by thinkers such as H.M. Hare, M.T. Singer, and Allan Gewirth. On some of these differences see Onora Nell *Acting on Principle: An Essay on Kantian Ethics* (New York, Columbia

causality whereby reason exercises its practical sovereignty over objects in the natural world. Theoretical objectivity rested in a distinction between outer and inner experience, a distinction dependent both on something 'given' to sensation and on the Transcendental Object. Without encountering resistance both on the sensible and the most abstract level, reason could not experience objects, indeed could not experience at all. The limits of reason were defined by this fundamental resistance, less visible than tangible. Unable to intuit its object immediately, reason was forced to construct its knowledge by projecting a form onto an imposing matter, forced to illuminate by its own artificial light stuff fundamentally opaque. This opacity erected a wall around reason, for ever preventing it from casting its light on things as they are. To us, 'intelligibles' remained unintelligible. In practice reason determines its objects by determining itself. In practice the one thing-in-itself to which reason has access is reason itself. The never-never land of intelligibles, vacant in theory, is populated in practice by a kingdom of intelligent beings.[9] The transition from intelligibility to intelligence marks the difference between theoretical and practical objectivity, between an objectivity grounded in the conflict between subject and object and one grounded in self-conflict, communal co-operation, and ultimate self-mastery.

In making this transition from theory to practice reason embraces its proper vocation. In the first *Critique* Kant showed how profoundly limited reason is in its pursuit of knowledge, the unconditioned knowledge that it seeks being for ever denied to it, and its conditional knowledge being a mere by-product of that pursuit. Kant showed that reason is in essence less a faculty of knowledge, for which it is dependent on the given, than a capacity to set itself tasks through the generation of principles or laws for which it is dependent only on itself. 'Everything in nature works in accordance with laws. Only a rational being has the power to act in accordance with his idea of laws.'[1] How then, according to Kant, do theoretical and practical task-setting differ? Not at all, in so far as theory is regarded as a purposive activity. All rational activity, in which reason takes an interest in something, is ultimately practical.[2] To set

---

University Press 1975) 14–31. Hare insists (contrary to Kant) on the 'moral neutrality' of his principle. Singer supplements his with utilitarian premises that Kant would not admit. Gewirth attempts to derive a principle of universal right from the 'necessity' of our desire for certain general means, a necessity that Kant would find inadequate as a basis for the moral obligation that right entails.

9 Kant's move from being to being*s* is helped along by his understanding of the theoretical category of 'community' as a '*commercium* of substances.' On the articulation of substance into substances see below, 136–7.

1 *Groundwork*, IV 412 (80)
2 *Crit. prac.*, V 121 (126)

73 The moral turn

oneself a task or purpose is to take an interest. The purposiveness of reason is itself a kind of self-necessitation. In theory as in practice reason accomplishes its tasks through rules or imperatives which reason itself generates. Imperatives are statements 'that express a possible free action by which a certain end is to be made actual.'[3] Not all ends, however, bind unconditionally. Ends which aim to satisfy human needs are, to this extent, conditioned by these needs and bind only subjectively. As finite rational beings we in fact adopt such purposes as our own; but we do not choose them in a full and uncompromising sense. Those ends which we adopt responsively are conditional on our susceptibility to forces outside ourselves. Their necessity depends in part on conditions over which we have incomplete control. It follows that only self-necessitation in the strictest sense can bind us unconditionally.

Conditional necessities are expressed by 'hypothetical imperatives.' Such imperatives presuppose some end as given and then command us to do all that we can to achieve it. Kant calls such imperatives analytic because they express what is already contained in our willing of an end as an effect, namely, 'the causality of [our] self as an acting cause' or 'the use of means.'[4] Hypothetical imperatives express the analytic rationality of an acting being: 'Who wills the end, wills also (necessarily, if he accords with reason) the ... means which are in his power.'[5] Hypothetical imperatives exhibit reason's power to generate procedures which lie dormant until stimulated from without. Like other practical rules, hypothetical imperatives are, in what concerns the will, tautologies of practical reason.

Unconditional self-necessitation requires more than practical analyticity. Imperatives which enjoin unconditionally, or categorically, require an *a priori* synthesis, in which (negative) freedom from the dictates of nature is combined through the moral law with (positive) freedom or 'autonomy.'[6] The *a priori* synthesis contained in the moral law implies self-unity, much as the *a priori* synthesis of understanding implied a 'transcendental unity of apperception.'[7] Kant calls this self-unity personality, a term which designates the integrity of the self as a morally responsible agent. The transcendental unity of apperception described the self merely as it appears to us and must appear for experience to be possible; personality on the contrary characterizes the self as it truly is. This objective unity of self asserted through the moral law 'stands against' the subjective duality of self which affords access to that law. It is

---

3 Immanuel Kant *Logic*, IX 86 (94)
4 *Groundwork*, IV 417 (85)
5 Ibid. For a discussion of some difficulties with Kant's formulation, see Beck *Kant's Critique of Practical Reason* 86.
6 *Crit. Prac.*, V 43, 48 (44, 49)
7 Cf. *Reflexion* #7204.

because of this duality that the moral law confronts us as an imperative, obliging us to do what a pure rational being would do without being told. If the characteristic mode of pure practical reason is unity, or obedience to the law it makes, the characteristic mode of human reason is duality, or choice. We experience our objective power of self-determination as a subjective conflict between duty and desire, esteem and happiness. Before it can join in a community of rational beings sovereign over objects in the world, reason must objectify itself.

3 / THE PROBLEM OF HAPPINESS

Happiness is less an end for reason than an insoluble problem. 'To be happy,' says Kant, 'is necessarily the desire of every rational but finite being.'[8] The rational 'being of need' naturally desires the satisfaction of those needs and finds in his neediness a ground and guide of action. These needs, however, are inadequate as guides of rational action; for finite reason cannot adequately comprehend them.

Life, according to Kant, arouses a succession of desires neither entirely foreseeable nor entirely satiable.[9] Extrapolating from his endless succession of needs and desires, man imagines a state in which such impositions would cease and calls it happiness. It is, indeed, the special gift of man to be able so to imagine. Man's deepest grievance against nature stems not from pain (which he shares with the beasts) but from his own capacity to anticipate pain. The Hobbesian fear of violent death is for Kant only a most extreme example of man's general anxiety (*Sorge*) about the future, brought on by his capacity to imagine consequences.[1] To the aches and pains of animal existence is added a specifically human anxiety about miseries to come. The aches and pains are feelings, and can, at the level of feeling, be satisfied. The general anxiety, however, is unrelievable; to such relief no feeling could be adequate. Reason

---

8 *Crit. Prac.*, V 25 (24)
9 Man's 'own nature is not so constituted as to rest or be satisfied in any possession or enjoyment whatever' (CJ, IV 430 (part 2, 93)); cf. Hobbes *Leviathan* chapter 11.
1 'Conjectural Beginning,' VIII 113–14 (57–8): 'Conscious expectation of the future,' that is to say, our 'capacity for facing up in the present to the often very distant future, instead of being wholly absorbed by the enjoyment of the present, is the most decisive mark of the human's advantage. It enables man to prepare himself for distant aims according to his role as a human being. But at the same time it is also the most inexhaustible source of cares and troubles, aroused by the uncertainty of his future – cares and troubles of which animals are altogether free.' Cf. *Anthropology*, VII 276 (142): the greatest sensuous enjoyment, that involves no element at all of aversion, is resting after work, when we are in good health.

75 The moral turn

can neither relieve its anxiety nor dismiss the conscious dependency which is its source.[2]

Happiness for man means carefree expectation of the future. Since the future is out of man's control, however, he has good reason to fear it. What one cannot control it is rational to distrust. That reason can solve any problem of its own making was the slogan of the first *Critique*. That we cannot depend on the beneficence of external powers could well be the slogan of the second.

Happiness requires not merely the satisfaction of this or that desire, but a totality of satisfaction. At the highest level of abstraction happiness implies a power to satisfy all possible desires, a consciousness of self-sufficiency. To finite reason such power is denied. Its finitude in thought and in action stem from the same source: dependency on the given. All desires (except rational desire) arise out of the contingencies of experience on which the satisfaction of these desires depends. All the elements of our concept of happiness are in fact empirical.

Kant did not always regard happiness as wholly empirical. 'The matter of happiness,' he stated in early reflections, 'is sensible, but the form is intellectual.'[3] Nor did he always regard happiness *per se* as antipathic to morality. On the contrary, Kant for a time hoped that the form of happiness could itself serve as a practical law of reason. In early reflections he presented self-contentment as the formal or *a priori* condition of happiness. 'Happiness,' he wrote, 'is properly not the [greatest] sum of pleasures, but rather the pleasure [*Lust*] in consciousness of contentment with one's own power [*Selbstmacht*].'[4] This rational happiness, or pleasure in *Selbstmacht*, Kant for a time took as an end-in-itself. Virtue, he argued, may have the privilege of bringing about the greatest happiness: its highest worth, however, lies not in its serving as a means but in its leading to self-contentment.[5]

In later reflections, however, Kant distinguished between happiness and the worthiness to be happy, identifying only the latter as truly moral.[6] Kant's final teaching lies far closer to these later reflections. His moral theory comes

---

2 *Crit. Prac.*, v 22 (20)
3 *Reflexion* #7202
4 Ibid.
5 Ibid. 'Happiness is not really the [greatest] sum of amusements (*Vergnügen*] but rather pleasure [*Lust*] to be content in consciousness of one's own power [*Bewusstsein seiner Selbstmacht zufrieden zu sein*]; at least this is the essential formal condition of happiness, although other material (as through experience) is necessary.' Kant also speaks of 'principles of ethics from the agreement of freedom with the necessary conditions of happiness in general, i.e., from the general self-acting [*selbstthätigen*] principle of happiness' (*Reflexion* #7200). The notion that happiness itself has some power to move us never disappears entirely from Kant's analysis.
6 *Reflexion* #7242

to emphasize the discontinuity between happiness and self-contentment. His abandonment of his efforts to understand happiness as a synthesis of both these parts should refute critics who explain his moral theory as a eudaimonism of autonomy.[7] But these efforts also suggest that non-eudaimonism is a rather late development in his moral thought, the final and successful solution to a problem with which he had long struggled. Kant's final teaching separates the two elements which at an earlier time he yoked together as the form and matter of a single idea. Ultimately he construes happiness as just that sum of pleasures which he once called the material of happiness. He comes to argue that happiness is empirical through and through. As the 'consciousness of the agreeableness of life which without interruption accompanies [one's] whole existence' the 'ideal' of happiness suggests the self-contentment which he once took to be its 'form.'[8] Even this ideal, however, is only the outer limit to an (indefinite) sum of pleasures for each of which we depend on something other than ourselves. By setting uninterrupted agreeableness as an upper limit to pleasure, Kant suggests the radical deficiency of even our most pleasurable experiences. Either these pleasures are themselves not quite agreeable or they represent a surfeit which only serves to glut us.[9] Happiness does not lie in one (or many) ecstatic moment(s), but in the extended 'agreeableness' or 'acceptability' (*Annehmlichkeit*) of life. It is not an ecstasy but merely contentment with our lot.[1] That such acceptability should set an unreachable limit to our pursuit of happiness suggests how far from acceptable Kant thought the natural condition of man to be.[2]

---

7 See, for example, Ralph Mason Blake 'Why Not Hedonism? A Protest' *International Journal of Ethics* 37 (October 1926): 1–18.

8 *Crit. Prac.*, v 22 (20); *Groundwork* IV 418 (86)

9 Cf. *Anthropology*, VII 105 (237) where Kant urges young men to ration enjoyment so as to keep it as much as possible in prospect; 'The ripeness of old age,' he observes, 'which never lets us regret having done without a physical gratification, will guarantee you, even in this sacrifice, a capital of contentment that does not depend on the contingencies or on the law of nature.' Kant later adds that more men die suddenly from unrestrained joy than from grief (255 (122)).

1 *Crit. Prac.*, v 25 (24)

2 According to Kant, pain predominates over pleasure. Not pleasure but pain directly prompts us to move; and movement, given the flux of time and experience, is the precondition of life. This pessimistic physiology helps to explain his statement in the *Critique of Judgment* that the 'value of life for us, if it is estimated by what we enjoy ... sinks below zero' (v 434n (part 2, 97n)). It also clarifies somewhat his puzzling argument in the *Groundwork* (v 421–2 (89)) that a policy of committing suicide whenever life promises more pain than pleasure could not be a law of nature. For, according to Kant, life *always* promises more pain than pleasure. The universalization of such a policy would be incompatible, given Kant's understanding of

77 The moral turn

We may regard our demand for happiness as a formal law of action. In fact, however, this demand determines nothing specific concerning what is to be done.³ Happiness is an ideal not of reason but of imagination. It does not systematically guide the will, but merely randomly incites it. The aspect of our ideal of happiness which incites us to action is not its so-called form, but rather the innumerable particular and unforeseeable desires whose satisfaction constitutes its 'matter.'

In its pursuit of happiness, the faculty of desire 'is determined by the agreeableness which the subject expects from the actual existence of [some] object.'⁴ The name of this feeling or expectation which incites to action is 'pleasure' (*Lust*). Unlike cognitive sensations, feelings are essentially subjective. They refer not to the objective constitution of things, but to our subjective 'susceptibility.'⁵ The colour or hardness of a thing pertains to it, its pleasurableness (or painfulness) to us. Sensations express our transcendental receptivity to something beyond experience, feelings our empirical susceptibility to things within experience. Feelings indicate the relationship between our own body and other bodies in the world. Unlike sensations, they are immediate calls to action, responses to the presence (*Dasein*) of an object to which we are vulnerable. The feelings of pleasure and pain express our dependence on things; indeed they constitute our most direct experience of this dependence.

Unlike cognitive sensations, feelings contribute nothing to our knowledge of the objective world. At the level of cognition we are the legislators of nature; at the level of feeling we are merely its dependents. At this level the necessity of natural laws, laws of our own making, is overwhelmed by the contingency of their effect on us as natural beings. The duality of man amounts to just this, that the objective world has a necessity and certainty that

---

physiology, with life as such. (Cf. H.J. Paton (*The Categorical Imperative: A Study in Kant's Moral Philosophy* 154) who mistakenly relies on teleology rather than physiology to substantiate Kant's argument.) Few passages illustrate more clearly what Kant takes to be the fundamental irrationality of eudaimonism. In pursuing our own happiness, we are like businessmen who strive to minimize their losses, knowing they can never turn a profit. On the bodily 'economy' and the relation between pleasure/pain and profit/loss, see *Anthropology*, VII 230–2 (99–100); and Kant *Menschenkunde* (Hildesheim, Georg Olms Verlag 1976) part 1, 45. The comparison is first made in Kant's 'Essay to Introduce into Philosophy the Concept of Negative Quantity.' Pain is not, as the rationalists taught, a mere absence of pleasure (or of reality) but a real presence in its own right. Cf. Olivier Reboul *Kant et le problème du mal* (Montreal, Les Presses de l'Université de Montréal 1971) 81.

3 *Crit. Prac.*, V 25 (24)
4 Ibid. 22 (20)
5 CJ, V 204–5 (part 1, 42–3)

our own needs and feelings inevitably lack. Feelings, which belong exclusively to inner experience, lack the external or 'spatial' component which characterizes experience of objects.[6] But if feelings are so radically 'subjective' how can they incite to action in the objective world? They can do so only because experience teaches us to associate our feelings with natural objects which imagination allows us to anticipate. This conjunction of feeling and imagination raises the faculty of desire from instinct to genuine (if not yet fully rational) choice.[7] Because its object is maintained and extended by imagination, desire can subsist after the external stimuli which aroused it have abated. Imagination, like free choice, is uniquely human. Unlike the beasts, whose action is a foregone conclusion, man can choose among his desires, forgo present for the sake of future pleasures and so live according to a self-chosen plan.[8]

So long, however, as our plans are grounded in the pursuit of pleasure, we lack an objective law to guide our actions. 'We cannot know, *a priori*, of the idea of any object, whatever the nature of this idea, whether it will be associated with pleasure or displeasure or will be merely indifferent.'[9] Happiness can supply to practice no objective principle. For 'where one places his happiness is a question of the particular feeling of pleasure or displeasure in each man, and even of the differences in needs occasioned by changes of feeling in one and the same man.'[1] Practical objectivity requires not just unanimity but necessary unanimity. Even if 'finite rational beings were unanimous in the kind of objects their feelings of pleasure and pain had ... they could not set up the principle of self-love as a practical law, for the unanimity itself would be merely contingent.'[2] Necessary unanimity is the test by means of which we free ourselves from practical subjectivity and the egoistic pursuit it renders futile.

Kant decisively rejects his early understanding of *Selbstmacht* as a component of objective law. According to his ultimate understanding, *Selbstmacht* is like all other pleasures, which differ from one another only in degree. No kind of joy is privileged over any other.[3] *Annehmlichkeit* is the common denominator which reduces all pleasures, from the coarsest to the most refined, to a common measure. Kant plays out the calculus of rational

6 See A/802 = B/830, A/28–A/31, B/44–B/45.
7 'Conjectural Beginning,' VIII 110–11 (54–5)
8 Ibid. 112 (56)
9 *Crit. Prac.*, V 21 (20): 'thus any such determining ground of choice must always be empirical ...'
1 Ibid. 25 (24–5)
2 Ibid. 26 (25)
3 Ibid. 23 (22)

79 The moral turn

hedonism to its mercantile conclusion. If agreeableness is the final measure, there can be no higher and lower agreeableness, only more and less. The one-dimensionality of hedonism is related to its subjectivity. To the ardent pleasure-seeker, the nature of his object, independent of the pleasure it can afford him, is irrelevant.[4] Nor does he consider the subjective source of his pleasure:

As the man who wants to spend money does not care whether [its matter] the gold was mined in the mountains or washed from the sand, provided it is accepted [*angenommen*] everywhere as having the same value, so also no man asks, when he is concerned only with the *Annehmlichkeit* of life, whether the ideas come from sense or from the understanding; he asks only how much and how great is the pleasure which they will afford him over the longest time.[5]

Like money, *Annehmlichkeit* provides a common measure of value. Value resides not in the source of the material, be it pleasure or gold, but in its 'acceptability.'[6] Planning his life like a ledgerbook, the rational hedonist defines a personal economy which purports to measure all things but cannot establish unconditioned worth. 'Self-loving,'[7] he appears to measure all things in relation to himself; hedonism is also egoism (*Selbstlieb*). The hedonist measures all things in terms of their agreeableness or acceptability to him. But this measurement begs the question of what he ought to accept. The egoist maximizes pleasure as a merchant maximizes profit and a nation wealth.[8] Like money, the objects he pursues derive their value from an 'acceptability' that is merely contingent. His calculus cannot establish the

---

4 CJ, V 205–7 (part 1, 44–6)
5 *Crit. Prac.*, V 23 (22)
6 For a discussion of the difference between desire and mere approval, see CJ, V 204–11 (part 1, 42–50).
7 *Crit. Prac.*, V 22 (20)
8 The indistinctness of the boundary between Kant's personal and interpersonal or political economies presages the assumption by later utilitarians of the intersubjective commensurability of pleasure. Even modern economic theorists who reject such commensurability (e.g., A. Downs, J.M. Buchanan, G. Tullock) assume intrasubjective commensurability, as embodied in their model of 'economic man' who maximizes utility through the 'rational' ordering of preferences. Rawls' *Theory of Justice* is a moral theory based in part on such a model. Kant and eighteenth-century economic theorists such as Turgot, with whose physiocratic school Kant was acquainted, recognized that both personal and political economy begged the question – for Kant ultimately a moral question – of objective or true worth. (See Turgot *Ecrits économiques* [Paris], Calmann-Lévy [1970] 233–49.) For Kant on the physiocrats Necker, Schmalz, and Schlettwein, see letter to Johann Heinrich Tieftrunk, 12 July 1797, GS XII 183; letter to Johann Schultz, 9 January 1798, GS XII 231; XII 362–8; letter from Conrad Stang, 2 October 1796, GS XII 100; *Reflexion* #6345.

value of the self which grounds it. This incapacity to establish the objective value (or worthiness) of the self renders the principle of happiness in any form unsuitable to serve as practical law. Happiness, as Kant noted, is not the same as worthiness; self-love is not self-esteem; and good reputation is not real worth.[9]

According to Kant, every object which can be an end for us has either a 'worth' or a 'price.' All ends whose value is relative to universal human needs and inclinations have a 'market price'; those ends whose value stems not from universal need but rather from idiosyncratic taste have a 'fancy price.'[1] What all such objects share is their dispensability. To have a price is to have an equivalent, or a counterpart of equal value.[2] For Kant, much as for Adam Smith, whose works he studied carefully,[3] universal human need establishes a natural market whereby objects of desire are priced according to the cost of the human labour which produced them. This price fluctuates according to demand, that is, according to the degree to which potential customers prefer to meet their needs in less costly ways. Each potential customer weighs the utility of the good against the burdens of its cost and so calculates the value of the good relative to his own ends. The utility of goods depends upon the subjective needs of the potential buyer, the cost upon the amount of labour spent to produce the good: 'Wealth, in so far as it can be acquired by money, is properly only the sum of the industry or applied labour with which men pay each other ...'[4] Thus labour, too, has a price,[5] and likewise human beings in their capacity as labourers. Fifty years before Marx, Kant bemoans the reduction of men to the status of commodities, interchangeable with other instruments and deriving their value from the contingencies of human desire. In such a system all values are relative. In the market system established by a subjective willing, everything – including ourselves – receives a market price.[6]

---

9 *Reflexion* #7242
1 *Groundwork*, IV 434–5 (102)
2 Ibid.
3 See, for example, DR, VI 289; *Reflexion* #1355; see also Ritter *Der Rechtsgedanke Kants nach den frühen Quellen* 140, 243, 272.
4 DR, VI 288
5 Kant has Smith in mind when in the *Doctrine of Right* he writes that 'price is the public judgment about the value of a thing' in relation to the abundance of some universally agreed upon substance, making possible the universal interchange of the products of human labour (VI 289; see *Groundwork*, IV 434–5 (102).
6 Cf. Hobbes *Leviathan* chapter 10: 'The ... WORTH of a man, is as of all other things, his price; that is to say, as much as would be given for the use of his power: and therefore is not absolute; but dependant on the need and judgement of another.'

81 The moral turn

For Kant, however, the problem of value is not economic but moral. Neither nature nor art can give anything intrinsic value or 'worth.' Only morality, 'and humanity so far as it is capable of morality,' has worth; for 'morality is the only condition under which a rational being can be an end in himself.'[7] What is subjectively unsatisfactory about egoism is not its vagueness as a principle but rather its inability to provide any touchstone for esteem. The egoistic will measures all potential aims in terms of its own happiness; but, like the wealth of nations,[8] the happiness of individuals lacks intrinsic worth. The egoist may act efficiently and systematically; but he cannot rationally justify those acts. The egoist acts out of selfishness. His selfishness does not, however, make him an end in himself. I am an end in myself, not in so far as I respond to subjective needs, but only in so far as I participate in a community of beings who make and are governed by objective law.[9] Only through its subjection to self-made law can the will be an end both in and for itself. Only through the moral law can willing ground itself; reason, describing a perfect if opaque circle, has the end it is.

4 / TYPIFICATION OF THE MORAL LAW

'All the difficulties in metaphysics,' Kant records in an early reflection, 'arise in connection with the reconciling of empirical principles with Ideas.'[1] The great problem of the metaphysics of morals is to connect the *a priori* principles, which morality requires, with the empirical realm in which such principles must be expressed. Practical philosophy must both separate the *a priori* from the empirical (anthropological) and show how they are joined. For practical purposes this means translating the formal *a priori* moral law into directives which enjoin specific actions in the world; for a practical principle which we could not practically apply would be for us no practical principle at all. In effecting this translation, Kant's understanding of 'typification' plays

7 Ibid. See also *Doctrine of Virtue*, VI 435 (101); Beck *Kant's Critique of Practical Reason* 176-81; and Hardy E. Jones *Kant's Principle of Personality* (Madison, University of Wisconsin Press 1971) 133. Cf. J.G. Murphy *Kant: The Philosophy of Right* 85: Murphy's distinction between the intrinsic moral worth of good men and the intrinsic non-moral worth of men as such does not take sufficiently into account Kant's insistence that the only source of intrinsic worth is morality.

8 DR, VI 284-6

9 'For nothing can have any value other than that determined for it by the law' (*Groundwork*, IV 436 (103)).

1 *Reflexion* #1260

an essential role. The typic expresses the abstract and objective moral law in terms subjectively concrete and comprehensible. Like the *tupos* or stamp, which translates force into image, the typic translates the moral law, which 'forces itself' on our consciousness, into a figure we can 'see' or 'imagine' (*einbilden*).

In the case of theory, principles were separable from the empirical data from which the principles derived. In the case of practice, the principles *are* the data. In the *Groundwork* Kant showed that even the commonest use of practical reason rests on *a priori* principles which ordinary reason recognizes as pure.[2] The distinction which arises in theory between ordinary and scientific experience does not arise in practice. Instead, common reason itself distinguishes between the rational principles which constitute a moral metaphysic and the empirical principles which do not.

Like the geometer, the moral researcher must treat *a priori* concepts, but unlike the geometer, he cannot rely on intuition. He is aided, however, in what would otherwise be a transcendent and even holy task by an experiment which he can arrange with the practical reason of any man, 'in order to distinguish the moral (pure) determining ground from the empirical.'[3] This he accomplishes by 'adding' the moral law to an empirically affected will, a step which allows self-respect to combine with reason and 'precipitates' the isolation of advantage, thus enabling him to view indirectly what he cannot observe directly.

What makes it possible for the moral researcher to examine what he can neither directly observe nor reconstruct is the internal and subjective violence precipitated by the law itself. The moral law 'forces itself' (*drängt sich aus*) upon us as a synthetic *a priori* proposition combining the concepts of positive and negative freedom, a proposition which would be analytic if freedom of the will were given independently. (This, however, would require an accompanying intuition precluded by our finitude.)[4] The moral law is not grounded in feeling; but men do feel its necessitating character. The necessitating or obligating character of the law is a function of the way in which it penetrates our consciousness. Reason in us is not fully transparent to itself and must resort to force, exercised against our bodily inclinations, in order that we may feel what we cannot see. We experience the moral law as inner resistance (*Widerstand*), the only opposition we ever meet whose source is not external to ourselves.[5]

2 *Groundwork*, IV 427 (94)
3 *Crit. Prac.*, V 92 (96); cf. ibid. 30 (30).
4 Ibid. 31 (31)
5 Ibid. 32 (33); see also ibid. 92 (95).

83 The moral turn

The moral law guides our judgment through an ideal which reason itself supplies. Kant call this edifying ideal a model (*Urbild*) or archetype.[6] The force of reason is first made visible through our ideal of pure practical rationality, which the moral law 'constantly and rightly holds before [our] eyes.'[7] The inner opposition which we feel is thus transformed into an aim which we can 'view.' By holding up the will 'to the pure will, i.e., to itself regarded as *a priori* practical,' men pass judgment on the lawfulness of their acts and thereby see what they must do. The ideal or archetype of self-sufficient reason is thus intimately bound up with our consciousness of the moral law.[8] Through it that law is held 'before the eyes' and autonomy put forward as 'the sole principle of all moral laws and of the duties conforming to them.'[9] In order to regard this law 'without any misinterpretation as given, one must note that it is ... the sole fact of pure reason, which by it proclaims itself as originating law (*sic volo, sic iubeo*).'[1] Through the moral law we extend to ourselves the ideal of a self-legislating being, 'self-sufficing' and pure, which we are and are not, or rather are not and ought to strive to be.

An ideal, like an idea, is reason's projection of a task. An idea, as we have seen, projects a task to which reason can never be entirely adequate. In it 'reason aims only at a systematic unity, to which it seeks to approximate the unity which is empirically impossible, without ever completely reaching it.'[2] The ideal is even further removed from objective reality than is the idea. For by 'ideal' Kant means the idea *in concreto* and *individuo*, that is, as an 'individual thing, determinable or even determined by the idea alone.' Through its ideals reason seeks not to determine an abstract unity, but rather to actualize some concrete and individual thing. Ideals, then, have an essentially practical rather than theoretical use. Although the determination of a concrete object, without recourse to the given of sensation, is beyond the reach of theory, it is at least within the gaze of practice, which makes the

---

6 Ibid. 32 (33), 83 (86); *Groundwork*, IV 408 (76)
7 *Crit. Prac.*, V 32 (33); see also *Groundwork*, IV 403 (71). The first *Critique*, although it demonstrated that reason, if it is to be consistent, must *think* of *noumena* (or intelligibles), also cut them entirely off from 'view' (*Aussicht*). The second *Critique*, although it cannot provide such a view, does give 'to hand' a fact, 'inexplicable from any data of the world of sense or from the whole compass of theoretical use of reason,' which 'points to [*Anzeige gibt*] a pure intelligible world' and 'enables us to know something of it, namely a law' (*Crit. Prac.*, V 43 (44)).
8 Immanuel Kant *Religion within the Limits of Reason Alone*, VI, 60–1 (54) (hereafter cited as *Religion*).
9 *Crit. Prac.*, V 32–3 (33)
1 Ibid. 31 (31), 6 (6)
2 CR A/567–A/568 = B/595–B/596

actualization of concrete objects its end. Whereas ideas supply a rule, ideals furnish a concrete and individual archetype for 'the complete determination of the copy.'[3] Theory aims at a systematic and all-embracing whole which it can never render individual and concrete. Hence for theory, ideas and the abstract rules they furnish suffice. Practice, however, which concerns the actualization of concrete things, requires, if it is to bring its actions to the greatest possible perfection, archetypes as well as rules. If, for example, we are to achieve the greatest possible virtue in ourselves, we need a model by which to gauge our progress. Such a model does not exist as an object in the world. But neither is it a '[figment] of the brain,' for '[it] suppl[ies] reason with a standard which is indispensable to it, providing ... a concept of that which is entirely complete in its kind, and thereby enabling [reason] to estimate ... the defects of the incomplete.'[4] To such ideals of reason Kant contrasts the so-called ideals of imagination (such as happiness), which yield not archetypes but only monograms, 'mere set[s] of particular qualities determined by no assignable rule.' Reason, on the contrary, aims, 'in its ideal, at complete determination in accordance with *a priori* rules' and accordingly 'thinks for itself an object which it regards as being completely determinable in accordance with principles.'[5] The ideal, a model from which can be made an unlimited number of copies, is a means of regulating and perfecting our practical activity.

To his ideal of reason Kant also contrasts the ideas of Plato. Plato's ideas are 'archetypes of things themselves, and not, in the manner of the [Kantian] categories, merely keys to possible experiences.'[6] For Plato there are theoretically creative archetypes of human knowledge, objects of divine intuition which are the most perfect of every kind of possible thing and the model of all copies in the field of appearance.[7] For Kant there are only regulative archetypes, whose source lies not (as for Plato) in the generosity of a divine intelligence, which bestows its ideas on human reason, but in the neediness of human reason, which can aspire to virtue only by 'thinking for itself' an ideal.[8]

3 CR A/569 = B/597
4 CR A/569–A/570 = B/597–B/598
5 CR A/570–A/571 = B/598–B/599
6 CR A/313 = B/370
7 CR A/313–A/316 = B/370–B/372. Plato recognized reason's dissatisfaction with the realm of mere appearances, but failed to recognize that reason could transcend this realm in practice only. Carved from the field of practice, his own examples – the ideas of virtue, wisdom, the perfect city, the good – indicate the defect of his theory. But his ideas serve as models which can 'bring the legal organization of mankind ever nearer to its greatest possible perfection' (A/317 = B/374).
8 CR A/570 = B/598. Practical philosophy must 'go where examples fail ... up to the ideas' (*Groundwork*, IV 412 (80)).

85 The moral turn

Early in his life Kant entertained an avowedly Platonic theory of ideas. 'The idea,' he wrote in an early reflection, 'is single [*individuum*], self-sufficient and eternal. The divinity of our soul is its capacity to form the idea. The senses give only copies or rather *apparentia*.'[9] 'As the understanding of God is the ground of all possibility, archetypes, ideas, are in God ... The divine *intuitus* contains ideas according to which we ourselves are possible; *cognitio divina est cognitio archetypa*, and His ideas are archetypes of all things.'[1]

According to Plato as represented by Kant, nature consists of imperfect ectypes or copies which derive the material of their possibility[2] from an archetype or ideal of reason.[3] In Kant's critical thought the archetype and ectype have moral rather than ontological significance, leaving to human practice the relating of model and copy accomplished according to Plato through divine intellection. Stripped by criticism of divinity, the ideas do not create their objects but merely pose determination or actualization of the object as a task of reason.[4] Kant's critical use of Platonic concepts emphasizes what we men lack, namely, an '*intellectus archetypus*' which, joining theory and practice, creates through its own thought the possibility and necessity of the real. At the same time his language reassures us of our power to carry out a moral synthesis which approximates the activity of the divine intellect. Although we cannot, like that intellect, legislate 'the greatest possible ... purposive unity,'[5] we can, unlike nature, legislate purposively.

Critical philosophy rejects Plato's suggestion of a divinely intuited archetype to which thoughts in our mind and things in the world ectypally correspond. Critical archetypes are not theoretical and constitutive but practical and regulative. Our moral synthesis approximates but cannot equal the Platonic *intellectus archetypus* in which intuition (*Anschauung*) and concept (*Begriff*), 'seeing' and 'grasping,' are not merely combined but perfectly united.[6] The critical archetype is not a means to knowledge but a tool to regulate and standardize the products of our moral labour.

In our awareness of the moral law we ourselves join the intelligible and sensible realms. Precisely because it reaches beyond the realm of ordinary knowledge, the nature of this juncture remains opaque to us. For practical

---

9 *Reflexion* #1240
1 Kant *Vorarbeiten*, XXVIII. 1, 328–30. See Norman Kemp Smith *A Commentary to Kant's 'Critique of Pure Reason'* 448–9.
2 CR A/578 = B/606; see also A/316–A/320 = B/373–B/377.
3 *Vorarbeiten*, XXIV. 2, 560–1
4 *Groundwork*, IV 417 (84)
5 CR A/694 = B/722
6 See above, 83, note 7.

purposes, however, we do need to know, if not the nature of the juncture, the acts to which it leads. To this end Kant draws upon the archetype already derived from the moral law and upon the notion of its ectypal counterpart. In his 'deduction' and 'elucidation' (in the Analytic) of pure practical principles, Kant argues that the moral law 'should [*soll*] give to the sensible world, as sensuous nature (as this concerns rational beings) the form of an intelligible world ... without interfering with the mechanism of the former.'

> The sensuous nature of rational beings in general is their existence under empirically conditioned laws, and therefore it is ... heteronomy. The supersensuous nature of the same beings, on the other hand, is their existence according to laws which are independent of all empirical conditions and which therefore belong to the autonomy of pure reason ... The law of this autonomy is the moral law ... the fundamental law of supersensuous nature and of a pure world of the understanding, whose counterpart must exist in the world of sense without interfering with the laws of the latter. The former could be called the archetypal world (*natura archetypa*) which we know only by reason; the latter ... the ectypal world (*natura ectypa*), because it contains the possible effect of the idea of the former as the determining ground of the will.[7]

The ideas of a *natura archetypa* and a *natura ectypa* anchor at both ends the span of moral action. The moral law entails ideas of an autonomously legislated nature and of the effect of such a nature in the world of sense, ideas which represent an otherwise incomprehensible moral process. As the idea of autonomous reason constituted an archetype, so a system of autonomous beings constitutes a *natura archetypa*. As we were required to assume the possibility of our subjective will conforming to an archetype of autonomous reason, so we must assume the possibility of a system of material effects, a *natura ectypa*, conforming to a *natura archetypa*.

The archetype (*Urbild*) and ectype (*Nachbild*) are connected by a kind of visible construction (*Bild*).[8] In the first *Critique Bild* refers to the visible constructions of the lower faculties. It refers, for example, to the 'hand' or 'figure' which allows us to add numbers,[9] and to the 'drawing of a line' in intuition which enables us to represent time and substance.[1] *Bilder*, our own working constructions made visible, substitute at the level of imagination (*Einbildungskraft*) for the divine union of intuition and conception.[2]

---

7 *Crit. Prac.*, v 43 (44) (my translation)
8 CR A/316–A/318 = B/373–B/375, A/569 = B/597. Cf. *Reflexion* #4983 on the typus as a kind of *Sinnbild*.
9 CR B/16
1 CR B/137–B/138
2 CR A/780 = B/808. See also A/569 = B/597; 'As the idea gives the *rule*, so the ideal in such a case

87 The moral turn

Even for the theoretical purposes of human reason, however, the *Bilder* are insufficient. Reason also needs some way to connect the *Bild* of imagination with the *Begriff* of understanding. The representation of such a universal procedure of imagination in providing an image for a concept Kant calls a schema, and it is schemata, not *Bilder* of objects, which underlie pure sensible concepts.³ No image (of a triangle or a dog) could ever be adequate to the concept (of a triangle or a dog) in general. Schemata provide rules according to which imagination can draw the form of the object in general, without being limited by the concrete characteristics of any image in particular. Only through schemata are images connected to concepts, and so only through schemata are images of objects possible at all. It is in the mysterious relation between *Bilder* and schemata that the juncture, critical to all experience, between intuition and concept, the sensible and the *a priori*, occurs.

In applying *a priori* law to sensible experience, practical philosophy requires a counterpart to what *Bilder* accomplish for perception and schemata for conceptualization. Kant calls this counterpart the typic.⁴ In one sense, theoretical reason had things easier, because 'everything depended upon intuitions to which pure concepts of the understanding could be applied.' The morally good, on the contrary, is something which, by its object, is supersensuous; nothing corresponding to it can be found in sensuous intuition; consequently practical judgment 'seems to be subject to special difficulties,' for it must apply a law of freedom 'to actions which are events occurring in the

---

serves as the *archetype* for the complete determination of the copy; and we have no other standard for our actions than the conduct of this divine man within us, with which we compare and judge ourselves, and so reform ourselves, although we can never attain to the perfection thereby prescribed.' The role of archetype as conduit between the sensible and intelligible realms suggests that of symbol in Kant's pre-critical essay *Dreams of a Spirit-Seer*: 'Spiritual ideas can pass over into the personal consciousness of man, indeed, not immediately, but still in such a way that, according to the law of the association of ideas, they stir up those pictures [*Bilder*] which are related to them and awake analogous ideas of our senses. These, it is true, would not be spiritual conceptions themselves, but yet their symbols' (*Dreams of a Spirit-Seer*, II 338-9, [69]). In this work Kant also compares poetic symbolization (e.g., through personification of the virtues) to that of the geometer, who 'represents time by a line, although time and space have conformity only by relation and therefore agree, indeed, according to analogy, but never according to quality' (ibid. 339 (69-70), cf. CR B/16, B/137-B/138). In his *Dreams* essay, symbols serve a representational function later reserved to *Bilder* themselves, a development made possible through Kant's Transcendental Deduction. In his critical thought, symbolization is restricted to the level of analogy and approximation as distinguished from conceptualization proper (see, for example, CJ, V 351-3 (part 1, 221-3)). Typification, as we shall see, falls somewhere between schematization and symbolization, both kinds of 'hypotyposis.'

3 CR A/140-A/143 = B/179-B/183
4 For an excellent discussion of schema and typic see Krüger *Philosophie und Moral* 79-89.

world of sense and thus, to this extent, belonging to nature.' Here we require not the schema of a particular case 'occurring according to laws,' but a 'schema' of a law itself. The schemata of understanding had a basis in intuition. 'But to the law of freedom ... and consequently to the concept of the absolutely good, no intuition and hence no schema can be supplied for the purpose of applying it *in concreto.*' The moral law thus has no other cognitive faculty that can 'mediate its application to objects of nature than the understanding (not the imagination); and the understanding can apply to an idea of reason not a schema of sensibility but a law.'[5] Reason cannot supply itself with an object of intuition. It can, however, give a law for intuition through its concept of causality, which 'contains a relation to a law which determines the existence of the many in their relation to one another.'[6] Moral and physical causality are in turn mediated by the concept of a law of nature. This concept can, for the purposes of moral judgment, 'be used only in its formal aspect' and is called the typus of the moral law. The resulting typic of the moral law asks '*whether, if the action which you propose should take place by a law of nature of which you yourself were a part, you could regard it as possible through your will.*'[7]

The moral law does not directly yield any material ends; instead it furnishes (through the concept of causality) an archetype and an ectype of nature. That archetype is the community of autonomous beings who, governing themselves and being governed by the same law, enjoy a harmony of purpose which Kant calls a kingdom of ends. We do not know what these ends materially may be: we only know that they are harmoniously shared. The ectype is the counterpart such a kingdom ought to have within the empirical world, subject to the restriction that such a counterpart leave intact the laws of natural causation.

We know of the archetype only its form, and of the ectype only its matter.[8] The form of the archetype is that of a community of universally self-legislating beings (that is, of autonomy itself). The matter of the ectype is constituted by the natural world. From this form and matter which the moral law supplies it is possible to determine what material ends the formal law prescribes. One cannot, however, determine these ends directly. The archetype and ectype are themselves pre- and post-constructions. To connect them we need something which, like the schema, can generate the rules and describe the conditions of their juncture. To put it plainly, we must do the joining. What is more,

5 *Crit. Prac.*, v 68–9 (70–1)
6 Ibid. 89 (92); see also 103 (107).
7 Ibid. 69 (72) (emphasis added)
8 Ibid 43 (44–5)

89 The moral turn

we must do the joining with deliberation. Schematization was a condition and not an object of consciousness. Typification, however, must be consciously grasped, for its accomplishment waits upon our own deliberate act. But the juncture of archetype and ectype cannot simply be willed. We need a tool, which, making use of our own faculties and powers, yields a result not possible through those powers alone. The typic is such a tool, enabling us to join two image-worlds which we cannot imagine, by inviting us to hypothesize a third world which we can.

This third world is a nature which we could legislate through our own maxim. The typic invites us to hypothesize a world which we ourselves govern. In this it seems to replicate what is already performed theoretically by our faculty of understanding, whose structures and concepts supply the laws of nature. That legislation, however, was not government in the fully human sense. Unlike human laws, the laws of nature lack all purpose or intention. They are made by us but not for us. Practical is distinguished from theoretical legislation by its unqualified purposiveness. Through cognitive law-making we appear to ourselves as means in a system which lacks inherent ends. Through such legislation our own laws ironically entrap us. This self-tyranny is a function and, indeed, a response to our inevitable duality as subjects who know themselves only as objects.

The typic calls upon us to imagine ourselves legislating for nature not theoretically but practically, not through categories but through our maxim. If our maxim is one that could serve as a law of nature of which we were at the same time a part, it furnishes an end which is morally permissible; if its contrary cannot serve, it furnishes an end which is morally proscribed. In making use of the typic we ask not what could be a purpose of nature (for nature lacks purpose), but what could be my purpose in legislating for nature.[9] The hypothetical world of the typic is a purposeful world, not because nature is inherently purposeful, but because through it nature is infused with the purposiveness of my maxim. The typic injects into nature the purposiveness inherent in human willing.[1]

---

9 Ibid. 43–4 (45)
1 Both Paton and Beck mistakenly attribute the purposive character of Kant's 'typical' world to nature strictly understood, rather than to the mechanics of the typic, which infuses that nature with the purposiveness of human willing. (See Paton *The Categorical Imperative* 146–50; Beck *Kant's Critique of Practical Reason* 160–1.) How far Kant is from attributing a teleological character to nature strictly understood is revealed by his admission that a 'system of nature could indeed always subsist under a universal law [of idleness].' It is not the character of nature but that of reason, which wills the means to all and any of its ends, that prevents my consenting to such a natural law. For as there is no rational limit to the quantity and scope of

But even as it makes me into a hypothetical legislator of nature, it also makes me a part of nature subject to the law. In this the typic parallels the epistemological disjunction of the self, trapped in experience by the laws of understanding. Here, however, the legislation is wilful, and the subjugation a matter not of entrapment but of consent. Kant uses the epistemological disjunction implicit in the theoretical legislation of nature as a platform for the typifying of practical self-legislation in which the fundamental unity of the self is asserted and upheld.

Our hypothesis is limited by the condition that we legislate a world in which we could experience our subjugation with the self-same will. If, for example, my maxim is selfishness, I conceive a world in which all, including myself, are selfish. I then ask if I, as a part of such a world, would willingly consent to such a natural law of universal selfishness. I immediately see that such a law does not serve my selfish purposes; far better for me that at least some be benevolent. Hence I do not consent to the law to which my own will has made me subject.[2] The conflict between my will as legislator and my will as subject reveals the moral inadequacy of my initial maxim.[3] Similarly, a maxim to lie when it suits my purposes would no longer suit my purposes if through it I legislated a world in which every one lied and hence the word of no one could be trusted. Benevolence, on the contrary, would remain acceptable to me in a world in which everyone was benevolent; I am thus able to conclude that it is a suitable end of moral action. Some maxims and their contraries, on the other hand, are equally typifiable (or untypifiable) and hence morally indifferent.[4]

---

our ends (subject to the moral law) there is no rationally pre-established limit to the powers in ourselves which we ought to cultivate (see *Groundwork*, IV 423 (90–1). On the example of suicide, see above, 76, note 2.

2 Kant's application of the Categorical Imperative is not fully comprehensible apart from his theory of human happiness as general (it is the only principle other than that of duty for duty's sake), indeterminate, and not fully rational (it is an ideal of imagination, not of reason). The fundamental human fact essential to an understanding of the application of the Categorical Imperative is man's status as a 'being of needs.' This fact rules out for Kant both the (Stoical) goal of self-sufficiency and the (Epicurean) goal of contentment as rational ends for man. On the 'Stoical' alternative, see Robert Paul Wolff *The Autonomy of Reason* 170–1. On deriving man's radical insufficiency from the 'fact' of moral duty, see Julius Ebbinghaus 'Interpretation and misinterpretation of the Categorical Imperative.' That the moral law impinges on man's consciousness as a duty is itself an indication of his finitude and 'neediness.'

3 See Paul Dietrichson's analysis of the typic in 'Kant's Criteria of Universalizability.'

4 Typification works best when confronted with maxims of appropriate specificity. The problem of selecting the proper maxim for a given action is to some extent simplified for Kant by his assumption that all maxims are ultimately conformable to either the (autonomous) principle of duty or the (heteronomous) principle of self-love. An obligatory end (such as the happiness of

The typic is not identical to the moral law, but rather renders it intuitively graspable. In the *Groundwork* Kant presents the typic, or 'formula' of the moral law, as a concession to human frailty, permissible but better done without.[5] In the *Critique of Practical Reason* he seems no longer to consider it expendable.[6] Reason, he there insists, '[has] a right and is even compelled' to 'use nature (in its pure intelligible form) as the type of [moral] judgement.'[7] The typic meets the two charges that might be levelled against it, namely that it is empirical or mystical; for it 'takes no more from sensuous nature than that which pure reason can also think for itself, i.e., lawfulness, and conversely transfers into the supersensuous nothing more than can be actually exhibited by actions in the world of sense according to a formal rule of natural law in general.'[8] In the *Critique* Kant presents the typic as the only means by which the moral law can attain the material concreteness necessary if it is to guide our actions. In obliging us the moral law 'in fact transfers us ... into a nature in which reason would bring forth the highest good were it accompanied by sufficient physical capacities; and it determines our will to impart to the sensuous world the form of a system [*Ganze*] of rational beings.' 'The least attention to ourself,' says Kant, 'shows that this idea really stands as a model for the determination of our will.'[9]

We experience ourselves as purposive; the moral law tells us that we also ought to be and can be autonomous. Human moral activity lies in the conformity of the self which we experience in practice (that is, the self which chooses among ends) with that self which we are required to assume, the self which spontaneously generates the moral law. The typic merely 'types' the conformity between will as legislator and will as subject which the moral law as a fact of reason already presupposes. The typic shows us how to obey the law that we ourselves have made. Out of our felt heteronomy it furnishes a visible model of practical causation and so (it is hoped) finally brings our underlying autonomy to light.

---

others) renders an action morally worthy only if its underlying principle is that of duty or respect for the moral law. See *Groundwork*, IV 440-1 (108-9); *Crit. Prac.*, V 35-6 (36-7); cf. *Religion*, VI 21-2 (36). On the problem of morally relevant description of actions, see Nell *Acting on Principle*. See also M.G. Singer *Generalization in Ethics* (New York, Alfred A. Knopf 1961). Cf. Paton *The Categorical Imperative* 136-7 and T.C. Williams *The Categorical of the Categorical Imperative* (Oxford, Clarendon Press 1968) 13-21.

5 *Groundwork*, IV 437 (104)
6 *Crit. Prac.*, V 69-70 (72)
7 Ibid. 70 (73)
8 Ibid.
9 Ibid. 43 (45)

5 / THE INCENTIVES OF REASON

The form of moral willing lies, as we have seen, in objective law; its content is furnished by material principles which men cannot renounce but ought to subordinate to the law. These material principles are the stuff out of which the typic generates tangible ends, making it possible for us to apply purely formal law to the material world. Unlike the law itself, which applies equally to every rational being, the ends of human reason are relative to our condition. Our duty to pursue our own perfection and the happiness of others is generated by the moral law in conjunction with human duality and finitude.[1] Our moral ends, while (unconditionally) obligatory for us, are subordinate to the moral law which holds for every rational being.

'How a law in itself can be the direct determining ground of the will' is for human reason an 'insoluble problem.'[2] We are, however, entitled to ask how the moral law can '[affect] the mind' subjectively as an 'incentive' (*Triebfeder*), which it evidently does and must.[3] For it is a subjective and experiential correlate to pure practical activity which first lends us access to the moral law.

In the first instance we experience duty only as a negative incentive, which 'affects feeling' by checking inclinations, which are based on feeling. The sum of inclinations whose complete satisfaction would constitute happiness[4] is called self-addiction (*Selbstsucht*). This self-addiction consists either in self-love (*philautia*) or in self-satisfaction (*arrogantia*). 'Pure practical reason merely checks selfishness, for selfishness, as natural and active in us even prior to the moral law, is restricted ... to agreement with the [moral] law; when this is done selfishness is called rational self-love. But it strikes self-conceit down, since all claims of self-esteem which precede conformity to the moral law are null and void.'[5] Self-love, which proceeds from our unavoidable neediness, is compatible with the moral law. Duty requires only that self-love give it precedence, not that self-love entirely disappear. Self-satisfaction, on the other hand, is always contrary to the law. Self-satisfaction is a pretension

---

1 See Paton *Categorical Imperative* 155. Paton's emphasis on a substantive teleology is not unrelated to his insistence on the priority for Kant of goodness over obligation, but cf. *Crit. Prac.*, v 62–3 (65–6): 'The concept of good and evil must be defined after and by means of the law.' Cf. Wolff *Autonomy of Reason* 65.
2 *Crit. Prac.*, v 72 (75)
3 Ibid.
4 Ibid. 73 (75–6)
5 Ibid.

93 The moral turn

to self-worth independent of the moral law, a false claim through which we wrong ourselves. When the 'matter' of desire 'press[es] upon us,' we find our pathologically determined self 'striving to give its pretensions priority and to make them acceptable as first and original claims, just as if it were our entire self.'[6] 'This propensity to make the subjective determining grounds of one's choice (*Willkür*) into an objective determining ground of the will (*Wille*) in general' is self-love. 'When it makes itself legislative and an unconditional practical principle,' it is self-conceit.[7] Evil is an unjustified claim, lodged not against others but against ourselves. At the level of subjective feeling, morality reveals itself in a juridical struggle between competing portions of the will. Like Christianity and like Rousseau, Kant makes pride the basis of his analysis of evil. The essence of Kantian pride, however, lies not in crimes against God or other men but against oneself.

In practice the theoretical opposition between subject and object turns inwards. The subject which could not hold an object in its grasp becomes an object for itself. Duty impinges on our awareness as the self-generated self-opposition of a dual self. The painful pleasure of moral feeling can be explained as a self-overcoming: negatively speaking, we feel ourselves checked; positively speaking, we feel an obstacle give way.[8]

Esteem (*Achtung*) is the positive feeling through which we pay homage to the moral law and with it to our higher selves.[9] As such it is Kant's answer to the effrontery of nature (which created man worthless). Esteem applies only to persons, never to things. The sea, volcanoes, beasts of prey can awaken fear but not esteem.[1] We overcome nature by assuaging the longings which made its valueless economy so fearful.

Morality consoles us not only with esteem but also with the promise of happiness itself. The highest good includes not only virtue but also the happiness which is its due. Nature does not promise man happiness. The relation between human desire and its satisfaction is, by nature, wholly contingent. The self-generated necessities of reason do not connect it with the object it desires, but merely set possession of the object as a task. Reason grasps as necessary only that which it imposes on itself.[2] The desire for happiness, however, arises out of our neediness or dependence on things external to ourselves. Unlike reason's desire for ideal satisfaction, its desire

---

6 Ibid. 74 (77)
7 Ibid.
8 Ibid. 74 (78); *Groundwork*, IV 403 (71)
9 *Crit. Prac.*, V 73 (76), 76 (79)
1 Ibid.
2 See chapter 2, part 2 above.

for happiness implicates reason directly in the material world. Reason understands its limitation no longer as a self-enclosing ideal boundary, but rather as a material susceptibility to forces in the external world. In pursuing unconditioned knowledge reason was guided by *a priori* principles; in pursuing happiness it is denied even this limited necessity. Yet in pursuing happiness, its very dependence on nature (and feeling) permits it to imagine a satisfaction which in its pursuit of knowledge was unthinkable.

Happiness is a mode not of knowledge but of feeling; and it is at the level of feeling that there emerges a connection between happiness and the desiring self. This nexus is rooted in our moral sense of worthiness or desert. Our sense of desert re-establishes at the level of moral feeling the rational connection, missing in nature, between human need and satisfaction. Kant's moral theory depends on a conflation of worth as a measure of value and worthiness as a measure of desert. Virtue implies both worthiness of happiness and unconditioned worth. Thus while good will is good in itself, only good will together with happiness constitutes the supreme good for rational finite beings. The desire for happiness, which the Analytic (of the second *Critique*) carefully excluded as a ground of choice, the Dialectic reincorporates as a morally acceptable object of choice. The moral notion of desert legitimates our unavoidable concern with happiness. For Kant the conflation of worth as a measure of value and worthiness as a measure of desert is fundamentally mysterious: 'In practical principles a natural and necessary connection between the consciousness of morality and the expectation of proportionate happiness as its consequence may be thought at least as possible,' but 'it is by no means known or understood.'[3] From the time of his earliest scientific essays Kant rejected as naive the belief that nature rewards virtue and punishes vice. Yet his final writings retain the reward of virtue and the punishment of vice (if not in nature, in a world hereafter) as a hope. The old, nagging problems of theodicy re-emerge in Kant's postulates of practical reason, God and immortality. Excluded from moral willing, the old demand for cosmic justice reasserts itself in moral feeling, where it constitutes the basis of Kant's doctrines of history and religion.

The 'synthesis' of happiness and the worthiness to be happy, which together constitute the highest good, provokes in us a conflict or 'antinomy,' which sets the requirements of nature and science against those of morality.[4] It seems that either happiness must lead to virtue as its incentive (a position which morality denies) or virtue must lead to happiness as its efficient cause (a

---

3 *Crit. Prac.*, v 119 (123)
4 Ibid. 110–1 (114–15)

position which nature and science do not support). We resolve this antinomy by recognizing that for moral purposes the support of nature is unnecessary. The reward of virtue is necessary only as a moral hope, which nature cannot undermine. We can thus hold forth the highest good as an end, even in the face of nature's morally indifferent dispensation of pleasure and pain. Nature's moral indifference cannot refute the practical postulates of God and the Immortality of the Soul; and in these postulates we can ground a hope sufficient to permit us to adopt desert combined with happiness as a rational end.

Reason resists futility. It insists on the possibility of that which it takes as its aim.[5] In the case of theory, this insistence led to an illegitimate postulation of the unconditioned, resulting in dialectical illusion and a false metaphysic. In the case of practice this insistence leads to a legitimate and morally supportive belief in God and immortality. The tendency of reason to assume that it can complete its task, a tendency which in theory had to be fought, can in practice be indulged. Morality holds forth an object whose possibility reason cannot disprove. For once, reason is the beneficiary of its own limitation.

Reason cannot act without hoping to succeed. All rational activity, then, entails some kind of belief in the possibility of success. In his *Logic* Kant defines belief (*Glaube*) as the subjective property of cognition as it relates to rational activity. Belief is not 'a special source of cognition' but 'a kind of holding-to-be-true with consciousness of its incompleteness.' It is distinguished from opinion 'by the relation it has as cognition to action.'[6] Kant explains this distinction by comparing reason to a merchant, who 'in order to make a deal, not only needs to have the opinion that something is to be gained thereby, but also needs to believe it, i.e., that his opinion is sufficient for an undertaking freighted with uncertainty.'[7] Belief is an expectation of success sufficient for rational action. As the merchant must believe, before he acts, that he will make a profit, so must the will believe, before it acts, that it will have a good effect. *Glaube*, which means 'credit' as well as 'belief,' permits us to assume a kind of moral capital before we have actually earned it. If we did not so credit our plans we could not begin to act on them.

In what may be an allusion to Pascal's wager,[8] Kant compares different sorts of belief in terms of what we would be willing to give up or to wager (*wetten*) on their behalf. On pragmatic beliefs we would take only a relative

---

5 Ibid. 49 (51), 122–7 (126–32)
6 *Logic*, IX 67n (75n)
7 Ibid. 67n–68n (75n)
8 Lucien Goldmann *Le Dieu caché* (Paris, Gallimard 1959) 331–7

and limited risk; on doctrinal beliefs we would wager our life; on moral beliefs, however, we cannot properly speaking gamble at all.[9] Moral belief is a '*free holding-to-be-true* ... of what I adopt on *moral* grounds ... so that I am certain that the opposite can never be proved.'[1] Although we do not need to believe in God (that is, a 'highest wisdom') in order to act according to the moral law, which is given by reason alone, we do need to accept (*annehmen*) 'a highest wisdom for the sake of the object of our moral will toward which, beside the mere legality of our actions,' we must direct our ends. 'Although *objectively* this would not be a necessary relation of our choice, the highest good is yet the *subjectively* necessary object of a good (including a human) will, and belief in its attainability is necessarily presupposed.'[2] Belief in the attainability of the highest good, and hence belief in God, are subjectively necessary corollaries of the moral law.

Kant's understanding of the relation of reason to belief sheds light on his understanding of the difference between theory and practice. Belief is, according to Kant, a kind of 'middle term' between cognition of an object and its mere presupposition. 'Between the acquisition of a cognition through experience (*a posteriori*) and through reason (*a priori*) there is no middle term.' However, between 'the cognition of an object and the mere presupposition of its possibility there is something intermediate, namely a ground, empirical or from reason, for adopting this possibility in relation to a necessary expansion of the field of possible objects over and above those whose cognition is possible for us.' This necessity exists only in respect to that object which is cognized as practically necessary, 'for the assumption of something for the purpose of merely expanding theoretical cognition is always *contingent*.'[3] Reason's theoretical object – knowledge of the unconditioned – and its practical object – the highest good – are both necessary relative to reason's purpose. What gives practice its edge over theory is the unconditional necessity of moral purpose set against the contingency of that purpose which aims only at rational cognition. It is well to recall that the first *Critique* attributes reason's belief in the unconditioned (and consequent dilemmas) not to reason's (freely chosen) purpose but to its nature and condition. Reason escapes the dilemmas seemingly imposed by its nature through a change of purpose which in turn redirects its interest.

Kant specifically associates interest with motion and extension, with

---

9 CR A/824–A830 = B/852–B/858. On betting and illusion see Kant's *Reflections on Anthropology*, XV. 2, 860.
1 *Logic*, IX 67 (74–5)
2 Ibid. 67–8n (75n)
3 Ibid. 68n (75n–76n)

97 The moral turn

synthetic self-expansion rather than mere analytic self-consistency. Only reason's 'extension, and not the mere agreement with itself, is reckoned as its interest.' 'That which is needed in general for the possibility of any employment of reason, i.e., that its principles and assertions not contradict one another, is not part of its interest but is rather the condition of having any reason at all.'[4] Like Hegel Kant attributes to reason a dynamic power of synthesis which allows it to move beyond mere analytic self-identity. Unlike Hegel, however, Kant argues that logic and interest, rather than uniting dialectically, remain essentially distinct.[5] In Hegel's logic self-identity is a dynamic rather than a static principle. For Kant it is not a logical principle of self-identity that has the power to move the world, but a moral principle of self-obedience. Moral interest is the subjective correlate of this self-legislating power. In the last analysis, speculative and moral interest may be identical; we should recall, however, that in the first analysis they were not.[6]

When compared with the theoretical antinomies, which Kant called the spring and source of criticism, the antinomy of practical reason seems artificial and contrived. In truth, however, the practical antinomy is more an echo than an afterthought, indicating the same problematic but in a new situation. Reason's misplaced belief led it wrongly to postulate both its own omnipotence and a conflicting 'transcendental physiocracy.'[7] This conflict could be resolved and reason's interest satisfied, or partly satisfied, only through thorough-going criticism of pure reason and acceptance of the priority of practice over theory. Resolution of the practical antinomy, on the other hand, lies in demonstrating that reason's interest can generate rather than be generated by reason's need.[8] This demonstration, however, effectively requires that reason adopt a new interest, or rather, that reason's theoretical interest be understood in the light of and as subordinate to reason's interest in the moral law.

---

4 *Crit. Prac.*, V 120 (124)
5 Kant's transcendental logic comes closer to Hegel's concept of a dynamic logic. For Kant, however, the activity of transcendental logic remains a wholly synthetic one, dependent on some correlate, or transcendental object, from without. For Hegel, for whom reason generates its own object, logic moves beyond principles of self-identity and combination to self-negation and its negation.
6 Cf. Jürgen Habermas *Knowledge and Human Interest* 203. Habermas' otherwise informative examination of Kant's notion of rational interest fails to treat with adequate care Kant's notion of speculative as distinct from moral interest, a notion which Habermas dismisses as incomprehensible.
7 CR A/449 = B/477
8 *Crit. Prac.*, V 125–6 (130–1)

98 The Rights of Reason

In the second *Critique* Kant discusses interest in relation to the primacy of practice:

To every faculty of mind an interest can be ascribed, i.e., a principle which contains the condition under which alone its exercise is advanced. Reason, as the faculty of principles, determines the interest of all the powers of the mind and its own. The interest of its speculative use consists in the knowledge of objects up to the highest *a priori* principles; that of its practical employment lies in the determination of the will with respect to the final and perfect end.[9]

Kant's description of rational interest in the second *Critique* differs from his description of it in the first. Reason, which had aimed extravagantly at knowledge of the unconditioned, knowledge which would for ever end its toil, now settles for a more moderate 'knowledge of objects up to the highest *a priori* principles.'[1] Reason reformed adapts its belief to its limitations and only insists on that which it can have. Its old demand for the unconditioned has been tamed by a more pressing interest. Theory submits to practice because 'every interest is ultimately practical' and particularly because 'that of speculative reason [is] only conditional and reach[es] perfection only in practical use.'[2] The old speculative interest of reason could not find satisfaction, because it was not fully an interest of reason's own making. In accepting the priority of morality over speculation, reason embraces an interest which can reach perfection because it is fully reason's own. The need to 'limit reason in order to make room for faith' is in itself a kind of choice.

The dynamic or interested properties of reason have a nature of their own. Reason attains to action by setting before itself an object which it purposes to effect. Expectation of success is not a condition of all action; for if it were, speculative reason could not assume its endless task. It is, however, the condition of self-expansion to possession of the object as an end. If 'we want to expand ourselves through action to the possession of the end thereby possible, we must adopt [*annehmen*] this end as being possible throughout.'[3] If we do not wish to foreclose success, we must assume its possibility from the beginning. The incentives of theory belong to reason's 'nature' but are not, properly speaking, 'chosen' by reason. The theoretically transcendental 'how' of speculative activity is therefore not open to inquiry. The free incentives of practice, however, can be understood from a practical point of view.

9 Ibid. 120 (124)
1 Ibid. 119–20 (124)
2 Ibid. 121 (126)
3 *Logic*, IX 67–9 (75–6)

99 The moral turn

What is more, unlike the inscrutable incentives of theory, the incentives of practice permit us to expect success. Reason cannot freely choose an end without believing that it can be attained. Without this *casus extraordinarius*, practical reason could not 'maintain itself in respect to its necessary end.' Logic and static resistance are not enough. Through logic reason cannot gain possession of its object, but can only 'resist what hinders' reason in the use of that which already 'practically belongs to it.'[4] Practical activity consists in coming into real possession of that which ideally already belongs to us.

By ceasing to esteem success, reason becomes entitled to expect it. Kant likens this expectation to our belief or 'faith' in the fulfilment of pacts and promises. '*Fides* is actually fidelity in *pacto*, or subjective trust in one another, that one will keep his promise to the other – good faith [*auf Treue und Glauben*]. This means faithfulness when the *pactum* has been made, and faith when it is to be concluded. By analogy practical reason is, as it were, the *promisor*; man, the *promisee*; the expected good from the deed, the *promissum*.'[5] Neither the merchant nor the will can act without trust. Unlike the exchanges of nature,[6] those of human economies depend on security.

The demand for satisfaction, which theoretical reason was forced to renounce, is reincorporated by morality as a hope.[7] Morality supplies what nature denies – the trust or credit necessary for productive action. The moral contract which guarantees that justice will eventually prevail anticipates the social contract, which (as we shall see) makes possible the moral and material transformation of the world.

6 / THE PSYCHOLOGY OF FREEDOM

Moral experience, as we have seen, begins with our assessment of a good will as unconditionally good. Moral philosophy uncovers the underlying objective principles of this experience and derives the *a priori* conditions of its validity. The typic makes possible the practical application of these principles to human affairs, and returns us to the realm of human judgment, praise and blame – in other words, to the subjective aspect of choice. The moral law leads

---

4 Ibid. 67n–9n (75n–7n); cf. *Crit. Prac.*, V 128 (133): the 'impartial observer' has become 'a wise and omnipotent dispenser' who alone can promise happiness. 'In this manner the moral law ... leads to religion' (V 130 (134)).
5 *Logic*, IX, 69n (77n); cf. *Crit. Prac.*, V 128 (133).
6 See A/452–A/455 = B/480–B/483.
7 See *Logic*, IX 25 (29); CR A/805 = B/833.

us both to recognize our own noumenal self and to assume a God. The moral law is will projecting itself beyond the human through the sheer energy of self-opposition. Scientific experience is grounded in outer opposition, or the imposition of some given upon the senses; moral experience is grounded in inner opposition, or the imposition of the will upon itself.

According to Kant's conjectural psychology,[8] morality begins with (sexual) refusal and self-denial.[9] That this beginning is also a social moment only serves to emphasize the prominence of self-opposition as distinguished from social opposition. What makes sexual refusal a first moral moment[1] is not the fact that one will should deny another, but that one will should accept that denial as binding on itself. Here human relations cease to be merely animal; for although animals may have the power to refuse each other, they lack the power to deny themselves. According to Kant the first moral moment is social, although not yet contractual. It springs not from pride, as with Rousseau, but from shame (*Sittsamkeit*), that is to say, from 'an inclination to inspire others to respect ... by concealing all that which might arouse low esteem.'[2]

---

8 See Kant's 'Conjectural History' (1786), and his discussion of psychology in the *Metaphysical Foundations of Natural Science* (published in the same year): Kant compares psychology with chemistry, which can become nothing more than 'a systematic art of experimental doctrines, but never science proper ... But not even as a systematic art of analysis or as an experimental doctrine can the empirical doctrine of the soul even approach chemistry, because in it the manifold of internal observation is separated only by mere thought, but cannot be kept separate and be connected again at will ... It can, therefore, never become anything more than a historical (and as such, as much as possible) systematic natural doctrine of internal sense, i.e., a natural description of the soul.' (IV 470–1 (7–8)). About the necessarily conjectural and narrative, or historical, character of psychology Kant is emphatic. For the relation between psychology and anthropology, see CR A/849 = B/877; psychology will remain a pendant to the empirical doctrine of nature 'until it is in a position to set up an establishment on its own in a complete anthropology.' See also Alfred Hegler *Die Psychologie in Kants Ethik* 5–7.
9 'Conjectural Beginning,' VIII 113 (57)
1 Ibid.: 'Refusal was the feat which brought about the passage from merely sensual [*empfundenen*] to spiritual [*idealischen*] attractions, from mere animal desire gradually to love, and along with this from the feeling of the merely agreeable [*Angenehmen*] to a taste for beauty, at first only for beauty in man but at length for beauty in nature as well. In addition, there came a first hint at the development of man as a moral creature. This came from the sense of decency [*Sittsamkeit*], which is an inclination to inspire others to respect [*Achtung*] by proper manners, i.e., by concealing all that which might arouse low esteem [*Geringschätzung*]. Here ... lies the real basis of all true sociability [*Geselligkeit*].'
2 Ibid. On the contrast here between Kant and Rousseau see Galston *Kant and the Problem of History* 96–7: 'For Kant, the desire to be respected or esteemed is ultimately admirable because it is linked to a divination of morality.' But cf. Lewis White Beck *Essays on Kant and*

101 The moral turn

The moral turn is stimulated by an anti-erotic impulse; the attainment of esteem (*Achtung*) is tied to a renunciation of desire. However much Kant later denounces such conditions, which allow men respect only at the cost of happiness, he never denies them. The ideal of a progressive history and, even more forcefully, of an afterlife in which worthiness and happiness combine in just proportion, merely salves a demand for satisfaction which would otherwise stand bare.[3]

The first moral moment is stimulated by, but does not consist in, opposition from without. The acceptance of refusal is an inward movement, which eventually enables us even to take pleasure in the object which refused us, a pleasure Kant calls beauty. At the same time, these early glimmerings of morality turn desire inwards to ideas. Thus the moral and rational impulses go hand in hand. Ideas are objects which reason internally projects, thereby generating principles or laws. Only by turning inwards can reason move from the 'abyss' of lawlessness to lawfulness generated through ideas.[4]

In this moral moment, the self for the first time encounters others as other selves. Unlike Rousseau, for whom wilful denial was the first and greatest threat to self, Kant finds in it the first instance of external opposition which is not perceived as hostile. The moral turn entails a differentiation between the otherness of nature and the otherness of men, a differentiation which makes sociability possible. In time, of course, antagonisms between men will spring up which almost obliterate this initial sociability.[5] The pacificity of men's initial recognition of each other, however, sets a standard for the peace which Kant holds to be always possible (if not actual) in human relations. The tensions inherent in society do not stem from potentially limitless demands upon others (as with Rousseau), but rather from potentially limitless demands upon the self. Kant's aborigine does not win esteem through contests of skill and fancy, contests which only a few can win, but through a self-control in principle possible to all. With morality, the human revolt against nature becomes co-operative.

Society implies collective self-limitation. Each man can rise above nature – including his own nature – only to the extent that he grants to every other man

---

Hume 200. Kant also calls love of honour a mere 'simulacrum of morality' and as such no more than 'glittering misery.'

3 'Conjectural Beginning' VIII 120–1 (66). Cf. *Anthropology*, VII 239 (107): 'The most thorough and readily available medicine for soothing any pain is the thought ... that life as such ... has no intrinsic value at all.'

4 'Conjectural Beginning,' VIII 111–12 (55–6)

5 See, for example, 'Conjectural Beginning,' VIII 118–20 (63–5); cf. 'Perpetual Peace' and 'Idea for a Universal History.'

an equal privilege. This collective self-overcoming, implicit in the earliest society, the typic re-enacts against nature as a whole. The typic invites us collectively to conspire to a usurpation of nature, imaginatively completing the human ascendency which theoretical philosophy began. For fully rational beings, such usurpation would be unnecessary; finite rational beings, however, must win respect through a conquest of nature which is essentially self-conquest. The typic is an objectification of our own internal battle. Furnishing judgment with an apparently external guide, it lends to our subjective struggle the objectivity and clarity of the moral law. At the centre of the typic stands the notion of human willing universalized, a willing-for-myself whereby I also will for all other men. The typic hypothesizes a perfect human legislation. The unity of will which links the self as legislator with the self as subject must, by extension, be attributed to all other men. What I do could be done equally by all. Thus my maxim loses what in it is peculiar to myself, though it cannot slough off that neediness which is endemic to humanity. I can, for example, will my own happiness, but only because it constitutes a part of the general happiness of humanity, a happiness which, owing to our incorrigible neediness, can never be complete. This incorrigibility may arouse an indignation we cannot stifle. This indignation must, however, be passed off onto a more-than-human, cosmic observer, to whose judgment alone the realms of nature and freedom subject themselves as part of a fully unified whole.[6] As hope is permitted us only when we cease to value it, so such indignation is permitted only when we cease to express it in our own name.

Men are born angry.[7] But their anger takes on a moral dimension only when they recognize themselves as free. Recognition of freedom makes possible a transmutation from anger to blame, whose first object, internal rather than

---

6 *Crit. Prac.*, V 110–11 (114–15); *Groundwork*, IV 393 (61); CR A/810–A/813 = B/838–B/841. The 'impartial observer' of Kant's critical writings calls to mind several of his earlier moral reflections in which he considers the 'impartial observer' as a guide to moral judgment, a technique developed by Adam Smith in his *Theory of Moral Sentiments*. Smith put forward his technique as a mechanism for arriving at just decisions. Kant questions the value of non-participatory neutrality, wondering how such a one would know the general good, and why he would care to serve it (*Reflexion* #6864; cf. *Reflexion* #6628, #7078). In fact, the categorical imperative seems to have occurred to Kant as, among other things, a solution to the problems posed by Smith's mechanism. The critical guide to moral judgment is based in universal self-legislation, rather than in a neutrality fostered by non-participation. It is not the negation of interest but its universalization that yields results in touch with the interest of all men. Nevertheless, the impartial observer, excluded from moral deliberations proper, re-emerges in Kant's critical works as the indicter of nature before the human race in general (cf. *Reflexion* #7093).

7 See *Anthropology*, VII, 269n (136n).

103 The moral turn

external to the will, is reason itself. Reason is the first object of blame; the use of reason is the first crime.[8]

The immediate cause of this self-condemnation is that new relation to our mortality which Kant calls care (*Sorge*). With his discovery of care man brings down his anger, heretofore vented externally, upon himself. He does not first condemn nature's ills but knowledge of those ills. He perceives how reason relinquishes happiness in the pursuit of it and, for a brief moment, prefers oblivion to a consciousness of his finite power.

In the first instance 'freedom is a subjective lawlessness. One does not know according to what rule one should judge one's own acts and those of other men.' Without objective practical laws, Kant records in a note, men are lower than the beasts and 'worthier of hate.'[9] In attributing his misery to himself, and thus in recognizing his own capacity for self-frustration, man moves from the pre-moral world of anger to the (properly) moral world of (praise and) blame. Primitive man achieves unwittingly that rational frustration of desire which the fully developed moral will later accomplishes deliberately. But why should what is after all an unwitting error, an abuse by no means intentional, warrant moral blame? Because, Kant seems to say, the first step towards self-emancipation occurs only when we cease faithfully to heed nature and recognize reflectively a power of opposition in ourselves which permits us to direct our anger inwards. Yet this very inwardness immediately establishes outward relations on a new plane. What distinguishes blame from anger is not only its inner dimension but also its implication of a community of like-minded beings. In blaming, one implicitly appeals to a standard independent of oneself, and in which one expects others to concur. In blaming oneself, one appeals to standards equally appropriate to blaming others. Thus self-condemnation provides the foundation for moral relations with others, incorporating the blame due a man in place of the anger due a thing. According to Kant we blame ourselves before we blame others. In blaming ourselves, however, we already implicitly recognize others apart from nature and like ourselves. The emancipation which we instigate by condemning ourselves is already, *in potentia*, a collective enterprise. Our capacity to choose our own end, a capacity which distinguishes us in our minds from the beasts, who are ruled by instinct, makes it impossible for us to expect, in making this choice, the objective guidance of nature. There is a discontinuity between the laws of nature and our experience of human wilfulness. We are free to choose, but we lack a natural standard by which to judge

---

8 'Conjectural Beginning,' VIII 113 (58); cf. *Groundwork*, IV 395 (63).
9 *Reflexion* #6960, #7202

our choice. Theoretical judgment did indeed find objectivity in the laws of nature. Practical judgment is threatened by the possibility that no objective laws exist for it at all.

Practical judgment requires an objectivity which takes its bearings not from nature but from reason itself, precisely what for theoretical reason was impossible. In exercising practical judgment we can escape an otherwise unavoidable contingency by taking our bearings not in what is peculiar to ourselves as men but in what must be true for every rational being as such. This abstraction (from what is peculiar to oneself to what must be true for every rational being), the most important moment in Kant's practical thought, is already contained in his initial discussion of a practical principle. Principles are subjective when 'regarded by the subject as valid only for his will,' objective 'when recognized as valid for the will of every rational being.' To assert the existence of an objective practical principle is to posit the existence of a community of unanimous rational beings. It is, moreover, to posit the existence of a community of beings for whom moral judgment and moral action are one and the same.

Subjectively men distinguish between what they do and what they ought to do, that is, between action and moral judgment.[1] Action entails determination of a single will. 'How should I act?' is a question which, strictly speaking, I can decide only for myself. I cannot will another man to lift his arm. In judging, on the other hand, I partially 'objectify' an act, which as an object of judgment could as readily be another's as my own. In so far as I choose judgment at all, I implicitly place myself on a par with others.

In so far as they have any bearing on our own action, practical principles grant us access to a community of purely rational beings. Theoretical objectivity was grounded in our relation to an alien and imposing matter; practical objectivity arises from our relation to a community of friendly and likeminded wills.[2]

The crime of our fathers is one of which we are all guilty, because we recognize that in like circumstances we would have done likewise.[3] By identifying ourselves, both individually and collectively, with hypothetical progenitors in their rebellion against nature, we dissipate an anger towards

[1] See *Reflexion* #6960.
[2] There is also a 'social' dimension to theoretical knowledge. In theory as well as practice, an objective judgment is valid for others as well as for myself. But see *Crit. Prac.*, v 26 (25).
[3] 'Conjectural Beginning,' VIII 122–3 (68)

105 The moral turn

nature which would otherwise devastate us.[4] The source of guilt[5] and blame lies in humanity's rebellion against no human paternity but nature itself. Yet self-hatred would soon replace our animosity towards nature, could not the moral law redeem us. Our own sacrifice makes us worthy. The harshness of Kantian morality retains his vision of man whose lawlessness is so hateful that he must be compelled to obey the moral law, forced to be free.[6]

With the issue of compulsion we enter the arena of external freedom and right as such. Even in their emancipation from nature men remain its creatures, able to exercise a restraining force on the actions of one another. This power, in Kant's view, is by no means wholly destructive. Indeed the systemization of men's power to compel one another provides Kant with his first working-models or types of the moral law,[7] and his first example of a moral archetype. Our capacity to compel one another supplies at least the formal basis for an objective constraint which nature no longer provides us. The paradoxes of a theory which derives restraint from freedom and freedom from restraint will play a role in my consideration in the following chapter of Kant's *Doctrine of Right*.

---

4 See, for example, ibid. 120–1 (66), 122–3 (68).
5 *Schuld*; see also CR A/555 = B/583, A/552n = B/580n, *Reflexion* #2125.
6 See *Reflexion* #6960
7 *Reflexion* #7260, 7269

4

The Doctrine of Right:
A selective commentary

Everything goes past like a river and the changing taste and the various shapes of men make the whole game uncertain and delusive. Where do I find fixed points in nature, which cannot be moved by man, and where I can indicate the marks by the shore to which he ought to adhere? Immanuel Kant *Bemerkungen* xx 46

The human condition is vexing, humiliating, and fearful. There is in nature nothing certain or determinate, and our desires, which we have not the power to satisfy, place us at the mercy of this natural flux. Reason desires, above all else, substantiality and permanence, either in reason itself as subject or in some object with which it might be completely and inseparably joined. But reason's longings deepen rather than solve the problem which arouses them. Seduced by its desire to natural but vain expectations of success, reason plunges into confusion and error. Critical philosophy extricates reason by showing it the futility of its longings for knowledge of absolute being, and so prepares reason for the new direction indicated by the moral law.

The assertion and elaboration of the priority of practice over theory marks a turning-point in the development of Kant's philosophy, and a fundamental redirection of rational interest. Hereafter, philosophy aims not at absolute knowledge, but at an understanding of reason's limitations; and this not for the sake of knowledge, but in order to save morality from reason's unwarranted pretensions. This turn is, moreover, no simple *fait accompli*; it is instead an ongoing task. The submergence of desire for the sake of autonomy and self-consistency continues to invigorate Kant's critical philosophy, constituting for this philosophy both the decisive moment in human history and the ultimate focus of all rational activity. The subordination of desire to duty and happiness to esteem is the most important and fundamental task of reason.

The concept of right (as we shall see) lies at the heart of this task. It is the recognition of this concept which Kant says set him straight[1] and which he calls the final and most important step in the development of human reason.[2] Through man's concept of right he first opposes nature and begins to discover his own freedom. Man first expresses his sense of right in anger and resentment against the resistance which his will naturally encounters. Unlike other creatures, man is almost from his first breath required to labour, an activity he is naturally disinclined to enjoy. He is a needy creature whose desires exceed his powers and who therefore meets opposition everywhere. Man's primal indignation represents his unhappy and almost unsupportable awareness of

---

An earlier version of portions of chapter 4 appeared in *Political Theory*, vol. 6, no. 1 (Feb. 1978): 75–90; they are printed here by permission of the publisher, Sage Publications, Inc.

1 *Bemerkungen*, xx 44; see above, 21.
2 'Conjectural Beginning,' VIII 113–15 (58–9)

his condition. Morality fortifies and rechannels this indignation while dissipating its initial cause. Morality turns anger inwards against the self, then outwards against other selves: the first movement sparks virtue, the second informs a systematic doctrine of right. Right, properly understood, is rational indignation, anger objectified. Righteous anger implies an acceptance of standards applicable to all including oneself; right and duty, self-assertion and self-limitation thus go hand in hand.

Having turned away from nature in order to establish moral bearings, the doctrine of right returns to nature and, carrying out in practice a project begun by theory, lays a foundation for the appropriation and material transformation of nature. The notions of possession and acquisition, and with them the experience of physical force and counterforce, prove essential to this effort. In the judicial community, defined both out of and against nature, the individual finds practical substantiality. As a physical creature, he is vulnerable to the opposition of nature; as a moral being, he is vulnerable only to the rectifiable opposition of other wills. The doctrine of right must come to terms with the ineradicable doubleness of man's relation to nature. Although its principles are rooted in *a priori* grounds, the doctrine of right must also defer to human limitation by, for example, cloaking the irreducible arbitrariness of political power, and by accommodating certain unavoidable inequalities of human nature. Perhaps Kant's most striking concession to nature is his admission of the impossibility of world government, and hence the impossibility of establishing a truly juridical condition on earth. This limitation is balanced, to be sure, by the hope of perpetual progress based on the material transformations which the doctrine of right should encourage. History, coinciding eventually with a rational world economy, appears to lead politics in a morally favourable direction. In the end, however, material progress is no substitute for moral progress. The moral necessity of the principles of right contrasts with the contingency and moral inconclusiveness of its material results. The power of right lies not in its results but in its foundation, which, teaching men to appreciate the necessity of their limitations, permits them to defy and to make peace with nature in a single breath.

In the course of Kant's exposition of right, there are suggestions that the concept may not always be equal to the ground-breaking tasks Kant would have it fulfil. The strain is most obvious when a formal and even scholastic rigour seems at odds with practical common sense. Some of these problems will emerge in the course of my consideration of the *Doctrine of Right*. My major concern, however, will remain the concept of right in relation to Kant's thought in general and to the tensions which the critical edifice as a whole must bear.

III *The Doctrine of Right*: A selective commentary

1 / RIGHT AND OPPOSITION (DR INTRODUCTION)

The *Doctrine of Right* (*Metaphysische Anfangsgründe der Rechtslehre*), published in 1797 as part I of *The Metaphysics of Morals*, partially fulfilled Kant's long-standing intention to demonstrate systematically how *a priori* moral principles apply to the realm of experience. The *Doctrine of Right* consists of 'principles of application.'[3]

Like the 'typic' of practical reason, the concept of right displays or schematizes the relation between nature and the will. The typic sets forth as a hypothesis the collective usurpation of nature; the concept of right replaces this radical usurpation with a less radical but real 'appropriation.' The doctrine of rights treats the encounter between the will and matter not as a hypothesis but as a fact. The typic asserts the ascendency of will over nature; the doctrine of right must conceptually reconcile this ascendency with the will's felt experience of natural opposition.

The doctrine of right schematizes in a conceptual but practical way the encounter between will and matter which is felt but cannot be theoretically comprehended. That will must meet resistance (that subject must encounter object) is, as the Transcendental Deduction of the first *Critique* established, the primary datum and condition of human consciousness. The activity of understanding can be understood as a never-ending effort to 'combine' the double elements of this encounter. Labouring to comprehend the 'given,' understanding informs and so transforms it. In theory and practice alike, mind's goal is, in the words of one critic, 'to shape its world rationally by dissolving natural resistance or "otherness."'[4] Combining its own formal categories with the 'matter' given to it through sensation, understanding produces concepts of objects, and so renders intelligible an externality, or otherness, which sensation can only blindly confront. The labours of understanding constitute a kind of appropriation, which is, however, necessarily incomplete. The concepts are reason's own; the objects continue to limit and oppose. Through the activity of understanding, reason transforms the externality felt through sensation into the externality of an objective world, calculable and even manipulable, but beyond the power of reason fully to control.[5] The ultimately inaccessible thing-in-itself conditions all of reason's appropriating and transforming activity. The instability of Kantian dualism lies in the attempt of reason as subject to unite itself with the object; the stability of the

---
3 DR, VI 217 (16)
4 George Armstrong Kelly *Idealism, Politics and History: Sources of Hegelian Thought* 11
5 Cf. *Bemerkungen*, XX 91: '[Man] is the administrator [*Verweser*] of nature, not its master [*Meister*].'

system lies in the futility of that attempt. The dynamic unity of the system derives from the attempt of reason to overcome the opposition which is the precondition of its own activity, the source, so to speak, of its furious energy.

The concept of right also has its source in this oppositional relation. Despite the specifically human and social context of the doctrine of right, the concept of right first emerges out of our primary experience of objects as such. To encounter objects is already to have some sense of right. Even the young infant manifests such a sense. Kant attributes the infant's cries to an indignation aroused by his apprehension of constraint.[6] Injury first awakens our sense of justice.[7]

In describing the outrages of infancy, Kant begins with a moving passage from Lucretius:

[The child, like a sailor cast forth by the cruel waves, lies naked on the ground, speechless, in need of every kind of vital support, as soon as nature has spilt him forth with throes from his mother's womb into the regions of light,] and he fills all around with his doleful wailings; as is but just, seeing that so much trouble awaits him in life to pass through. [*De rer. nat.* V 227–8][8]

Lucretius' doleful infant cries out of a praeternatural sense of the evils which await him in later life. Kant's angry infant cries from his experience of the world here and now. Barely freed from his mother's womb, the child already senses his incapacity to make his limbs serve him. It is his own body which first resists him and prompts the 'announcement of his claim to liberty.' To this pretension is added irritability and anger when, approached by objects, or compelled to alter his condition, the child feels hindered. 'This drive to have his own will and to take as an injury [*Beleidigung*] every hindrance is shown by his tone, which reveals a nastiness which his mother feels obliged to punish, but to which he generally replies with yet more violent cries.'[9] The human child is distinguished from young animals both by his cries and by his idea of liberty.[1] Both are awakened by opposition and expressed through anger.

---

6 *Anthropology*, VII 268–70 (135–7): see also *Reflexion* #1211: if one wishes to understand human nature it is important to observe children (and savages) closely.
7 Cf. J.J. Rousseau *Emile* 63.
8 *Anthropology*, VII 268 (136); the text in brackets is omitted from Kant's quotation (translation of Lucretius by W.H.D. Rouse *De rerum natura* (Cambridge, Mass., Harvard University Press 1924))
9 Ibid. 269 (136) (my translation)
1 Ibid. 327 (188)

113 *The Doctrine of Right*: A selective commentary

Our concept of right is initially awakened by natural objects which push against the will and resist it. Right is itself a revolt against nature, a revolt in which no other creatures share. 'The young of animals play; those of men quarrel very early, and it is as if a certain concept of right (which pertains to external freedom) develops at the same time as animality, without having to be progressively learned.'[2] Our concept of right develops along with but apart from our animality. It develops along with our capacity to perceive objects, and so along with our capacity for experience in the proper sense. In his earliest infancy, the child neither weeps nor perceives objects (though his visual attention to things prepares him to perceive them).[3] In order to perceive objects, the sense of sight must be related to the more fundamental sense of touch.

Our first experience of objects is mainly tactile, a function of our ability to sense pressure and resistance. Touch is the only sense which belongs to *immediate* outer experience; it is also the sense which first gives us a notion of form or shape (*Gestalt*). By experiencing obstruction we first conceive of form. Reason grasps a thing not through its idea or 'looks' (as with Plato) but through its shape or 'feel.' Knowledge is not most fundamentally related, as with Plato, to sight – the sense Kant calls the noblest – but to touch – a sense which Kant admits is baser, but calls most important and unique to man.[4]

The primarily tactile nature of our perception of objects suggests deeper connections between Kant's understanding of objectivity and his concept of right. His understanding of the origins of right is related in important ways to his theory of matter and the relation between bodies in space. Kant presents his theory of matter and body in the *Metaphysical Foundations of Natural Science*.[5] According to Kant's *Natural Science*, we first become aware of objects when they press against and resist us as we compete with them for the same space. Objective experience implies material opposition. Matter is 'substance' as we encounter it in experience. It 'reveals its existence to us through our senses, whereby we perceive its impenetrability ... hence, it reveals its existence only in relation to contact ...'[6] Matter first reveals itself to

---

2 Ibid. 269n (136n) (my translation)
3 Ibid. 127–8 (9–10)
4 Ibid. 154–7 (32–4)
5 DR, VI 205 (3). In his preface to the *Metaphysics of Morals* Kant calls the *Doctrine of Right* (*Metaphysische Anfangsgründe der Rechtslehre*) the 'counterpart' (*Gegenstück*) of the *Metaphysische Anfangsgründe der Naturwissenschaft*. Both works define a system of external relations (as distinguished from psychology and the *Doctrine of Virtue*, which concern internal relations).
6 Kant *Metaphysical Foundations of Natural Science*, IV 510 (59) (hereafter cited as *Natural Science*)

us as something real through its 'impenetrability,' itself a function of the power of matter to repel us.[7] It fills a space, not by its mere existence, but by a 'special moving force.'[8] Matter, according to Kant, is not passive and inert (as Newton maintained) but actively resists all that would penetrate its space.[9]

An object feels hard when our efforts to displace it are matched by its power to repel us. Repulsion is that force through which a body assaults the position of another or defends its own. While acknowledging (Newtonian) attraction as important, Kant insists on the priority of repulsion for our experience of the objective world. The force of attraction gives us no sensation and no determinate object of sensation.[1] Pressure and impact, on the contrary, are influences – and indeed the only influences – we can immediately perceive.[2] In so modifying Newton, Kant also decisively rejects Aristotelean mechanics, to which attraction as a kind of hierarchical desire was fundamental.[3] For Kant, attraction is never a direct, felt constituent of objective experience. The force of attraction is a scientific construct, necessary to mechanics, but never directly experienced. Repulsion, on the contrary, is directly felt and crucial to our earliest knowledge of the objective world. Man's felt experience of the objective world is unequivocally negative and repellent.[4] From the moment he makes contact with the world, he must meet force with force. From the moment the child affects and is affected by the world, he begins to labour. It is no wonder that the child, inclined to indolence,[5] finds nature vexing.[6]

Freedom is first grasped as unencumberedness, the unresisted activity of the child's own wilful drive. The child grasps this state only negatively; the unencumbered will is only an ideal, for all experience implies resistance. And yet the child grasps this ideal state as properly his; the child *is* free, and only this allows him to claim encumbrance as an injury. It is as if in claiming freedom, to which none of our experience can be adequate, we were remembering and regretting some previous life. By means of this claim to freedom, which transcends all our experience, we first propel ourselves beyond the state of bodily nature.

The first signs of a concept of right manifest themselves long before a child

7 Ibid. 508 (56)
8 Ibid. 497 (41)
9 Ibid. 496 (40). Cf. *Opus post.*, xx 163.
1 *Natural Science*, IV 510 (59)
2 Ibid. 508–10 (56–9)
3 Cf. Aristotle *Metaphysics* 1072a–1073a.
4 See above, 76, note 2.
5 Cf. *Reflexionen* #1482, #1511.
6 See *Anthropology*, VII 328n (188n), 289 (155): the person of choleric temperament 'is the ... least happy, because he incites the most opposition.'

115 *The Doctrine of Right*: A selective commentary

has learned to distinguish between men and things, between willed and unwilled opposition. Opposition from whatever quarter stirs his anger. The very young child may even fail to distinguish between obstacles encountered from without and those posed by his own body. He does not at first perceive nature as a source of comfort nor his own body as a source of power. It is, indeed, only in so far as things obstruct his will that he perceives them at all.[7] The child's first movements are accompanied by an 'explosion of anger,' not because he is hurt, but because he is 'annoyed' and 'vexed.'[8] These vexing hindrances intensify his youthful energy and, through his anger, render it vindictive.

The 'passion for justice' (*Recht*) is from the beginning closely linked with the 'passion for revenge' (*Rache*).[9] The intentionally punishing blows which other human beings inflict on us increase our anger but do not change its character. Our primal personification of nature is not an anthropomorphic prejudice but an anthropological fact.[1] The experience of injury and anger with respect to things furnishes a basis for man's subsequent recognition of other rational beings. In recognizing others, a man attributes to them the rights he already senses in himself. The primal interconnection of self-awareness and anger makes it possible for Kant to explain the transformation of man from a purely natural to a social being. It is the key (which morality turns) to the 'asocial sociability' of man.[2]

Our early concept of right does not distinguish between will and thing.

---

7 The human ability to 'abstract,' essential to the development of reason, is bound up with our experience of power and impotence. Abstraction is a power to look or turn away (*absehen*). According to Kant, the effort (*Bestrebung*) to become conscious of our representations consists both in 'paying attention' (*attentio*) to a representation and in turning our attention from it. Abstraction is not merely omission or negligence, but a real act of rational power (*wirklicher Act des Erkenntnissvermögens*). By abstracting from 'the determination [*Bestimmung*] of a representation of an object ... it attains the generality of a concept, and is accepted by the understanding.' The capacity to abstract is also bound up with human freedom. 'The ability to abstract from a representation, although it imposes itself [*sich aufdrinkt*] on man through his senses, is a greater power than that of attention; for it reveals a freedom in man's faculty of thought [*Freiheit des Denkungsvermögens*] and a spontaneous power of spirit [*Eigenmacht des Gemüts*] to control the state of his representations [*den Zustand seiner Vorstellungen in seiner Gewalt zu haben*]' (*Anthropology*, VII 131-2 (13)). Consciousness, according to Kant, involves will (*Willkür*).

8 Ibid. 269 (136)
9 Ibid. 270-1 (137-8)
1 See ibid. 269-70 (136-7).
2 See Kant 'Idea for a Universal History from a Cosmopolitan Point of View,' VIII 20 (15). See also Georges Vlachos *La Pensée politique de Kant* 168 and *Reflexion* #1443: the word *cosmopolitan* signifies a judgment according to the idea of right.

Fully developed, however, our concept of right insists and, indeed, depends on this distinction. Man's primal indignation is merely the 'analogue' of right fully understood.[3] Between indignation and an assertion of rights in the true sense there must intervene a moral revolution, 'the most ... important in the interior world of man.'[4] Before he can have a 'genuine concept of right,' a man must come to recognize others as men apart from nature and like himself.

This revolution constitutes the final step by which reason raises man altogether above community with the animals.[5] This sublimation (*Erhebung*)[6] entails, however obscurely, the idea of man as an end in himself, and with it the notion of contrast (*Gegensatz*) between man and the other creatures of nature whom man is free to use as means (*Mittel*) and tools (*Werkzeuge*) for his chosen ends. Man leaves 'the womb of nature' by investing nature with his own ends.[7] If he would claim this investiture as a right, however, he must acknowledge the equal claim of every other rational being. In laying claim to nature as a tool, man must recognize all other men as co-owners and participants. The revolt against nature is completed when man appropriates nature not only on his own behalf but also on behalf of every other will. The revolt against nature begins with the individual; its completion is a collective enterprise.

Without the moral law, the anger which opposition engenders lacks all justification and objectivity. In his pre-moral condition man rages over his situation, but without support. From a pre-moral perspective, human life is nearly unbearable. Man feels himself assaulted and affronted but cannot set

---

3 *Anthropology*, VII 269 (136)
4 Ibid. 229 (97) (my translation)
5 'Conjectural Beginning,' VIII 114 (58)
6 For Kant, sublimation is a 'lifting up' preceded by surrender or sacrifice. As a category of aesthetic judgment, it prefigures, at the level of imagination, moral transcendence. See CJ, V, 257–64 (part 1, 105–14). Whereas the beautiful evinces the imagination in 'free play' (*vis à vis* the understanding) the sublime evinces the imagination 'tax[ing] itself to the utmost' (*vis à vis* reason). Kant likens sublime experience to a 'vibration,' i.e., to a series of 'repulsions' and 'attractions' towards a 'point' or 'abyss' (*Abgrund*) in which imagination 'fears to lose itself' (ibid. 258 (part 1, 107)). Imagination extends itself through sacrifice. By its own act 'imagination [deprives] itself of its freedom by receiving a final determination in accordance with a law other than that of its empirical employment. In this way it gains an extension and a might greater than that which it sacrifices. But the ground of this is concealed from it, and in its place it *feels* the sacrifice' (V 269 (part 1, 120)). Imagination recapitulates aesthetically man's primordial discovery of moral freedom. On the sublime as awareness of a power to overcome internal obstacles, see *Religion*, VI 183 (171). The sublime rescues us from what would otherwise be a dizzying and unsupportable height (see *Religion*, VI 197 (185); *Groundwork*, IV 425 (93)).
7 'Conjectural Beginning,' VIII 114 (59)

forth his complaint as an objective claim. Morality, in forcing him to turn his indignation back against himself, permits him to set forth such a claim. The moral law grants him rights, but only to the extent that he admits the rights of others. The system of right defines a community of wills, each of whom asserts his own rights and reciprocally recognizes the rights of all the others.

The categorical imperative makes this transformation possible. According to the categorical imperative expressed as a juridical postulate of reason, 'every action is right that in itself or in its maxim is such that the freedom of the *Willkür* of each can co-exist together with the freedom of everyone in accordance with a universal law.'[8] Right is thus the aggregate of those conditions under which the *Willkür* of one person can be lawfully conjoined with the *Willkür* of all the rest.

The juridical postulate suggests the 'formula' of the categorical imperative which enjoins us to treat every man not only as a means but also as an end.[9] Like that formula, the juridical postulate applies to the domain of nature and 'external freedom,' in which men have a natural power to use one another and are naturally susceptible to being used. Both the categorical imperative and the law of right assert an absolute distinction between things of nature, which may be used as a means (*Mittel*), and men, who as part of nature can be used as means, but who are also ends-in-themselves. 'Persons ... are not merely subjective ends whose existence as an object of our actions has a value *for us*: they are *objective ends*.'[1]

To treat another as an end-in-himself is to treat him as a being for whom our action, when it affects him, could also be an end. It is, in other words, to recognize him as a person with intentions like ourselves. Those activities through which we make use of other persons ought to serve their purposes as well. Our use of others ought to await their (rational) consent. The notion of reason as an end-in-itself translates practically into a duty to treat others in a way to which they can (prudently) agree. The ideal consensus of a rational community translates externally into a duty to secure the consent of others in all one's social dealings. We cannot establish the 'kingdom of ends' without first securing a juridical community of means. The moral idea of an end-in-itself entails the juridical notion of a means in general. Fully perfected, the concept of right implies a system of reciprocally related, equal selves. If we are to conceive of such equality, we must imagine the will as a power attributable to all. The juridical concept of the self therefore abstracts from all those particular ends and desires which make each self unique.

---

8 DR (introduction), VI 230 (35)
9 *Groundwork*, IV 427–8 (95)
1 Ibid. 428–9 (96–7). Thus: 'treat humanity ... never simply as a means, but always at the same time as an end.'

The juridical concept of the self therefore abstracts from all those particular ends and desires that make each self unique and focuses instead on the formal capacity for choice as such. Kant's name for this capacity is *Willkür*, which he distinguishes from the law-giving *Wille*.² Juridical community establishes the reciprocal relationship of one *Willkür* to another. *Willkür* is the faculty of desire 'considered in its relation to action.' It is the will directed outwards to a choice of objects as means by which the will may attain its ends. *Wille* furnishes the inner, determining ground of such ends; *Willkür* considers the means to achieve them. Thus *Willkür* is desire 'combined with the consciousness of the capacity [*Vermögen*] of its action to produce its object.'³ Juridical community involves consciousness of a power or means in general (*Vermögen überhaubt*) to make use of any object in the world.

The notion of a power in general, which defines our membership in the juridical community, also plays a fundamental role in our rational and moral development. It is crucial, for example, to the development of the passions, in which Kant locates the human propensity for evil.⁴ Passion, which Kant also calls formal (as distinguished from material) desire, does not relate immediately to a particular end or object, but rather to external freedom and a power in general. Both innate passions (for example, the passion for freedom) and acquired passions (for example, the passion for honour, for domination, and for wealth) concern 'the possession of means in order to satisfy all inclinations themselves directed toward particular ends.'⁵ Formal desire thus 'leads much farther' than do particular cravings. By pursuing power in general we are able to secure more of our material ends than would otherwise be possible. Having turned our attention to power in general, however, we are inevitably tempted to treat such power not as a mere means but as an end-in-itself. Thus does the special expedient of humanity become its special 'delusion' (*Wahn*).⁶

Passion is evil because it holds forth power, rather than man, as the ultimate end. Passion is desire in conflict with the rights of man. The human 'tendency toward freedom' becomes a passion when a man refuses to recognize the freedom of others. The tendency to freedom as a 'reciprocal pretension between men' is a decisive but short step away from unilateral and wrongful pretension.⁷

Passion is bound up with reason, imagination, the capacity to abstract and

---

2 DR, VI 213 (12)
3 Ibid.
4 *Religion*, VI 28–9, 93 (24, 85); *Anthropology*, VII 265–7 (132–4)
5 See Kant *Pädagogik*, IX 492; *Anthropology*, VII 270 (137).
6 *Anthropology*, VII 270 (137)
7 *Anthropology*, VII 268 (135). Cf. *Religion*, VI 42 (37).

to adopt a principle – in short, intellectual abilities that are specifically human. The human propensity for evil is directly linked to the capacity to reason. Passion has this much in common with reason, 'namely, that it entails the idea of a power [*Vermögen*] bound up with freedom, through which alone ends in general can be achieved.'[8] Passion involves severing desire from its immediate object through the intermediation of a 'maxim.' Natural inclination is extinguished when its object is achieved. Material desire ceases with its consummation. The existence and duration of such desire is determined by nature through the appetites it instils and the resources it provides for fulfilling them. Natural desire provides, with regard to its object, no constant or enduring connection or principle (*beharrliches Prinzip*).[9] To desire as nature dictates is to succumb to forces over which one has no control. To desire via a maxim, on the contrary, is to secure a hold over one's intention. Passion is desire mediated and extended by a principle or maxim. In expressing its desire as a maxim the will imagines and holds before itself an end that cannot be extinguished by the play of external forces.

It is through passion that reason first establishes a constant relation with its object, that is, sets itself a task.[1] By making power or a means in general its end, reason hoists itself beyond the flux of nature to which immediate natural desire subjected it. The objects of natural desire were satisfied more or less effectively by nature itself; the objects of reason are, on the contrary, *tasks* for reason to pursue. In electing to choose its own end, reason severs the natural connection between desire and satisfaction.[2] The natural connection between reason and the object of its desire, a relation reason was not in a position fully

---

8 *Anthropology*, VII 270 (137). The consciousness of a power and possession of means to satisfy one's inclinations evokes passion more strongly than does their actual use (ibid. 272 (139)).
9 *Anthropology*, VII 266 (133). Hobbes, too, links the human notion of power with the uniquely human capacity to imagine consequences (see *Leviathan*, chapters 3 and 5; Leo Strauss *What is Political Philosophy?* (Glencoe: The Free Press 1959) 176). Cf. Kant *Anthropology*, VII 182–7 (57–61). For Kant, however, imagination is not merely a passive receiver of sense impressions (as for Hobbes), but rather a productive and reproductive faculty, which, through its own spontaneous synthesis, mediates between sensation and the concepts of understanding. (See CR A/115). '*Imagination* is the faculty of representing in intuition an object that is *not itself present*' (CR B/151). As such it is not only a condition of experience in general but also crucial to the development of the passions.
1 Passion depends on imagination, which first develops as a capacity (sexually) to desire an object that is not present. As the source of our (aesthetic) experience of the beautiful and the sublime, however, Imagination also has an important socializing and moralizing effect. Sociability begins with disinterested pleasure in the opposite sex as an object of beauty; morality begins with a sublime overcoming of care and pain. Juridical society has more to do with sublime self-overcoming than with beauty and love. (See 'Conjectural Beginning,' VIII 113–15 (58–9); and *Anthropology*, VII 266 (133).)
2 Cf. Jean Starobinski *Jean-Jacques Rousseau: La transparence et l'obstacle*.

to control, is replaced by a new relation between reason and its tasks. This relation, however, unlike the object desired, is fully in the power of reason to secure.

Prudence (or 'pragmatic' reason) carries the formalization of desire one step farther than does passion. Prudence provides what passion lacks, namely, a principle for connecting power in general with the inclinations it was originally meant to satisfy. Prudence moves 'from the general to the particular' according to the principle that one 'not condescend to any single inclination, thereby placing all the rest in the shade, but rather see to it that it can co-exist with all the others.'[3] The emancipating principle of reason, a principle entailing the capacity to reconcile each of one's inclinations with all the others, is strikingly juridical in form. The prudent ego presides over its inclinations as a referee (and not, as Plato would have it, as a potentate). The self-consistency of the prudent soul prefigures the juridical harmony of the united will. When reason, surpassing prudence, makes self-consistency not only a means in general, but also an end-in-itself, reason attains true moral autonomy.

The idea of a power in general is a necessary element of that capacity to abstract from one's immediate object without which neither good nor evil (nor even knowledge) would be possible. It is also a most powerful historical force. With his recognition of nature as a means to his own ends, man also recognizes, however dimly, other men as capable of lodging similar claims. The determination to use things as means and tools for his own end instils a fear that others may do likewise with him. Alongside the desire for happiness there springs up a fear of depending for that happiness on the wills of others. Savage man expresses his passion for freedom by militantly repelling all other men who might try to make use of him. The passion for freedom first expresses itself in the uniquely human preference for independence over a happiness dependent on the will of others.[4]

The innate desire for freedom becomes a passion when it is directed against other men.[5] The Kantian war of all against all is initially defensive. In time, however, it occurs to man actively to attempt to make use of other men. The 'inclination to have a general power to influence others' becomes the acquired and specifically social passions for honour, domination, or possession.[6] The

---

[3] *Anthropology*, VII 266 (134) (my translation). Cf. ibid. 131–2 (13): Kant notes that many a suitor could make a good marriage if only he could abstract from his beloved's wart or missing tooth.
[4] Ibid. 268–70 (135–7)
[5] Ibid. 270 (137)
[6] Ibid. 271 (138)

tendencies which initially drove men apart begin to pull them together. Man has an 'inclination to associate with others, because in society he feels himself to be more than man.'[7] The power of the isolated individual extends no farther than his limited ability to place objects under his physical control. Human society gives far greater scope to his desire for power in general. Formal desire, and the concomitant capacity to abstract from the immediate object of one's inclination, is almost necessarily a social phenomenon. Along with Rousseau, Kant cites, as the first and fatal training of a future tyrant, that indulgence of infants which teaches them how to gratify their desires by exploiting others.[8] At the same time, man continues to fear in others the unsociable and tyrannical qualities he recognizes in himself. His desire to coerce others is matched by his fear of being coerced. This tension awakens 'all [man's] powers,' and teaches him for the first time to labour. It brings man to conquer his laziness and, 'propelled by vain glory, lust for power, and avarice, to achieve a rank among his fellows whom he cannot tolerate but from whom he cannot withdraw.'[9]

As attempts to use other men as means alone, the passions undermine the objective basis of one's own claim to worth. In one's passion one loses sight of and subverts the ends in pursuit of which one's passions originally developed. As a 'kind of delusion' through which one 'takes part of one's end to be the whole,' and 'the value of a thing' to be what others 'think it worth,' passion not only falls short of but actually negates the formal principle of reason.[1] Passions of pride and false pretension characteristically subvert the ends towards which they strive.[2] Those of revenge go even further, causing a man to lose sight of his own interest entirely. Through revenge, 'sweetest version of malicious joy,' one seeks to harm others even without advantage to oneself.[3] At its worst, passion makes a man forget altogether the end that he is in himself, in order to rectify some real or imagined injury. The fury of revenge makes one willing to destroy oneself in order to destroy one's enemy.[4] The maxim of self-love is not only contradictory but ultimately self-destructive.[5] As vengeance (egoism at its most violent), self-love becomes suicidal.

---

7 'Idea for a Universal History,' VIII 20–1 (15–16)
8 *Pädagogik*, IX 461. As noted above, Kant's treatise on education is strongly influenced by Rousseau's *Emile*; Kant, however, speaks less of happiness and more of principle, self-consistency, and moral training generally than does Rousseau.
9 'Idea for a Universal History,' VIII 21 (15)
1 *Anthropology*, VII 266–70 (133–7)
2 Ibid. 266, 272–3 (134, 139)
3 Kant *The Doctrine of Virtue*, VI, 459
4 *Anthropology*, VII 271 (138)
5 Cf. Hegel *History of Philosophy* III 451.

Vengeance is not only the most contradictory of the passions; it is also that most closely linked with right. The desire for revenge (*Rache*) 'issues irresistibly out of human nature,' along with the concepts of outer freedom and right. However evil vengeance may be, it is also the 'analogue' of a desire for justice (*Recht*).[6] Anger is our earliest expression of the capacity for self-forgetting which also underlies morality. By universalizing anger, right transforms a physically destructive self-forgetting into a morally constructive one. The rational alternative to self-destruction is the adoption as one's end of a universal legislation which serves all. In submitting to this legislation, the will reclaims itself, becoming indirectly the end in and for itself that it could not be directly. Man is liberated when he subjects himself ideally to the punishing force to which he would subject others. Carrying him beyond the range of that which first aroused his anger, this submission saves him from real annihilation.[7] In this one respect Kant and Nietzsche are, for all their differences, not far apart; for each the concept of *Rache* stands with *Recht* at the crux of moral evolution.

In his introduction to the *Doctrine of Right*, Kant calls external freedom, or 'independence from the constraint of another's *Willkür* ... compatible with universal law,' the sole and original right that belongs to man by virtue of his humanity.[8] The rights of man do not abstract entirely from the human weakness for which Kant would have them compensate. Our *Willkür* is 'free'; but it is also somehow 'capable of constraint.' (*Wille*, which is 'absolutely necessary,' and so 'incapable of constraint,' is 'neither free nor unfree.')[9] To be free is to be subject to resistance and limitation. Willing entails a consciousness of power (*Vermögen*) to achieve one's aims. But even the will which fails to achieve its aims must be accounted free. Thus, the consciousness of our 'means in general' (*Vermögen überhaupt*) may also entail a consciousness 'of our incapacity [*Unvermögen*] with respect to the external world.'[1] The *Willkür* is a function both of our self-sufficiency and of our neediness. Au-

---

6 *Anthropology*, VII 270 (137) (my translation)
7 According to Kant, even one's suppressed indignation poses a threat to one's life (ibid. 260 (127–8)). The proper way to deal with anger is not to 'hold it back' (*zurückhalten*) but rather to channel it into a 'legitimate desire for right.'
8 DR, VI 237 (43–4). Right is concerned not with inner freedom of choice but with the 'use of freedom' in the world, a use that man in exercising his inner freedom cannot help but intend. On some moral and logical problems with the notion of external freedom cf. Galston *Kant and the Problem of History* 200–1.
9 For a discussion of the political implications of Kant's distinction between *Wille* and *Willkür*, see Lewis White Beck, 'Les deux concepts kantiens du vouloir dans leur contexte politique.'
1 DR, VI 357 (131)

tonomous with regard to its ends, the will is dependent with regard to its means. The will is free precisely to the extent that it needs to make use of objects in the external world. To be free in this human sense is to be internally constrained, externally opposed. External freedom concerns the relation between the will and that opposition which, because it is a fundamental condition of human consciousness, cannot be abolished, but which can, through a system of right, be made 'acceptable.'

Kant expands the definition of right provided in his Introduction by describing the conditions of its application. The concept of right applies 'only to the external and ... practical relationship of one person to another in which their actions can in fact [*als Facta*] exert an influence on each other.' It 'applies only to the relationship of a will [*Willkür*] to another person's will, not to his wishes or desires (or even just his needs), which are the concern of acts of benevolence and charity.' And it applies only to a reciprocal relationship which ignores the content (*Materie*) of the will, that is to say, 'the end that a person intends to accomplish by means of the object that he wills.' For example, if someone buys wares from us, '[we] do not ask whether [he] will profit from the transaction.' Instead, in applying the concept of right, 'we take into consideration only the form [*Form*] of the relationship between the wills in so far as they are regarded as free, and whether the action of one of them can be conjoined with the freedom of the other in accordance with a universal law.'[2]

The juridical community is not a 'kingdom of ends.' It does not assume coincidence of motives nor does it abolish internal conflicts over ends. No person has any *rightful* concern with the inner motives of his fellows.[3] The laws of right require only that every action (whatever its moral incentive) which outwardly affects others gain their rational consent. In a juridical community, the means of each become, at least formally, the means of all.

The juridical community is also not (necessarily) a kingdom of happiness. Consent does not guarantee actual benefit.[4] It is the formal condition of mutual consent, not the material condition of mutual benefit, which binds the juridical community. The laws of right do not promise happiness but merely submit to our approval the wilful activity which may affect us. If an activity which we have approved turns out for the worst, we have only ourselves to

---

2 Ibid. 230 (34)
3 The distinction between externally and internally imputable motives, though not explicitly formulated by Kant, is essential to his distinction between the juridical and the ethical.
4 'No generally valid principle of legislation can be based on happiness' (Kant, 'On the Common Saying: "This May be True in Theory, but it Does not Apply in Practice,"' VIII 298 (80) (hereafter cited as 'Theory and Practice').

blame. Kant's conception of juridical community tends to deflect our indignation inwards. When we approve the actions of another, they become, in a sense, our own.

The laws of right are objects of what Kant terms a 'perfect' moral duty. Unlike pragmatic maxims of happiness, laws of right, and the juridical community they define, provide the will with an objective and determinate end.[5] In this regard they surpass even benevolence and self-perfection, which as objects of 'imperfect' duty, cannot determinately guide the will. Without the principle of right as a moral end, no supreme and determinate principle could be found for reason at all.[6] Having broken away from its immediate end, the will as member of a juridical community attains an objective and determinate end of which the will is itself a part. Through its participation in juridical community, the will becomes the end in and for itself which it otherwise could not be.

Although it is the object of moral duty, right is also separable from duty; the system which it defines abstracts from inner motivation, moral and otherwise. The relation between wills which right defines is a purely external one. As both an end to the moral few and a means to the immoral many, the doctrine of right is both co-ordinate with and separable from the doctrine of virtue. 'Just as right in general has as its object only what is external in actions, so strict right, in so much as it contains no ethical elements, requires no determining grounds of the will besides those that are purely external; for only then is it pure and not confused with any prescriptions of virtue.'[7]

Juridical community, Kant argues, does not depend on moral motivation. As a strictly external system, it relies on external grounds for determining the will. Right therefore implies the possibility of external 'coercion.' Strict right, as Kant states in his introduction, can 'be represented as the possibility of a general reciprocal use of coercion that is consistent with the freedom of everyone in accordance with universal laws.' Right is bound up with 'authority to compel.'[8]

The notion of authorized compulsion makes possible, according to Kant, a

---

5 DR, VI 240 (46)

6 *Groundwork*, IV 65 (96). Unlike perfect duties, imperfect ones do not specify precisely 'what and how much one's actions should do toward the obligatory end.' See Kant *The Doctrine of Virtue*, VI 389 (49). In the *Doctrine of Virtue*, Kant discusses determinate duties towards oneself, or 'inner juridical duties' following from the 'right of humanity in one's own person.' For both outer and inner relations, juridical duty provides morality with its only determinate standard. See Mary J. Gregor 'Translator's Introduction' in Kant *The Doctrine of Virtue* xxix.

7 DR, VI 232 (36) (my translation)

8 DR, VI 231–2 (35–7)

kind of 'construction' of right in pure intuition.⁹ What heretofore has been purely conceptual now becomes accessible to intuition. The enforceable character of right renders it intuitable. The construction of right as a system of external relations resembles that of physics (the science of body), another system of external relations to which Kant explicitly compares right.¹ The model of reciprocal coercion 'exhibits' the concept of right in pure intuition. The possibility of reciprocal coercion makes palpable the law of right, just as geometric figures and mechanical formulas 'construct' the laws of mathematics and physics. The possibility of reciprocal coercion 'exhibits [the concept of right] in pure *a priori* intuition, on the analogy of the possibility of free movement of bodies under the law of the equality of action and reaction.'² The same construction which makes possible an *a priori* mechanics enables us to grasp the properties of right.³

The possibility of a reciprocal exercise of force constructs in intuition an ideal system of free, lawful activity. Our ability to construct in intuition a (mechanical) system of action and reaction, force and counterforce, enables us to make sense of right. Opposition is bound up with right, not only psychologically, as the source of the child's first indignant cries, but also logically, as the condition of a complete exposition of the concept. Lawful coercion goes hand in hand with external freedom; for by means of it lawless and unjust opposition may be opposed and thereby negated. Granting the reality of external opposition to one's freedom, authority to use coercion follows from the law of contradiction. 'If a certain use of freedom is itself a hindrance to freedom ... then the use of coercion to counteract it ... is

---

9 DR, VI 232–3 (37–8): 'The law of a reciprocal use of coercion that is necessarily consistent with everyone's freedom ... may in certain respects be regarded as the *construction* of this concept [of right] ...'
1 See above, 113, note 5. Cf. *Reflexion* #6667, in which Kant likens the juridical common will to the 'focal point' of interaction between physical bodies.
2 Cf. *Bemerkungen*, XX 165: 'Analogy: by attraction a body fills its own space, as every man fills his. By attraction all parts join into one.' The 'free' movement of bodies is analogous to that activity by which a person fills a space and thereby (physically) constitutes himself.
3 The impersonality of mechanics, as (an external) system of body, is paralleled by the impartiality of right, as an external system of wills. Both abstract from the special experience and perspective of the individual. Mechanics turns our attention from our subjective experience of bodies (in which our own body is special and paramount) towards a uniform system in which our own body is like any other. Similarly, right turns our attention from our personal situation (that which restrains *us*, or which *we* would restrain) towards a uniform system of mutual restraint. In such a system of juridical 'equilibrium,' according to Kant, the opposition of one will neutralizes or 'cancels out' (*hebt auf*) the opposition of another. Juridical coercion is 'opposition' of the 'opposition' of external freedom. Unlike the *Aufhebung* and double-negation of Hegel, that of Kant achieves equilibrium, not transcendence.

consistent with freedom.'⁴ The authority to coerce follows from the fact that we are in a position to oppose each other.⁵

External freedom implies a kind of external self-limitation. Men are beings in a position to oppose one another, but also beings who can, through a reciprocal act of will, cease to oppose one another. Out of the possibility of such an act of will arises the system of right. The laws of right erect, through the mutual agreement of all, external barriers to the activities of each. The barriers of nature are imposed on us without our leave; the laws of right, on the other hand, erect barriers to which we consent or ought to consent. Laws of right regulate and legitimate our tendency to oppose and our susceptibility to being opposed. Through right, external resistance becomes acceptable (*annehmlich*), remains external, and yet becomes our own. The innate right to outer freedom cannot abolish outer opposition; it does, however, submit such opposition when it is wilful to the condition of our approval. Through this condition, physical opposition can, at least ideally, cease to oppose.

The doctrine of right asserts a fundamental distinction between willed and unwilled opposition. Against the forces of nature we may struggle with greater or lesser success. Ultimately, however, we are at the mercy of overwhelming powers, the ends of which we can neither know nor share. Juridically, on the other hand, we can demand that what affects us be acceptable to us. The capacity to exercise certain and objective power over nature is necessarily a moral power, which physical force can heed only when it is imbued with human wilfulness. We properly assert our rights, not against nature, but against other wills. But just as duty implies a power to exercise an absolute causality over nature, so right asserts a power, in imbuing nature with our ends, to make it our own. The corollary of the immunity of nature to our claims is its susceptibility to our appropriation. Right concerns will as or acting through body, will in its capacity to influence and to be influenced. The realm of Kantian justice consists of wills (that have rights) and things (that can be owned).⁶ As we shall see, Kant's theory of right is substantially a theory of property.

---

4 DR, VI 231 (36)
5 A right is the objective ground to 'stand against' another *Willkür* (*Vorarbeiten*, XXIII 302).
6 'The worth of the humanity in one's own person is personality itself; if one is an end in oneself ... one can set oneself an end. That which cannot set itself an end has only the worth of a means' (*Reflexion* #7305).

127 *The Doctrine of Right*: A selective commentary

2 / PROPERTY AND SUBSTANCE (DR PART I)

Kant's treatment of property is complex, involuted, and condensed. To make matters even more difficult for the reader, he often implicitly refers to and relies on arguments presented in other works. In examining Kant's theory of property I shall draw attention to such arguments when they clarify the structure and intention of the whole. In general, however, I shall consider Kant's doctrine of property in the order in which the *Doctrine of Right* presents it.

POSSESSION (DR I I)

The laws of right apply to wills in their capacity to affect one another. Men affect one another by affecting nature, of which they are a part. The relation of right to human affairs is thus bound up with the relation between nature and the human will. Through their desire and power to make use of things, men come into conflict with one another. According to Kant, such conflict between free agents brings freedom 'into contradiction with itself.' If this contradiction is to be avoided, the claims of everyone must be reconciled according to some universal law. The primary purpose of Kant's doctrine of right is to provide the principles necessary for such reconciliation.

The first encounter between nature and the (human) will involves the human body, physical *locus* of men's double capacity to use and to be used. Each human will is, by virtue of its body, not only before the world but also in it, and hence susceptible, like any natural object, to the exploitation of other wills. Inborn (*angeborne*) right is effectively a right to the use of one's body.[7] Anyone who, without my consent and contrary to universal law, physically restricts me, that is to say, obstructs my body, violates this right.

Inborn right may also be regarded as innate property, or 'that which is internally my own,' as distinguished from external property, which must be acquired (*erworben*).[8] Kant devotes only a short section of his introduction to the presentation of inborn right, or inner property; for according to Kant its articulation is 'analytic' and unproblematic. Innate property is, as it were, divided and distributed by nature; we possess our own bodies as a birthright that is naturally and exclusively ours. With regard to inner property, there is no doubt as to what is and what is not one's own.

Inner property, however, also implies the use of outer objects, and hence

---

[7] On our inborn right to 'the place we fill,' see *Vorarbeiten*, XXIII 286–304.
[8] DR, VI 237 (43)

the need – if conflict is to be avoided – for a division of outer objects into 'mine' and 'yours.'[9] 'Mine,' Kant records in his notes, 'is that the alteration of which also alters me.' 'Mine is internal when it only belongs to my determination in time, external if it is outside me but so bound to me that its alteration at the same time alters me.'[1] Just as we cannot experience time without space, or our bodies without a world beyond, just as inner implies outer experience, so we cannot will to use our bodies without also willing to make use of objects in the external world. 'Without external objects of the will [*Willkür*] we could not be aware of possession of our own determinations, and of the inborn right to the use of ourselves. Thus, the right to serve ourselves through outer objects must be seen.'[2] The body is both a means of power and the badge of our dependency; in either capacity, it implies a will directed beyond itself towards objects in the world. Both moral duty and natural need direct man beyond himself. A man must make use of things to effect his ends, whatever they may be. In using something, however, he withholds it from the use of others. Hence there must be a law concerning the distribution of things, lest persons enter into conflict over what each may use. In the case of outer (as distinguished from inner) property, there is no simple, naturally articulated answer to the question, 'What is mine and what is yours?'

Kant devotes the first half of his *Doctrine of Right* to the subject of external or acquired property. The problem of external property stems from the relation between the will and its (external) objects, a relation which is always externally contingent and physically insecure. If the will is to claim an outer object as its own, it must establish some secure connection between that object and itself. Earlier thinkers associated the right to property with the rational or divine nature of things. According to Roman and scholastic jurisprudence, certain things or kinds of things were held to belong naturally to certain men or kinds of men. Caste, order, class, and all the other divisions of property and society were thought to reflect some natural or divine articulation of the world. According to Kant, on the contrary, the only necessary relations in nature are those put there by man. However, man in his capacity as a natural being is unable to establish any necessary connection between himself and any other natural thing; he is unable to secure any necessary relation between himself and the material objects of his will. If such a relation exists, human reason must supply its ground.[3]

---

9 Hence the title of part 1: 'Das Privatrecht vom äusseren Mein und Dein überhaupt'
1 *Vorarbeiten*, XXIII 334. See Mary J. Gregor *Laws of Freedom* 50–63.
2 *Vorarbeiten*, XXIII 310.
3 *Reflexion* #7701: 'Things are by nature free.' But cf. DR, VI 250 (54). Although Kant, with Hume, rejects Locke's labour theory of property, he also rejects Hume's associational

A will can unilaterally secure a necessary relation to its object only when the will is that of God and the object his divine creation. A will 'indisputably owns what [it itself] has substantially made [*der Substanz nach*].'[4] Such production, however, no human being can accomplish. For by substantial production, Kant means creation of something out of nothing, creation, that is to say, of being (*Substanz*) itself. The Lockean assertion of a right to the fruits of one's labour is a claim which Kant ascribes to God alone.[5] A being that can create its object holds that object wholly in its own power.[6] Its omnipotence and the necessity of the connection between the object and itself go hand in hand.

Human reason is not creative but recreative or 'reproductive.' Its practical power over nature, like its theoretical power over the 'given,' is finite. The connection between men and the objects of their will is based not on their omnipotence but on their vulnerability. As Kant said, that is mine the alteration of which alters me. For the human subject, itself the labouring and laboured product of an effort to hold change at bay,[7] property is always a defensive assertion. To have property is, at the same time, to be susceptible to injury. An object is *de jure* mine, the *Doctrine of Right* begins, if I am so bound to it that anyone else who uses it without my consent thereby injures me. For Kant, as for Locke and Rousseau, 'there can be no injury where there is no property,' and vice versa.[8] Injury is harm against which we may rightfully protest. Our rights testify both to our moral power and to our natural vulnerability: they fortify us without eliminating the source of our weakness. Rights are demands morally fortified but not necessarily satisfied. The concept of right captures the self wresting its own wholeness from forces beyond

---

account of causality and property (which Hume sees as a 'species of causation' and its best illustration), on the grounds that it cannot explain the necessity attributed to both causal and propertal relations. See Hume *A Treatise of Human Nature* (Selby-Bigge ed.) 310,505-6. Cf. James Moore 'Hume's Theory of Justice and Property' *Political Studies* 24 (1976): 103-19.

4 DR, VI, 345 (117)

5 Kantian 'substance' is a radical adaptation of the Lockean term for that which 'stands under' accidents (CJ, V 352 (part 1, 223)). Locke's analysis of substance was meant to show the empirical basis of a seemingly metaphysical idea. Kant's analysis is meant to show the *a priori* element in what Locke took to be wholly empirical. (See Locke *An Essay Concerning Human Understanding* chapter 23.)

6 *Vorarbeiten*, XXIII 306. See also DR, VI 265; cf. ibid. 345 (117) on natural products as 'artifacts' of the state.

7 See *Anthropology*, VII 134 (15).

8 DR, VI 245 (51). Possession is the only condition under which one can be injured (*gekränkt*) in one's freedom (*Vorarbeiten*, XXIII 222). Cf. Rousseau *The Second Discourse* 150; Locke *The Second Treatise of Government* chapter 5.

its control which threaten constantly to overwhelm it. The concept of right also captures the ambiguity of this achievement of a self who combines without creating and subsists without self-subsistence.

The juridical reach of the human will exceeds its natural grasp. This discrepancy gives rise to an apparent 'dialectic' or 'antinomy' concerning the claim to outer property.[9] The will claims (outer) objects as its own. But in order for the will to have something as its object it must be conscious of its power to use it. To have something as its object, then, the will must (physically) occupy or hold it. The human will, however, cannot secure this occupation against the power of nature and other wills. But an object no longer in one's power is, strictly speaking, no longer an object of one's will. An object taken out of one's possession ceases to be one's own. Thus injury with respect to outer property seems to be impossible.

Kant resolves this antinomy by distinguishing between physical and rational (or juridical) possession. For external property to be possible, there must exist some rational connection between the will and its object, one which prevails even when the physical connection is severed. An external thing is mine 'only if I can assume that it is still possible for me to be injured by someone else's use of the thing even when it is not in my (physical) possession.'[1]

To 'deduce' the possibility (that is, establish the conditions) of external property is, then, to deduce the possibility of non-physical, juridical possession. Rightful possession must be grounded in an intelligible connection of the object with the person. Since human reason cannot guarantee the existence of its own object, this connection cannot exist between wills and their (contingent) objects. 'The will that has an object in its power is its creator. If, however, the thing must be assumed to exist independently, one cannot by oneself, even through the greatest power, make it one's own.'[2] A rational connection between men and things can only be established indirectly and collectively. A direct rational connection cannot be established between wills and things, but only between wills. 'To attempt to appropriate something unilaterally is an arbitrary act,' and 'nothing external can be acquired arbitrarily.'[3]

It is the rational connection between finite wills – a connection that resembles what Hegel will later call recognition – which furnishes the rational foundation for external property. Property implies a collective usurpation

9 DR, VI, 254–5 (63–4)
1 DR, VI 245, 249 (51, 56)
2 *Vorarbeiten*, XXIII 306
3 Ibid. 319

whose ideal basis is the idea of a universal or united will (*allgemeiner Wille*). Outer property entails the idea of a collective will, united through the willingness of each to submit his use of things to limits approved by all.[4] 'Property depends on the [*a priori*] idea of a will ... united with regard to things, [a will] as originally and objectively necessary but also as if it existed.'[5]

The united will does not imply a harmony of ends, but only a collaboration over means in order to maximize that use of things which is compatible with external freedom. Unlike Rousseau's 'general will' (which is in part Kant's model), the united will does not imply an *identification* of self-interest with the interest of the collectivity.[6] In Kant's juridical community, only means need be shared; ends are always an individual and private matter. Kant's united will is a union of convenience, implying no ethical surrender of the self to the collective spirit. The moral and moralizing function which Rousseau assigned to the political community Kant locates in a moral community which, springing directly from the noumenal personality of the individual, bypasses politics altogether. Like Rousseau, however, Kant understands juridical unity to require the freedom of each from dependence, and from the humiliation of such dependence, on the arbitrary will of anyone else. 'Free is he who is subject to no one else. Subject is he the condition of whose happiness depends on the will of another.'[7] As a mutual collaboration over the means to happiness, the Kantian general will 'cancels out' (*hebt auf*) the subjection of each.[8] Through the idea of the united will, our dependency on the wills of others is balanced, and thereby cancelled, by their equal dependency on us.

The rational connection binding objects to our will is a function not of divine omnipotence but of human collaboration. Our purely exploitative relationship with things defines itself against our juridical relationship with other men. Through his concept of right and the juridical community it entails, man raises himself 'altogether above community with animals.'[9] The natural susceptibility of men to be used as things is countered by the assertion of an inalienable property of each in himself. The distinction between things (as means) and men (as means but also ends-in-themselves) is crucial to the juridical appropriation of nature. The juridical emptiness of nature, which

---

4 DR, VI 249–52 (56–60) (Kant's 'deduction' of the concept of the rational possession of an external thing)
5 *Vorarbeiten*, XXIII 306
6 Kant's 'united will' is an *a priori* condition of intelligible possession, not a historical fact, dependent on space and time.
7 See *Vorarbeiten*, XXIII 307
8 Ibid. 328
9 'Conjectural Beginning,' VIII 114 (58)

assigns itself to no one, is filled by an act of wilful legislation that appropriates nature for one and all.

Unlike inner property, outer property is acquired 'synthetically.' The united will unifies itself in appropriating nature, and appropriates nature in unifying itself. Each act of synthesis[1] implies the other: wills could not be combined without something to appropriate; nothing could be appropriated without a unity of wills.

Early drafts of the *Doctrine of Right* suggest a similarity between the function of the united will and that of the 'transcendental unity of apperception' discussed in the Transcendental Deduction of the first *Critique*.[2] Both the *Doctrine of Right* and the first *Critique* 'deduce' synthetic unity as necessary to rational possession. By 'deduction,' Kant means an argument supportive of a claim to property.[3] Both the juridical deduction and its transcendental counterpart establish how it is possible to 'possess' or 'have' something as one's own. Kant calls the Transcendental Deduction an 'explanation of the possession [*Besitzes*] of pure knowledge.'[4] The Transcendental Deduction concerns possession of the knowledge of objects; the juridical deduction concerns possession of those objects themselves.

The united will bears other similarities to the transcendental unity of apperception. This unity of apperception, roughly synonymous with 'self-consciousness,' is bound up with our capacity to attach 'I think' to all of our representations.[5] As the united will defines itself in appropriating nature, so the transcendental unity of apperception defines itself in appropriating the 'given.' For 'manifold representations, which are given in intuitions, would not be one and all *my* representations, if they did not belong to one self-consciousness. As *my* representations ... they must conform to the condition under which alone they *can* stand together in one universal self-consciousness, because otherwise they would not all without exception belong to me.'[6] Unity of consciousness is bound up with the capacity to call representations one's own. The business of (theoretical) understanding is the acquisition (*Erwerbung*) of knowledge.[7]

---

1 DR, VI 250 (57)
2 *Vorarbeiten*, XXIII 297, 299
3 CR A/84–A/86 = B/117–B/118
4 CR A/87 = B/119
5 CR B/131
6 CR B/132–B/133; theory is concerned with what is 'mine,' practice with what is 'mine' and what is 'yours.' Cf. Dieter Henrich 'The Proof-Structure of Kant's Transcendental Deduction' *Review of Metaphysics* 22 (1968/69): 640–59.
7 CR A/87 = B/119

133 *The Doctrine of Right*: A selective commentary

For Kant consciousness is, as Hegel observed, distinctly proprietary.[8] In the Transcendental Deduction, Kant expresses in terms of a kind of mental ownership the unity of consciousness implicit in all knowledge. The elementary but fundamental point from which he begins is the fact that we regard mental representations – if they are anything at all to us – as our own. By uncovering the conditions of this ownership, Kant thinks he can establish the *a priori* laws which govern human thought. His task resolves itself into two questions: a/ How is mental ownership possible (that is, what are its conditions)? and b/ What have my representations to do with the objects of my knowledge? Kant's response may be broadly summarized as follows. The fact that I regard all these representations as my own implies, and is implied by, the unity of self-consciousness. For I am conscious of myself at a certain moment in possession of a particular representation; but I could not conceive all such representations as 'my own' without the concept of a single self united through time to which they all belong. What then is to explain the affinity of these

8 See G.W.F. Hegel, *Encyclopedia of the Philosophical Sciences*, Part Three (*Philosophy of Mind*), trans. William Wallace and A.V. Miller (Oxford, Clarendon Press 1971) #453-4, #456 *Zusatz*, #528.

In his *Philosophy of Mind*, Hegel characterized Kantian mind as a subconscious 'mine or pit' (*Schacht*) in which is 'treasured up a world of infinitely many images and representations.' According to Hegel, such images are at first ours only in a formal manner; like the hidden contents of land over which one holds mineral rights, they cannot at will be called forth. Mere property in the image becomes actual possession when the image is combined with memory or recollected existence, a combination which Hegel calls 'representation proper.' For Hegel, these progressive stages of consciousness imply the actual unity of mind, both as 'universal mine' in which all images are treasured up, and as 'possessor' of representations as its own. The unity of image and concept is to be understood not, as it was for Kant, as a '*neutral*, so to speak *chemical* product,' of the 'particular and the general,' but rather as the 'generalizing of the image' and the 'imaging of the universal' by the idea 'actively proving itself to be the *substantial* power over the image ...'

Similarly, the three substantial correlatives of civility for Kant – land, money, and the exchange of ideas – were translated by Hegel into hierarchical estates (*Stände*). The first Hegel describes as the '"substantial," natural estate' to which 'the fruitful soil and ground supply a natural and stable capital.' The second is that of social capital, created by individual industry and exchange. The third, 'thinking' estate, has both subsistence (like the second) procured by its own skill and 'certain subsistence' (like the first) because it is 'guaranteed through the whole society.'

In their politics as in their theories of mind, the assertions of unity and substantiality which Kant made equivocally were absolutized by Hegel. Hegel would breach the ambiguous but necessary distinction in Kant's thought between theory and practice, demand and satisfaction, actual and ideal. Similarly, the actual state whose authority for Kant cannot be directly opposed, but which can and ought to be improved by other means, assumed in Hegel's thought the rigid and final – even tomblike – perimeters of the Prussian monarchy.

diverse representations, alike in their one and all belonging to me? Kant excludes the possibility that this affinity derives from an external source, be it God or the nature of the objects represented. Instead, he assumes that it must derive from the affinity-conferring, or synthetic, power of the mind itself.

The foundation of the unity which we attribute both to the world and to our various states of perceiving it is an underlying *a priori* act of combination or synthesis, which Kant refers to as the transcendental unity of apperception. 'Apperception' means the awareness of perception (which itself originally connotes a taking of possession); the unity of apperception is thus the unity of all possible states of (actually or potentially) self-conscious perception. The identity which one attributes to oneself as subject and the order which one attributes to the objective world both have their source in a transcendental appropriation of the 'given' as 'one's own.'

The mind's appropriating and self-unifying synthesis furnishes the pure form of all possible knowledge. To its laws and categories all one's representations must conform. The regularity of experience reflects the combination of all its elements according to the same *a priori* rules. The laws of nature correspond to laws of reason; and the flux of nature is informed by categories of our own mind.

Lacking direct access to the transcendental synthesis which underlies the unity which informs experience, the mind expresses this synthesis through its concept of an independent object to which knowledge corresponds, an object which is regarded as preventing thought from being haphazard or arbitrary. Although reason is proprietary, it is also limited in its appropriating power. Its representations of objects are its own; the objects themselves elude its synthesizing grasp. In conferring on representations their affinities, understanding must refer them to an 'object in general,' which, alien and apart, is nothing to reason at all.[9] Even self-knowledge is subject to these limits. The mind's transcendental synthesis is, paradoxically, expressed in the grounding concept of something utterly alien. Self-awareness and critical philosophy cannot penetrate beyond this seeming negation. In a world whose affinities the mind has itself conferred, reason remains a partial stranger to itself.

Like its epistemological counterpart, juridical possession requires a transcendental synthesis. Juridical synthesis entails a unity not of apperceptions, however, but of wills. This unity, which Kant also calls the united or general will, confers on men the right to make use of things.

As the individual ego was constituted by an appropriation of that which is given to sensation, so the social unity of men is constituted by an appropriation of the natural world. The right of each of us to anything presupposes a transcendental and ideal but nonetheless necessary moment in which all as members of the general will appropriate the earth. According to Kant's deduction, this contractual communion or community gives private property its only conceivable justification and foundation. At the same time, such community must be construed in terms of the myriad individuals each of whom wills to appropriate things for himself. Although private property implies an ideal and primal community, so, too, community implies an indissoluble right to private property.

Unlike Locke, who argued that the right to property precedes contractual community, Kant argues that the right to property requires it. Unlike Marx, who equated true community with communal property, or communism, Kant argues that the general will appropriates in common only so that each member may possess in private. Both moral communalist and economic capitalist, Kant contends that our rights to property are at once individually and socially derived. The ideal community, which each private act of possession implies, but which none can instate, is like the transcendental ego, which each separate state of consciousness implies, but which none can embrace.

For both the theoretically united understanding and the practically united will, synthetic unity is bound up with property. And in both theory and practice, rational possession is distinguished from empirical possession according to the mode in which it is acquired. Unlike empirical possession, which is always accidental and insecure, rational possession is connected with an *a priori* synthesis. As unity of consciousness makes possible a combination of *a priori* categories with the 'matter' of sensation, so unity of will makes possible a combination of *a priori* categories with that 'matter' furnished by the natural world. As synthetic unity of consciousness entails both formal *a priori* concepts and the matter supplied by the 'given,' so the united will entails both a shared formal concept of proprietary rights and a sharable material relation to the world. We are bound together juridically both by our common concept of rights and by our common relation to the world.

Kant describes this sharable relation to the world as 'common possession of the soil.' Private possession is based on the *a priori* ideas of a united will and on the 'innate common possession of the earth's soil corresponding to it.' Like the united will, original community of the land 'is an idea that has objective (juridical-practical) reality.' Kant distinguishes this original community in the soil (and that which it holds) from individual occupation (or squatting) and from primitive communism, each of which, Kant insists, already presupposes the existence of private property.[1] Original community derives neither from unilateral usurpation nor from a contract in which each gives up what is already his; rather, it makes such actions possible.

Original common possession of the soil follows in part from our common dependence on nature. 'All men are originally and before any juridical act of will in rightful possession of the soil; that is, they have a right to be wherever nature or chance has placed them without their will.'[2] This immediate and unchosen dependence on the soil provides the material basis for the community of rational beings who share the earth. In practice as in theory, men share their dependence on something given. In practice, our shared relation to the soil supplies individual experience with a common substrate. By virtue of the fact that each of us makes use of some portion of the earth, we are all (potentially) interdependent. Juridical community is a function of our common will, united with regard to the earth on which we all depend and which we all would possess.

Having deduced the ideal foundation of juridical property, Kant proceeds to an elucidation of the *a priori* categories and laws which govern its acquisition, distribution, and exchange. In this elucidation, which replicates with baroque symmetry the categories and laws governing theoretical knowledge, the concepts of community, substance, and reciprocity play a special role. By community, Kant means a *commercium*, or 'state of reciprocal interdependence,' in which substances are mutually co-existent and co-determinate. By substance, he means the 'permanent,' or the 'substratum of all change.'[3] Through its category of substance, the mind conceives both of its own substantiality as a subject and of the substantiality of the world of objects. As the 'object in general,' or unpredicated being, substance is the necessarily assumed substrate against which change is perceived and without which experience would not be possible.[4]

Kant is careful to distinguish his own theory of substance from that of Leibniz, for whom substances are at once things-in-themselves and objects in the world.[5] For Kant, 'substance' refers not to things-in-themselves, but rather to the way in which *we* perceive relations. Matter, according to Kant, is 'phenomenal substance' (or substance as it appears in space and is 'experi-

---

1 DR, VI 251 (58–9)
2 DR, VI 262 (Ladd's translation omits sections 10–35, 37–40).
3 CR B/6, A/414 = B/441
4 CR A/182–A/189 = B/225–B/232, A/204 = B/250: 'Wherever there is action – and therefore activity and force – there is substance.'
5 CR A/264 = B/320

enced').⁶ Matter consists entirely of external relations. Matter, as we can experience it, has no 'inner' being at all. Purely inward objective substance, a substance, that is to say, which is, so far as its existence is concerned, related only to itself, is not to be encountered in experience.

Man is tempted, however, to apply his concept of substance to what he seems to know as 'inward being,' that is, himself. Everyone 'necessarily regard[s] himself as substance' and regards his thought 'as (consisting) only (in) accidents of his being, determinations of his state.'⁷ But the fact that we necessarily conceive of ourselves as something absolutely permanent does not save us from the fact that as part of nature we 'arise [and] perish.' 'Consciousness is, indeed, that which makes possible all representations to be thoughts; and in it, therefore, as the transcendental subject, all our perceptions must be found. But beyond this logical meaning of the "I," we have no knowledge of the subject in itself, which as substratum underlies this "I," as it does all thoughts.'⁸ The conception of our own permanence which underlies consciousness does not imply our actual substantiality. The only permanence we know empirically is the outward permanence of matter. Only to the relative permanence of the objects we encounter in experience 'can the concept of substance be applied in a manner that is empirically serviceable.'⁹

The fact that I, as a logically simple subject, can accompany all my thoughts, does not mean 'that I, as *object*, am for myself a *self-subsistent* being or *substance*.'¹ For Kant (unlike Hegel), the subject cannot know itself as substance. That permanence which reason necessarily attributes to itself is a function of its relation to, and hence a badge of its dependence on, that which is external to itself.² Inner experience presupposes outer experience. If the subject, as soul, were a 'simple part of matter,' we might deduce its permanence and indestructability.³ As material beings, however, we are, like all other material bodies, destructible composites. The fact that we must con-

---

6 CR A/277 = B/333
7 CR A/349
8 CR A/350; B/278: 'The consciousness of myself in the representation "I" is not an intuition, but a merely intellectual representation of the spontaneity of a thinking subject. This "I" has not, therefore, the least predicate of intuition, which, as permanent, might serve as a correlate for the determination of time in inner sense – in the manner in which, for instance, *impenetrability* serves in our *empirical* intuition of matter.'
9 CR A/349
1 CR B/407
2 CR B/413; the ego is merely the appearance of substance.
3 CR A/401

ceive ourselves as permanent does not, Kant insists, protect us from the flux of the empirical world.

'Although the dictum of certain ancient [Heraclitean] schools, that everything in the world is *in a flux* and nothing is *permanent* and abiding, cannot be reconciled with the admission of substances, it is not refuted by the unity of self-consciousness. For we are unable from our own consciousness to determine whether, as souls, we are permanent or not.' We cannot know whether to an outside observer the 'I' which accompanies all our thoughts 'may not be in the same state of flux as the other thoughts which, by means of it, are linked up with one another.'[4]

Like other *a priori* concepts which structure the empirical world, substance derives its objectivity not only from reason's power but also from reason's dependence on the given. We could not experience the substantiality which we attribute to ourselves without experiencing external obstacles which threaten that substantiality. The existence of the obstacle furnishes the ground of all experience, including, paradoxically, that of our own existence. Our sense of inner permanence presupposes the permanence of an external world to whose forces we are vulnerable. The permanent 'cannot be an intuition in me. For all the grounds of determination of my existence which are to be met with in me are representations; and as representations, themselves require a permanent distinct from them, in relation to which their change, and so my existence in time wherein they change, may be determined.'[5] As subjects, we define ourselves in relation to what opposes us. The transcendental unity of consciousness combines the formal substantiality of the subject with the resisting material substantiality of the given. Nature, as a product of this combination, incorporates both permanence and change through the law of conservation of matter. Material change implies an underlying constant. The teaching of the ancient schools that 'all is flux' does not describe the world as we perceive it. Heraclitus is refuted, for purposes of science, by our experience of the natural world. This refutation, however, does nothing to bolster our security or ensure the permanence of man. Reason, whose experience depends on a permanence external to itself, cannot guarantee its own substantiality. From the perspective which matters most to reason, the claims of Heraclitus cannot be conclusively denied.

At least, they cannot be theoretically denied. Practically, however, reason can assure itself of the substantiality of its own moral personality. Morality establishes the absolute practical substantiality of the self. Moral personality

---

4 CR A/364; cf. *Reflexion* #1511, on the 'dark temperament' of Heraclitus.
5 CR B/xxxix

is both self-determining and self-determined; it owes its existence only to itself.[6]

Juridical personality is moral substance, externally conceived. Right is the outer aspect of moral personality. Virtue involves a person's inner relations with himself; right involves his outer relations with other persons and with the (natural) world. Through these external relations the juridical substantiality of the person is established. The idea of an original community in the land yokes together synthetically the ideal formal substantiality of the united will with the material substantiality of the land. For theoretical reason, the inner determinations which we experience presuppose the phenomenal substantiality of matter. For practical reason, phenomenal substance is the earth itself, or that which literally 'stands under' us. The soil is the permanent material foundation, the supporting resistance, in relation to which we conduct all our practical affairs.

As substance corresponds to land, so accident corresponds to that which the land supports.[7] Just as we perceive the permanent only in relation to change, so we use the land only by using what it holds. To meet the requirements of his metaphysical distinction between substance and accident, Kant adapts the distinction, fundamental to Roman and feudal law, between immovable and movable property.[8] We do not make use of the world apart from its accidental ways of existing. 'Movables' are these accidents, the objects and products of our individual labour.[9] Human experience is particularized as well as common. To use things we must alter them for ourselves.[1] As in theory we define nature with respect both to permanence and to change, so in practice we define ourselves with respect both to the (material) substance which unites us and to the (material) accidents which separate us.

Original community in the soil gives individual possession a substantial juridical foundation. The inability of the will unilaterally to appropriate its objects stemmed from its inability to produce them. The united will and the original community in the soil to which it corresponds give (external) property a substantiality which it would otherwise lack. The appropriating power of the united will substitutes for the creative power of divine will[2] and supplies both

---

6 Cf. Kant *Opus. post.*, XXII, 121: 'Substance is the thing-in-itself ... If it is conscious of its freedom, it is a person, it has rights.'
7 DR, VI 261, 265
8 DR, VI 261
9 DR, VI 265
1 Cf. Locke *Second Treatise* chapter 5.
2 Cf. Saner *Kant's Political Thought* 34.

the material and the ideal ground for all subsequent human labour and production.³

We use things individually and privately, but also in relation to one another and to a common material substrate. Just as the concept of right implies an intention to make use of things, so juridical community implies the possibility of reciprocally exchanging them. The contiguity of the surface of the earth, which makes us materially interdependent, also makes possible among us universal and potentially unlimited exchange. Juridical community is a *commercium* at once ideal and material.⁴

The synthetic unity of the united will combines the substantiality of moral personality with that of the material world. The theoretical gap between subjective and objective permanence, between the substantiality of the 'I' and that of the world, is spanned by the practical idea of juridical community. Like a material body, the juridical person can be determined externally; unlike a material body, however, he can appropriate these external determinations and thereby make them his own. 'Determination' refers either to the external forces which experientially determine us, or to the inner legislation through which we determine our own will.⁵ The dependency implicit in the first kind of determination is balanced by the autonomy of the second. These two kinds of determination can be combined if that which affects us elicits our consent. It is precisely this condition which the laws of right install. We have a right to consent to or to refuse, at least where other wills are concerned, that which can physically affect us. Through right that which 'determines' us becomes subject to our 'determination,' and that which was merely in or to us becomes for us. Our intentions are, to this extent, united with their realization. The

---

3 Cf. Locke *Second Treatise* chapter 5. Both Locke's theory of knowledge and his theory of property begin with 'gifts' which men 'join' or 'combine' to render useful. Kant's theories of knowledge and property also concern something 'given.' For Kant, however, the given is not a 'gift' (still less a gift of God) but rather itself entails 'combination' and labour. To be receptive to, and hence able to use, the 'given,' man must have completed a prior, transcendental synthesis. Thus whereas Locke effectively begins with simple (empirical) ideas, and with individual possession, Kant begins with the transcendental unity of apperception, and with the idea of a united will, as necessary *conditions* of empirical knowledge and private appropriation. According to Locke the 'ground' of simple ideas is, like the earth itself, 'God-given' and unproblematic, as is the ground of their suitability for human use. As Kant observes, however, Locke's empiricism undermines his arguments for the existence of God (CR B/127, A/854 = B/882). In Kant's view, neither Locke's 'accidental' account of having nor his 'physiological' account of knowing can account for their 'legitimacy.' Neither God, utility, nor labour can furnish grounds of right. (See CR A/86 = B/119; cf. Locke *An Essay Concerning Human Understanding* chapters 23 and 24; *Second Treatise on Government*, chapter 5.)
4 See DR, VI 352 (125).
5 Cf. *Vorarbeiten*, XXIII 310.

141 The Doctrine of Right: A selective commentary

doctrine of right asserts a power over objects otherwise reserved for their creator.

Juridical community partly overcomes the dualism inherent in the notion of natural community. As one student of Kant puts it: 'The unity of nature emerges in the observing subject exclusively; it is produced exclusively by him in the sense materials, and on the basis of sense materials which are themselves heterogeneous. By contrast, the unity of society needs no observer. It is directly realized by its own elements because these elements are themselves conscious and synthesizing units.'[6]

The idea of juridical personality spans the gap between man as natural and as moral being; it cannot, however, close the gap entirely. Material bodies destroy and are destroyed without doing violence to the law of mechanics. Juridical persons, on the contrary, enjoy an ideal integrity which cannot be breached without doing violence to the laws of right and to the integrity of every other person. The tension between our juridical substantiality and our natural vulnerability is a function of our dual participation in both the natural and the juridical community. The enforcing power of the civil state, as we shall see, can do much to alleviate the tension, but always imperfectly. By synthesizing natural and moral community, the concept of right both transcends and continues to express the doubleness of man. Juridical community consists of self-subsistent moral beings who also depend on the world. Through the idea of the social contract, men appropriate nature's substance as their own. Moral and natural exchange intersect in a consensus at once natural and ideal.

Having completed his juridical deduction, Kant turns to the question of application. According to Kant, the pure concept of right is applied to objects in the empirical world, through the concept of having something in one's power.[7] In applying the concept of right to objects of experience, we leave aside our empirical representations of possession and think of the object simply as 'in our power,' independent of all temporal and spatial conditions. This pure concept of having an object in my power (*in potestate mea positum esse*) translates between the power which we enjoy as moral persons and the power which we exercise as creatures of the natural world. Our concept of such a power mediates between rational and empirical possession, between moral authority and physical force. Our property in nature is made possible by our capacity to think (but never know) the object both as external, that is, as separate from ourselves, and as our own.

---

6 Georg Simmel 'How is Society Possible?' 7

7 DR, VI 253 (61); see also Kant's 'Deduction of the Conception of Original Primary Acquisition' (section 17), DR, VI 268.

External property makes possible in practice the ascendency over objects which in theory reason could not achieve. The nature of this ascendency is partly indicated by the concept of external 'possession' (*Besitz*) or 'having' (*Habe*). For reason in theory, there is no 'external possession.' Everything which can be theoretically mine (for example, representations, concepts, sensations) pertains to my inner experience. The object of outer experience to which my concept refers is just that which cannot be my own in the theoretical sense. Theoretical reason cannot possess that which is external to itself. Its representations of objects are its 'own'; the objects themselves, however, elude its synthesizing grasp. Thought defines itself against a never fully penetrable object. Theory presupposes an irreducible boundary between the 'inner' and the 'outer.'[8] The transcendental externality of the given re-emerges in the experienced externality of the natural world.

Theoretical reason encounters and transforms that which is external to itself but never fully appropriates it as its own. The boundary between 'inner' and 'outer,' a boundary which furnishes the ground for all theoretical objectivity, is surmountable only in practice, which derives its objectivity from the moral law. In practice, though not in theory, reason can 'have' that which is 'separate and different' from reason itself. In so far as reason is finite rather than infinite, representative rather than creative, it can have an object in its power only through the idea of a united will.

MODES OF ACQUISITION (DR I 2)

Acquired rights establish claims to outer property, claims to that which is external to ourselves and yet our own. Kant's 'division' of external property recognizes the diversity of human experience. Kinds of claims to external property vary with the nature of the thing appropriated and with the way in which it is acquired. Kant insists, however, that the divisions of external property be derived from *a priori* principles, rather than from contingent customs or empirical facts. He bases his division of acquired property on nothing less than the transcendental logic of pure reason. His division of acquired property therefore 'corresponds' to that of the *a priori* relational categories of pure reason (substance, causality, and community).

Real right and first appropriation (DR I 2 i)
Real right (*jus reale*), which Kant associates with the category of substance, is a right to the exclusive use of an external thing. Real right is acquired either orginally or through exchange. Original acquisition is that kind of appropria-

---

8 See, for example, CR B/275-9 (The Refutation of Idealism) and *Vorarbeiten*, XXIII 306.

tion which does not require the intervention of an actual juridical act or the specific consent of others.[9] Since no object is 'objectively ownerless' and every object is potentially of use, everyone is free to appropriate anything not already appropriated by someone else. 'Anything external may be originally acquired when no one else has yet made it his.'[1]

The elements, or moments (*momenta*), of original acquisition include: 1/ physical occupation or seizure, 2/ declaration of my will to have it as mine, and 3/ appropriation as the ideal act of a united will, whereby 'everyone is obliged to act in conformity with my faculty of choice.'[2] Through such appropriation, one acquires a right to oblige others to refrain from using that which they would otherwise be free to use. According to Kant 'being first' is the only conceivable ground for unilateral appropriation. 'The act of taking possession [*apprehensio*], as being at its beginning the physical appropriation of a corporeal thing in space ... can only accord with the law of the external freedom of all ... under condition of its priority with respect to time.'[3]

Locke argued that labour creates a natural and original right to a thing. Kant dismisses this argument as a false personification of things that suggests that things bind themselves to us in exchange for the labour we bestow on them. According to Kant, property does not arise out of an exchange with nature. Property rights do not hold against things, but only against other wills. Hence, to 'pay' nature with our labour earns us nothing. We must first gain possession of nature's substance, that is to say, the soil, which our labour can in turn transform.[4]

This substance is made 'mine' through a conjunction of will, physical power, and universal legislation. 'That is mine which I bring under my power according to the law of external freedom, which, as an object of my faculty of choice, I have the capability of using ... and which I will to become mine in conformity with the idea of a possible unified will.'[5] To make something mine, I must be capable of using it; that is to say, I must bring it under my physical power, and I must will that it be mine. For something to become mine, I must be conscious of my physical power to use it. Thus my acquisitions are effectively limited both by my desires and by my powers of defence.[6] Locke, who also argued that rightful acquisition in the state of nature is limited to that

9 DR, VI 259
1 DR, VI 258
2 DR, VI 259
3 DR, VI 263
4 DR, VI 265–6
5 DR, VI 258
6 DR, VI 265

which can be used, subjected acquisition to the additional condition that there be enough for all. Kant, on the contrary, holds natural abundance or scarcity to be juridically irrelevant. For Kant, the abstract concept of power over a thing, and not the natural environment, is fundamental. To be sure, he acknowledges that property can only be acquired through the application of this abstract concept to our peculiar situation. We must take physical possession of a thing to make it ours (though we need not retain possession to keep it ours). There must be an initial moment when the (rational) concept and the (natural) experience of 'having' intersect. According to Kant the right of taking possession of the soil extends as far as one's capacity to hold on to it. It extends, that is to say, just as far 'as he who wills to appropriate it can defend it, as if the soil were to say, "if you cannot protect me, you cannot command me."'[7] This personification apparently is valid (where Locke's was not) in that it compares the relation between man and thing not to that between buyer and seller, but to that between master and slave, a relation which can never properly obtain between two wills. To acquire rights over something, I must physically secure it, and so wrest it loose, if only momentarily, from the flux of nature.

In distinguishing between physical and intelligible possession, Kant adapts the Roman legal distinction between possession and ownership. According to the Roman tradition, possession (or having something) is conceptually distinct from ownership (or being entitled to have it).[8] According to Roman law, possession and ownership coincide when that which is occupied is not already owned by someone else. According to Kant physical and rational possession coincide under the same conditions. The Romans referred to things not previously owned as 'ownerless [*res nullius*].'[9] Kant, however, dismisses *res nullius* as an empty category. According to him, the right to occupy a thing does not follow from the nature of the thing, but rather from the permissive legislation of the united will, before which nothing can by its nature withhold itself.[1]

---

7 DR, VI 265

8 See, for example, Ulpian: 'Ownership has nothing in common with possession' (Barry Nicholas *An Introduction to Roman Law* 107). On the distinction in Roman law between *dominum* and *possessio*, see also R.W. Leage *Roman Private Law* rev. A.M. Pritchard (London, Macmillan 1961) 151. Kant's distinction between intellectual and physical possession also suggests the Roman distinction between intellectual possession (which implies the intention to use a thing) and physical possession (which implies actual occupation or detention). See Nicholas *Roman Law* 113.

9 See Nicholas *Roman Law* 130.

1 DR, VI 250 (58)

First acquisition of a thing is conditioned only by one's will to have the thing and by one's physical power to use it. The 'moments' of original acquisition include physical occupation, a declaration of intent, and the ideal corroboration of the united will. My act of will is thus a medium, connecting a thing in time and space with the *a priori* legislation of the united will. The act of appropriation captures the will in a moment of supreme power, when desire and capability, wish and fulfilment are one.

Personal right and exchange (DR I 2 ii)
In addition to real rights (rights *in rem*), which we assert against all, Kant recognizes personal rights (rights *in personam*) which we assert against single individuals. Whereas real rights are associated with the *a priori* category of substance, personal rights are associated with that of causality.[2]

Personal right is a right to oblige others not merely to refrain from using what we own, as in the case of real right, but rather to perform some positive action. In this sense, they confer a power to exercise 'causation' over another will. 'The possession of the free will [*Willkür*] of another person, as the power to determine it by my will to a certain action, according to laws of freedom, is a right relating to the external mine and thine, as they pertain to the causality of another.'[3] Real right, or the right to keep others from using what we own, follows directly from the ideal legislation of the united will. However, personal right, or the right to oblige others to some positive action, requires their individual consent.

All real acquisition, other than original acquisition, presupposes an exchange of personal rights. Only through such an exchange can one acquire goods which already belong to someone else. Here, once again, Kant adapts Roman law, which, in contrast both to the law of ancient Greece and to Anglo-Saxon common law, does not award title to contractually promised goods prior to their actual delivery.[4] Through contracts, one immediately acquires personal rights to the delivery of goods, and only mediately acquires real rights to the goods themselves.[5]

Rightful acquisition by means of the action of another is always 'derived from what the other has as his own.' This derivation cannot be affected by a mere negative relinquishment, through which the thing relinquished would

---

2 DR, VI 247 (54)
3 DR, VI 271
4 According to Roman law, the passing of title 'was, strictly, an effect not of the contract but of the consequent conveyance.' A contract could create rights *in personam* but not rights *in rem*. See Nicholas *Roman Law* 101–5, 173.
5 DR, VI 271

become available to anyone. The acquisition of a right to something owned by someone else requires a positive transference (*translatio*) or conveyance of his right to it, and this, in turn, is possible only through a shared (*gemeinschaftliche*) will, whereby what one relinquishes the other simultaneously receives. Such a transfer (*Übertragung*) is termed alienation (*Veräusserung*). The act of the two persons united as one will is called a contract (*Vertrag*).[6] Through the idea of a shared will, the empirically successive moments of the contract (namely, offer, approval, promise, and acceptance) can be conceived as happening simultaneously. Declaratory acts (such as a handshake, breaking of straws, and so on) represent empirically the ideal simultaneity of the transfer.[7] The contract implies, but does not include, the further moments of delivery and reception.[8] The juridical transfer of rights anticipates but does not assure actual delivery of the promised goods.

The distance, both intellectual and actual, between acceptance and delivery, promise and performance, suggests the necessity of providing to the promisee some guarantee that he will get what he is promised. Such is the function of the so-called cautionary contracts, which include pledges, deposits, and the like. Subjectively speaking, a contract would seem to require not two persons but three, that is to say, a promisor, a promisee, and a cautioner or surety (*Cavent*).[9] This cautioner is an embodiment of the 'common will' which obtains objectively but could not otherwise subjectively prevail. Kant's understanding of the private contract informs, as we shall see, his understanding of the public or social contract. The relation between private cautioner and 'common will' prefigures the relation between the political sovereign and the idea of a united will.

Kant considered contracts so important that he included a special supplement devoted to the 'systematic division' of contractual acquisition. Gratuitous (unilateral), onerous (reciprocal), and cautionary contracts constitute the major segments of this division. The need for cautionary contracts is, however, effectively removed in cases of reciprocal simultaneous acquisition in which delivery immediately follows acceptance.[1] This kind of immediate acquisition is presumably facilitated by monetary transaction. Money, which

---

6 DR, VI 271
7 DR, VI 274–5
8 DR, VI 284. Considered objectively 'every contract consists of two juridical acts: promise and acceptance.' Considered subjectively, however, 'it is clear that I have no assurance as to whether the acquisition, which ought to follow as a rational consequence, will follow as a physical fact.'
9 Ibid.
1 DR, VI 286

can 'represent' all exchangeable goods, is 'the greatest and most useable of all the means [*Mittel*] of human commerce with regard to things.'[2]

To the subject of money (*Geld*), which Kant defines as the 'general means by which men exchange their labour,'[3] much of his supplement is devoted. In Kant's view, money is not merely an empirical or accidental adjunct of juridical exchange, but 'rationally conforms' to the concept of right itself.[4] His treatment of money links the Roman understanding of contractual exchange (as an exchange of human performances) with Adam Smith's theory of price and labour. In Kant's view, all contractual exchange involves an exchange of labour. Men either transfer their labour directly (as do servants and wage-earners) or indirectly (as do artisans and merchants).[5] Money facilitates the exchange of human performances by providing a general measure of human labour, that is, by determining its price. The 'intellectual concept of money,' according to Kant, 'is that of a thing which, in the course of the public ... exchange of possessions ... determines the price of all other things [*Waaren*].'[6]

Money supplies a (relative) constant in relation to which the value of all other things can be measured. Monetary price is a 'public judgment [*öffentliche Urteil*] about the value of a thing relative to the proportionate abundance of what constitutes the universal representative [*stellvertretende*] means for the reciprocal exchange of *labour*.'[7] Price, then, is the function of two variables: men's subjective preferences and the relative abundance of that which constitutes the means of exchange. The first variable depends on the contingencies of human need and desire. The second depends both on such contingencies and on the natural availability of the 'material' which serves as a means of exchange. Kant considers precious metal (for example, gold) to be the usual material of exchange. Its abundance is a function both of nature, which hides the metal within the earth, and of the willingness of men to labour to discover it.[8] As 'material' the exchange of which defines a human *commercium*, money is a man-made counterpart of the earth itself.[9]

According to Kant the quantity of money in national circulation constitutes a nation's wealth.[1] What apparently enables money so to function is the fact

[2] Ibid.
[3] DR, VI 287
[4] DR, VI 289
[5] DR, VI 285
[6] DR, VI 288
[7] Ibid.
[8] DR, VI 287–8
[9] Cf. above, 79.
[1] DR, VI 288

that, unlike other goods, it is used without being 'used up' or consumed. The absolute quantity of money is not diminished by its use.

Money is, to be sure, a 'fungible,' or a thing exchangeable for some equivalent;[2] and fungibility usually connotes perishability.[3] Historically, fungibles were goods which were borrowed to be consumed (for example, corn) or which when borrowed were likely to break (for example, fragile crockery).[4] In order to be borrowed at all, such goods had to be returnable in kind and hence exchangeable for some equivalent. Unlike these other fungibles, however, money has no use apart from its capacity to be exchanged. Despite and indeed because it directly satisfies no human need, money is 'a means [*Mittel*] of the highest utility.'[5] The demand for money, unlike the demand for most goods, does not diminish the absolute supply. As a 'permanent' in relation to which all exchange can be defined, money is a man-made analogue of substance itself.

The amount of gold in national circulation furnishes an indication of the desirability of the nation's products. It might be objected that if this is so, a starving nation should be the richest of all; for in it, men would trade almost anything for a loaf of bread. Kant would reply that in such a nation there would be little incentive to increase the supply of gold, which measures national wealth, and every incentive to diminish it by trading it away to other nations. In Kant's view, national wealth seems to imply an expanding, luxury economy in which the increasing desirability of goods is matched by an increasing capacity to produce them. In a wealthy nation, the increased desirability of its products is not a function of the increased neediness of its people, but rather a function of their expanding appetite and power.

Kant's economics would rescue value from that anarchic relativism which equates the value of something with the intensity with which it is desired. Money measures value not only as a function of (subjective) desire but also as a function of men's (empirically objective) capacity to expand their power by exchanging their labour and so to satisfy their own ends by becoming means for others. A nation becomes wealthy by maximizing the productivity, relative to human want, of an increasable but finite quantity of labour. Economic value is relative, but advisedly so. By steering a course between subjective value and objective worth, money establishes a kind of external middle ground between the passions and the moral law. Because it measures subjec-

---

2 DR, VI 287–8
3 See DR, VI 360.
4 Nicholas *Roman Law* 167
5 DR, VI 287. See also *Vorarbeiten*, XXIII 282.

tive desire against the objective recalcitrance of nature, monetary value is both relative and pragmatically real.[6]

Money furnishes 'material,' or a permanent, in relation to which contractual exchanges can rationally and substantially be defined. As a representation of the sum of applied human labour, it abstracts from all but the pure form of contractual exchange. Money extends to society a 'means in general' like that which the concept of right extends to the individual will. Through a monetary system, society can determine the most useful way to expend its collective effort (relative to private inclination), much as the individual calculates the most useful means to his own ends. Money, however, furnishes a calculus which is, unlike individual calculation, neither deliberative nor deliberate.[7] Money can reconcile competing wills without relying on the authority of any will in particular.

Money is an impersonal and impartial sovereign, a warranted but unwitting version of the united will. In its material impersonality, the power of money approaches the ideal impartiality of the united will and establishes, as we shall see, a material sovereignty against which no man can rightly complain.

The sovereignty of money is a kind of culmination of the demand for independence from the wills of others. Money can meet this demand, however, only by submitting all men to an impersonal and unwitting force.[8] Marx denounces the power of money, accusing it of alienating men from their own products. For Kant, however, money, which represents 'the sum of human labour,' is a kind of collective human product, and thus a material 'representation' through which men can, it seems, properly and effectively rule themselves.

Personal right of a real sort (DR I 2 iii)

Kant recognizes a third kind of acquired right which he calls 'personal right of a real sort,' or the right to possess an object as a thing but use it as a person.[9] Personal right of a real sort combines the exclusivity of real right with the

---

6 The value-confusion associated with evil is externally resolved by money, which steers a course between subjective and objective worth. Money externally resolves the confusion (at the heart of evil) between 'the value of a thing' and that which people 'think it worth.' The lust for money is a passion which, although internally evil, need not be harmful or unjust in its external effects. See *Anthropology*, VII 270, 274 (137, 140). For a recent account of money along similar lines, see Charles Fried *Right and Wrong* (Cambridge, Mass., Harvard University Press 1978).
7 Cf. *Groundwork*, IV 395, 418 (62, 86); *Crit. Prac.*, V 24 (22).
8 Cf. DR, VI 314 (79) and 'Perpetual Peace,' VIII 365, 368 (111, 114).
9 DR, VI 276

individual focus of personal right. Like real right, it confers title to exclusive use; and like personal right, it implies a power to oblige individuals to the positive performance of certain actions. Unlike the first two kinds of acquired right, which have a counterpart in Roman law, personal right of a real sort is Kant's own discovery.[1] Adapting Roman law (and prevailing social and political practice) to the requirements of Kantian morality, it sanctions some political and social inequality while asserting the more fundamental equality of men as moral beings.

As real and personal right were associated with substance and causality, personal right of a real sort is associated with community. The key to Kant's concept of community is his notion of reciprocal – as distinguished from hierarchical – influence. Members of the community are separate but co-dependent, different but morally equal. Just as bodies in space constitute a whole, by 'mutually determining their positions,' so persons constitute a society through their reciprocal interdependence. It is not ruling and being ruled (as with Aristotle) but interdependence that supplies the formal basis of community, both natural and social.

The smallest version of juridical community is the household. Unlike juridical relations based on a coincidence of means alone, domestic society presupposes a common end. Thus, the subservience of the wife to the husband is justified by the 'natural' superiority of the husband in effecting their common interest, the subservience of the child by the responsibility of his parents for his welfare, and the subservience of the servant by his willingness to be used for the benefit of the household. In each case, subservience is limited by the 'rights of humanity,' assuring the fundamental moral equality of all members of the community. The 'legal supremacy' of the husband, so long as it is based in his superior aptitude for achieving their common ends, is derived not from any metaphysical or religious hierarchy, but rather from the juridical unity and equality of the married pair. Domestic society is based on the 'natural' commerce of the sexes, which results in procreation and leads to establishment of the family.[2] Personal right of a real sort represents a kind of concession to the natural interdependence of men, prefiguring at the level of right the moral interdependence of true ethical community. This natural

---

1 DR, VI 358-9. Kant's peculiar 'discovery' represents yet another attempt on his part to reconcile the conservative demands of moral obedience with the radical implications of moral autonomy. Kant's acceptance here of the labour and marital laws of his day, laws which gave a man physical custody over servants and wife, may offend modern liberal sensibilities. Yet by denying such inequalities their traditional metaphysical support, Kant did much to undermine their 'necessity,' a necessity which was even for Kant merely empirical.

2 DR, VI 277

interdependence is rendered juridical through lawful consent, explicit in the relations between spouses and between master and servant, implicit in the relation between parent and child, who deserves nurture and support (in recompense for having been brought into the world without his consent!).[3] Real personal right is an answer to the threat posed by nature to the juridical equality and independence of men. It is as close as men juridically come to being ends for each other by sharing each other's ends. Yet, despite this naturally based congruence of interest, members of domestic society retain the individuality and independence which constitute the basis of their juridical and moral personality. Domestic unity, like all other forms of society, is essentially contractual; morality demands a price for that which nature offers free. The price is monogamy, an exclusivity guaranteed by law. Personal possession of a real sort requires legal support in a way that personal and real property do not. Domestic status is acquired 'neither through arbitrary individual action (*facto*), nor through mere contract (*pacto*), but through law (*lege*).'[4]

Marriage, Kant dryly notes, is 'the union of two persons of different sex for life-long reciprocal possession of their sexual faculties.'[5] The purpose of sexual union viewed juridically is not to perpetuate the species, but rather to gratify the individual. Natural commerce, according to Kant, is an enjoyment for which 'one person is given up to the other.' The purpose of matrimony is to ensure that this surrender is perfectly reciprocal, thus restoring to each person the juridical personality of which he would otherwise be robbed. Marriage is therefore necessarily monogamous; and both concubinage and prostitution are precluded as an inherently unequal trade.

To treat another person (unilaterally) as a means of gratification is, according to Kant, to reduce that person to a *res fungibilis*, or thing exchangeable for some equivalent.[6] As juridical persons, men are non-fungible; they can neither be represented nor exchanged. The *Doctrine of Right* concedes a right to the possession of other persons (as things) but denies that such possession can be alienated or exchanged. Illicit sex is wrong, not because it makes use of others, but because in treating others as interchangeable it denies their unique and absolute worth. Personal possession of a real sort sanctions 'possession' of men but forbids those 'exchanges' which would call into question their juridical personality.

Sex out of wedlock turns men into fungibles by making them 'expendable'

---

3 DR, VI 281
4 DR, VI 276
5 DR, VI 277
6 DR, VI 359–60. See also *Vorarbeiten*, XXIII 358.

(*verbrauchbar*). Goods (with the exception of money) are rendered fungible because they can be consumed. To engage illicitly in sexual activity, a kind of exploitation of the body that literally consumes it, is to be dehumanized (*sich entmenschen*). Kant speaks of sex in terms of a dehumanizing exploitation similar to that which Marx associates with wage labour. According to Kant, sexual possession not only uses; it uses up, either by causing death in childbirth or by inducing physical exhaustion. 'There is merely a difference in the manner of enjoyment,' he astoundingly asserts, between such exhaustion and 'the consumption of bodies by the teeth and maw of the savage.'[7] It is not merely the interchangeability of men in their natural commerce that is morally abhorrent, but also the mortality which this natural fungibility connotes. What is merely change for nature is destruction for the individual, who exists only by resisting, reforming, and containing change.[8] In nature, to be exchangeable, to have an equivalent, is to be subject to destruction. Matrimony is a juridical assertion of unity and permanence out of and against the natural laws of alteration. In the Kantian universe there can be no utopia of erotic abundance. Kant's striking association of sex with 'cannibalism' and 'fungibility' underscores the connection in his thought between desire and mortality. It is desire which first subjects us to the economy of nature; and it is the renunciation or suppression of desire which makes possible our transcendence of nature and final metaphysical security.

3 / PUBLIC RIGHT AND JURIDICAL COMMUNITY
(DR PART II)

Kant's theory of justice is, substantially, a theory of contract. The categorical imperative enjoins us to treat other men as ends. We can do so, however, only by treating them as beings with ends, that is to say, by treating them so that they may share in our actions. This we do by eliciting their consent. The categorical imperative permits us to treat other men as means, so long as we obtain their (rational) consent and thus become means to them. The juridical postulate of the categorical imperative calls for an expansion of the means available for an aggregate of ends, whatever they may be. In this respect, justice is at once moral and prudential. This coincidence is not enough to keep the selfish just; hence there arises a need for force and penalties. It is, however, enough to guarantee the workability and perhaps even the perfecti-

---

7 DR, VI 359
8 See *Anthropology*, VII 134 (135).

153 *The Doctrine of Right*: A selective commentary

bility of the system, given men at their worst and not as they ought to be. The system of right gives grounds for hope regarding the legal, if not the moral, perfection of the species.

To be publicly enforced, laws must be publicly promulgated. The body of those laws which must be made universally known in order to produce a juridical condition Kant calls public right.[9] The primary purpose of public right is to secure innate rights, which in the state of nature are insecure, and to enforce contracts, which in the state of nature remain provisional. In its emphasis on security, Kant's teaching calls to mind earlier contractarian thought. The aim of government for Kant is, as with Hobbes, the preservation of life, and, as with Locke, the protection of property. According to all three, government is established in order universally to secure the means for the private pursuit of individual ends. But whereas Hobbes and Locke expected these ends to be rational in a narrowly selfish sense, Kant hopes they will be rational in a moral, universal, and objective sense. Upon politics Kant makes moral demands of which Hobbes and Locke would not have seen the necessity. They regarded politics as for the protection of humanity. But for Kant the only conceivable justification for politics is morality, which gives humanity its worth. Like Rousseau, Kant sees in self-legislation, or obedience to the law one sets for oneself, the highest expression of morality. For Rousseau political community was the primary medium for such expression. For Kant, however, self-legislation is a private affair for which political legislation is at best a preparation. Kant rejects Rousseau's homogeneous and virtuous political community, preferring, along with Hobbes and Locke, cosmopolitan diversity and a clear separation of public and private spheres. Kant conceives the state as an external means to an internal ethical commonwealth; the state remains, however, a purely external means, that is to say, a 'means in general' for the pursuit of ends – good, bad, and indifferent – which it is up to the individual to choose. Despite its moral foundation, the Kantian state externally resembles that of Hobbes and Locke far more than it does the moral community of Rousseau. In the external freedom of juridical community, morality and egoism intersect. The Kantian state is a means for all, but an end only for the virtuous.

What was for Hobbes and Locke primarily a selfish impulse to quit the state of nature becomes for Kant a non-selfish imperative of duty as well. We have a duty to protect ourselves from wrongful injury and to refrain from injuring others. We are thus obliged either to avoid all other men, or (if this is impossible, and the contiguity of earth's surface ultimately makes it so), to

---

9 DR, VI 311 (75)

quit the state of nature and enter civil society.[1] The state of violence that impels us into civil society is not merely a fact of experience, but also a necessary consequence of the human condition. One need not assume that men are bad (as Hobbes did) to conclude that the state of nature is a state of war. 'Even if we imagine men to be ever so good natured and righteous before a public lawful state of society is established, individual men, nations, and states can never be certain that they are secure against violence from one another, because each will have his own right to do what *seems just and good to him* ... independently of the opinion of the others.'[2] It is not men's empirical nature which necessitates civil society but rather reason itself, which is unable, even with the best intentions, unilaterally to establish externally the community which reigns as an ideal. Even the best of men, if they pursue an independent path, will disagree about what is just and good in the particular case. Whatever his intentions, man in the state of nature cannot avoid affecting others without their participation and consent. Man in the state of nature, whatever his will and temperament, injures and is injured. Virtue in the state of nature is indistinguishable from vice, benevolence becomes paternalism, and self-perfection turns into self-aggrandizement.

The necessity of conflict in the state of nature arises from the necessary indeterminacy of reason's end, excepting that of the juridical state itself. Morality tells us to be just and good, but does not tell us precisely how. Morality supplies the form, or procedure, while experience furnishes the matter and sharpens the judgment. Although these subjective conditions do not affect the form of willing, they can shape the result. Thus even the best of men, internally united by the purity of their intentions, could find themselves externally divided by the disparity of their means. To this extent Kant shares Hobbes' disbelief in a natural common end (which in Aristotle's view makes men sociable).[3] In Kant's view external harmony can come about only through the deliberate and contrived effort of each to adjust his own ends to the naturally disparate ends of others. External harmony requires laws, publicly promulgated and enforced, to speak where nature's voice is silent.

The doubleness of Kantian politics, yoking together what morality in its own sphere kept apart, has its source in the Kantian notion of right as at once prior to and dependent on morality. Morally speaking, right is based on duty. In the *Metaphysics of Morals* Kant derives right from the respect one owes oneself as a being who is subject to the moral law.[4] Anthropologically speak-

---

1 DR, VI 237 (43)
2 DR, VI 312 (76)
3 See Hobbes *Leviathan*, chapter 4; cf. Aristotle *Nichomachean Ethics* 1094, *Politics* 1252.
4 DR, VI 238 (45)

ing, however, our sense of right precedes our sense of duty,[5] and Kant's *Opus postumum* defines a person both as a being with rights and duties and (alternatively) simply as a being with rights.[6] Rights, as we have seen, are what we assert against that which resists us. To this extent, all experience is juridical. Like the dove 'cleaving the air in her free flight,'[7] the human will resents opposition. Philosophy, teaching the necessity of opposition, resigns us to the impossibility of satisfaction, be our object happiness or knowledge. The doctrine of right transforms our primordial indignation in the face of opposition into a moral indignation that distinguishes between opposition that we may claim as injury and opposition that we must accept with a calm spirit. Kant presents his theory of property as a theory of injury; its function is to establish the possibility of injury and to distinguish that opposition which injures from that which does not. This step has the effect of absolving nature from blame for human ills, even as it unleashes an unlimited human right to exploit nature and men themselves to the extent that they participate in nature. As we shall see, this step has the political effect of banishing indignation from whole realms of social activity, while reasserting it in others.

The doctrine of right does not abstract entirely from the physical economy. As a theory of property, it primarily concerns the acquisition and exchange of things. As the doctrine linked the idea of rational 'having' with the experience of physical power, so it combines the idea of a united will with the historical reality of force. The doctrine of right never ceases to concern opposition, either in terms of its legitimation or in terms of its 'cancellation' through counter-opposition.[8] Right never completely severs its connection with the palpable.

Just as the concept of external right required the intersection of the rational idea of having with the fact of physical possession, so the idea of a united will requires a physical power to enforce its laws. The idea of a united will can justify claims outside civil society. It cannot, however, itself guarantee obedience to its decrees. Unlike the categorical imperative, which commands all men at all times and with equal force, the united will commands only when each is assured of the compliance of all the others. To comply with the ideal dictates of the united will without such a guarantee would be to violate the rights of humanity in one's own person, by making oneself a mere means for others. Here morality and egoism reinforce each other. A bad bargain is, in Kant's view, not only foolish (as with Hobbes) but also immoral. Hence Kant,

---

5 *Anthropology*, VII 268–9 (135–6)
6 *Opus. post.*, XXI 12–14, 16
7 CR A/5 = B/8; cf. above, 52.
8 *Vorarbeiten*, XXIII 301; *Reflexion* #7915

like Hobbes, requires an overarching power to guarantee the social contract and all subsequent civil decrees, a power without which the united will could not effectively legislate at all.[9]

THE CITIZEN

Through an original contract, an aggregate of men constitute themselves a people and subject themselves as individuals to their united sovereignty. The civil community has from the beginning an inherent doubleness, setting citizen as sovereign against citizen as subject. The citizen gives up his external freedom in order to take it back immediately as a member of the commonwealth. He abandons a wild, lawless freedom in order to 'find his whole freedom again undiminished in a lawful dependency,' which comes 'from his own legislative Will.'[1] In entering civil society a person divides himself, much as his will is already internally divided. Juridical freedom, like its moral counterpart, means submission to laws one lays down for oneself. Juridical freedom is freedom externally focused, autonomy mediated by an external power.

Freedom and the material basis of juridical community

The defining qualities of the citizen are his autonomy, equality, and independence. The citizen need obey no law to which he has not (at least ideally) given his consent; he is juridically equal to all other citizens; and he owes his 'existence and support, not to the arbitrary will of another person in the society, but to his own rights and powers as a member of the commonwealth.'[2] In his essay 'Theory and Practice,' Kant describes the principles of civil personality as '1/ the *freedom* of every member of society as a *human being*; 2/ the *equality* of each with all the others as a *subject*; 3/ the *independence* of each member of a commonwealth [*gemeine Wesen*] as a *citizen*.'[3] The self-subsistence and support which the individual could not achieve alone are established juridically through a common will which guarantees to each what is his. In the communal relation interdependence and independence are inseparable. Juridical subsistence is not an absolute self-grounding; it does not solve the problem of man's neediness. It is rather a substitute for that solution, giving reason a substantial ground that it can have in no other way. As part of a substantial juridical community the individual is himself substantiated.

9 DR, VI 256 (65)
1 DR, VI 316 (81)
2 DR, VI 314 (79)
3 'Theory and Practice,' VIII 290 (74)

157 The Doctrine of Right: A selective commentary

This juridical independence implies that civil personality 'cannot be represented by another person' in matters concerning rights.[4] Because it is and must be grounded in his 'own' rights and powers, his civic personality cannot be represented by another person. Civic personality is inalienable and non-reproducible. Citizenship may be acquired or given up but never exchanged. Kant means it to be that 'possession' which, along with our inborn rights, is most fully and indissolubly our own. But civil personality is not innate. To be a citizen it is not sufficient that one be alive, or even that one live in a commonwealth; one must also be capable of voting (*Stimmgebung*).[5] Only through voting can one be not only a part of the commonwealth but also a member of it. By voting, the citizen submits to his own will, and is thus at once subject and free.

Not all members of the commonwealth, however, are eligible to vote. Kant distinguishes between active citizenship, which confers a right to vote, and passive citizenship, which does not. Like ownership, citizenship requires an exercise of physical as well as juridical power. Juridical substantiality needs a material correlate. The prerequisite for civic independence is a kind of material independence. This independence requires not so much property or wealth *per se* as a specific mode of subsistence. Servants, minors, all women, 'and generally anyone who must depend for his support (subsistence and protection) not on his own industry [*Betrieb*], but on arrangements by others (with the exception of the state) – all such people lack civil personality, and their existence is only in the mode of inherence.'[6] What is necessary for active citizenship is that one live by means of one's own alienable property. Thus the artisan, piece-worker, teacher, and farmer are eligible for active citizenship while the servant, tutor, and sharecropper are not. Any kind of (alienable) property, including a skill, trade, or science with which one can support oneself, can qualify one for full citizenship. What distinguishes the voting labourer is his ability to earn his living by 'selling that which is his,' rather than allowing others 'to make use of him.'[7] According to Kant, he who does his own work can alienate it (sell it to someone else) as if it were his own. But guaranteeing one's labour (*praestatio operae*) is not something alienable.[8] The voting labourer is distinguished from his non-voting counterpart by his

---

4 DR, VI 314 (79)
5 Ibid. *Stimmgebung* is etymologically related to *Bestimmung* (determination). In voting, the citizen participates in the determination of the united will, much as, in choosing, he determines his individual will.
6 Ibid.
7 'Theory and Practice,' VIII 295 (78)
8 Ibid.

ability to sell the products of his labour as his own, rather than merely to guarantee his labour. The non-voting labourer lives by making himself a means for the plans and projects of others.

The ability to exchange one's property or products with others is the 'material' condition of free civic personality. Kant distinguishes labour, which is not alienable, from the product of labour, which is. The artisan submits his products, rather than himself, to the use of others; the servant, on the contrary, loans out his own person for the completion of tasks set by others.

Kant was concerned that a voting citizen be 'his own master' (*sui juris*).⁹ But he interpreted this traditional principle, traceable to Aristotle, in a new way.¹ Self-sufficiency (*sibisufficientia*) was traditionally thought to imply leisure and independence from the pettier practical concerns of daily life. It was argued that landed wealth and station provided the best opportunity for such independence and ought accordingly to be favoured politically. That such arguments coincided with the feudal claims of the nobility made them all the more powerful. Kant emphatically rejected such claims of privilege, and with it the voting by class (or *Stand*) still prevalent in Europe (but already overturned in France). According to Kant, all active citizens, whatever their wealth or station, are entitled to an equal vote.² It is not leisure which defines the citizen but self-employment. Only the mode of acquisition and not the amount acquired has juridical significance. The active citizen, who works at tasks he sets himself, is the embodiment of reason, for which task-setting is the quintessential activity. In both theory and practice, to labour at self-imposed tasks is to be as free and self-sufficient as man can be.

Kant precedes Ricardo and Marx in attributing the radical dependence of the wage-earner, not to his poverty, but to the fact that he does not own what he produces or produce what he himself proposes. For all that (and contrary to Marx), the wage-labourer does not alienate himself; for labour is, by right, no alienable commodity. Material dependence does not jeopardize the integrity of moral and juridical personality. 'This kind of dependence on the Will of others and the inequality that it involves are by no means incompatible with the freedom and the equality that men possess as human beings, who together make up a people. Rather, only by conforming to these conditions can the people become a state and enter into a civil constitution.'³

9 Ibid.
1 See Aristotle *Nich. Ethics* 1097b; cf. Manfred Riedel 'Die Aporie von Herrschaft und Vereinbarung in Kants Idee des Sozialvertrags.'
2 'Theory and Practice,' VIII 295 (78)
3 DR, VI 315 (79-80)

Like the dependency of women and children, that of servants and wage-labourers is a matter of nature or chance to which the doctrine of right must to some extent concede.[4] The community needs women and servants; it needs passive as well as active citizens. The distribution of active and passive citizenship, however, cannot be objectively determined, but must be left to chance.

'Passive parts' of the state 'can still demand that they be treated ... in accordance with the laws of natural freedom,' laws which include the right to work up from a passive to an active status.[5] The state is not obliged to compensate juridically for inequalities which arise from natural forces, be they biological or economic. But natural inequalities aside, the state must place no obstacle in the paths of those who would by dint of their own efforts rise.

Kant radically distinguishes the realm of persons and their rights from the realm of things. A man can be considered happy (*glücklich*) 'in any condition so long as he is conscious that, if he does not reach the same level as others, the fault lies either with himself (i.e., his means, or his strength of will) or with circumstances for which he cannot blame others, and not with the irresistible will of any outside party.'[6] One may envy others for their talents and their goods; but one cannot blame them for one's own mediocrity or poverty. Inequalities of wealth, talent, and fortune do not in themselves constitute grounds for injury and so lie beyond the scope of right. Such inequalities are the result of chance and human effort; they are, that is to say, a part of nature, bent more or less imperfectly by human endeavour. Such inequality is understood by Kant as either earned through strength of will or won by chance.[7] Poverty is therefore less a social evil than a natural one. To be sure, Kant (along with Hobbes and contrary to later *laissez-faire* thinkers) urges the duty of the state to support the destitute, as it is obliged to protect the lives of all of its citizens.[8] Nevertheless, much like these *laissez-faire* thinkers, Kant treats economics as a part of nature, its cruelties and comforts like any other natural events for which men, so long as they respect themselves and others, cannot be praised or blamed. The inevitable material progress that Kant anticipates is a blessing to the human race but not a credit.

---

4 See 'Theory and Practice,' VIII 291–2 (75).
5 DR, VI 315 (80)
6 'Theory and Practice,' VIII 293–4 (76–7) (my translation)
7 Ibid.
8 DR, VI 320 (93–4). On the perfunctory character of Kant's welfare policy, see J.G. Murphy *Kant: The Philosophy of Right* 145. For Kant, our right to protection by the state includes a right to bare subsistence but no more than that. Cf. Hobbes *Leviathan* chapter 30.

So long as other wills remain formally 'resistible,'[9] so long as they grant my right to acquire whatever they may have, they can do me harm but never injury. It is enough if everyone can 'possess himself' and 'not depend on the absolute Will of another next to or above him.'[1] Kant opposes that social inequality, which, by laying claim to a rational or religious basis, calls into question the juridical equality of man. Distinctions of rank and caste are for Kant mere social conventions, which he trusts will in time disappear. Juridical equality precludes inheritance of rank or caste (for personal attributes are inalienable); it permits, however, inheritance of wealth. Formal equality is thus compatible with extreme material inequality. The 'uniform equality of human beings as subjects of a state ... is perfectly consistent with the utmost inequality of the mass in the degree of its possessions.'[2]

The state is bound to render all social opposition formally – but only formally – resistible. This condition satisfied, material obstacles to one's prosperity and comfort pertain to happiness and not to justice. One is for purposes of right assumed to be happy so long as one's situation is not the fault of others. Right 'has nothing to do with the end which all men have by nature (i.e., the aim of achieving happiness).'[3] The state is not obliged to make us happy, but only to protect us from injury and to avenge those injuries it cannot prevent. The doctrine of right does not solve the problem of happiness; it does, however, introduce a surrogate happiness. He may be accounted happy who thinks he has met with justice. The doctrine of right abandons the quest for happiness and instead takes as its goal the calming of outrage. The doctrine of right supplies balm for the angry heart. In a properly regulated society men would have no object for indignation but themselves. The doctrine of right is thus the necessary complement of that turning inwards of anger requisite for morality.

Equality and punishment

Enforcement of the law in a community of citizens who might break the law requires a system of punishment. The aim of juridical punishment, however, is not only to maintain the peace. Unlike the penal theory of Hobbes and utilitarian thinkers generally, that of Kant is explicitly retributive. Unlike Hobbes, who condemns all punishment which does not deter crime or re-

9 'Theory and Practice,' VIII 294 (77)
1 DR, VI 317 (82)
2 'Theory and Practice,' VIII 291–2 (75–6)
3 Ibid. 289 (73); cf. *Reflexion* #7854: the aim of the state is not to make the individual happy but to secure him against others who might hinder him.

habilitate the criminal,[4] Kant attunes his penal system to the 'law of retribution' (*jus talionis*).[5] 'Juridical punishment can never be used merely as a means to promote some other good for the criminal himself or for civil society.' The criminal must be punished 'only on the ground that he has committed a crime.'[6] To do otherwise would be to treat him as a means and not as a person. Condemned to lose his civil personality and even his life, the criminal cannot lose his right to the respect which attaches inalienably to his person. Retributive punishment is essential if the criminal is to be treated as morally responsible rather than as a thing to be manipulated for his own good or that of others. The end of Kantian punishment is not external restraint alone, but also an internal 'equalization.'[7] The state is obliged to rectify those inequalities which, unlike natural inequalities, are the 'fault' of men, that is to say, the result of morally imputable action. The principle of equality furnishes the rule of retribution. As the only proper basis for political equalization, *jus talionis* is the penal complement of Kant's economic *laissez-faire*.

Every injury ought to be balanced by the infliction on its perpetrator of an equal hurt. In cases such as rape or mutilation, where strict equality would violate humanity, an equivalent (in fines or labour) may be substituted. 'Whoever ... commits a murder,' however, 'must die.' 'In this case there is no substitute that will satisfy the requirements of legal justice'; for between death and remaining alive under even the most miserable conditions 'there is no sameness of kind.'[8] Because death has no living equivalent, murderers must be executed. Kant goes so far as to suggest that crimes and punishments are strictly equal only when death is matched by death.[9] The natural equalizer, death, weighs the character of the criminal and treats him accordingly: the courageous and stoical fare better in their final hour than do the cowardly and base.[1] Where execution is concerned, legal and natural punishment complement each other. Death, the dizzying centre out of which we arise and into which we perish, becomes for Kant the ultimate measure of punitive equality.

Kant takes issue with the jurist Beccaria, who argued that capital punish-

---

4 Hobbes *Leviathan* chapter 23
5 Cf. Murphy *Philosophy of Right* 140–4, and J.P. Day 'Retributive Punishment' *Mind* 87 (1978): 498–516. Day contrasts Kantian punishment with less 'vindictive' systems of retribution.
6 DR, VI 331 (100)
7 DR, VI 332 (101). See also Murphy *Philosophy of Right* 173.
8 DR, VI 333 (102)
9 DR, VI 333 (102–3)
1 See also *Anthropology*, VII 238 (106).

ment is incompatible with the original civil compact in that 'no one can dispose of his own life.' It is not the will to be punished that leads to punishment, Kant replies, but rather the willing of a punishable act.[2] 'The penal power comes not from our will to be punished,' he elsewhere states, 'but from our will to punish others.'[3]

Punishment is the morally mandated public expression of the private 'desire for justice' that is only one step away from the passion for revenge. It is the objective version of the anger that comes (naturally) to a man who feels himself wronged. Only through universalization, and with it a willingness to entrust punishment to a public power, can this desire be rationalized. 'Punishment is not a function which the injured party can undertake on his private authority, but rather the function of a tribunal distinct from him, which gives effect to the law of a supreme authority over all those subject to it.'[4] Submission to this tribunal ideally lifts a person beyond the range of that which first aroused his anger. Even the criminal condemned to die enjoys thereby external confirmation of his noumenal substantiality.

REPRESENTATION AND THE POWERS OF GOVERNMENT

The legislative, executive, and judicial powers of government express the relation between sovereign and citizen. Kant combines Rousseau's conception of government as mediator between the people and the general will with Locke's and Montesquieu's insistence on a tripartite separation of powers. For Kant this separation and the mediating role of government go hand in hand. The powers of government, which proceed out of the concept of a commonwealth (*gemeine Wesen*), are just so many relationships in the united will of the people, which originates *a priori* in reason.[5] Kant also refers to these powers as 'dignities' (*Würden*); for they command a respect analogous to that which the individual owes to his own sovereign and autonomous will.

These co-determinate powers of government form a community, a stable and autonomous whole.[6] As moral persons they are at once mutually complementary and mutually subordinate. This combination of relationships, in which none can 'usurp the function of those there to aid it,' secures to 'every

---

2 DR, VI 334–5 (104–5). Punishment must be both retributive and deterrent. Hence, where its deterrent effect is cancelled by 'necessity' or conflicts with 'honour,' the death penalty cannot legally be imposed (however morally culpable the deed). See DR, VI 106 (39–42); 233–6; cf. Montesquieu *The Spirit of the Laws* book XXIII, sec. 3.
3 *Reflexion #7994*
4 *Doctrine of Virtue*, VI 460 (130)
5 DR, VI 338 (109)
6 DR, VI 316 (81)

subject what is right.' At pains to establish the *a priori* foundation of his tripartite division, Kant compares it to a practical syllogism: one power makes the law; one power administers it; one judges its application to the particular case.[7] Kant insists that the three powers do not derive from mere maxims of prudence, but from the idea of government itself as the necessary means by which a state 'acquires its autonomy' and 'forms and maintains itself according to laws of freedom.'[8]

The legislative authority must come from the united will of the people, not because the people know best, but because 'he who consents cannot be injured.' The stipulation of self-legislation through universal consent provides a formal and unimpeachable ground for justice. Hence only the united will of the people, 'by which each decides the same for all and all decide the same for each,' can legislate.[9]

This legislative power, although sovereign, is by virtue of its very universality incomplete. The sovereign legislator cannot also execute the law or judge its application. 'Separation of powers' is required to insulate the universality of the law from the necessary particularity of its administration. The very purity of legislation requires distinct powers to carry out the dictates of the sovereign will. By the same token, the subordination of the ruler to the law implies that the sovereign of the people cannot at the same time execute the law. Government should create resistance within and against itself. Should it fail to do so, should the separation of powers collapse, government would return to the tyrannic, arbitrary, and ultimately anarchic state out of which it arose.

Hence 'the sovereign can take his authority from the ruler, depose him, or reform his administration, but cannot punish him,' for punishment is an executive function. Similarly, the legislative and executive powers may appoint judges to preside over juries elected by the people but may not themselves preside, for adjudication involves contingency and the indignity of potential injustice.[1]

Together, these three powers (*Gewalten*) make up the pure idea of a sovereign or head of state, an idea which has 'objective practical reality.'[2] This reality, however, remains merely ideal unless it is combined with effective force. The sovereign is only 'an abstract object of thought (representing the whole people)' as long as there is no physical person to represent the

---

7 DR, VI 313 (78)
8 DR, VI 318 (83)
9 DR, VI 314 (78)
1 DR, VI 317–18 (83)
2 DR, VI 338 (109)

highest power (*Staatsgewalt*) of the state and to procure an effective influence of this idea on the popular will.³ The relation between the sovereign and the people is one of 'representation.' The sovereign can be said to represent the people in so far as his laws can be thought to proceed from their very wills.

At a time, during and after the French Revolution, when the radical discourse of France interested him keenly, Kant nevertheless continued wherever possible to express his own revolutionary teaching in the enduring language of Roman and scholastic jurisprudence. In this respect his theory of representation is no exception.⁴ In preparatory notes to the *Doctrine of Right* Kant suggests that representation can be understood as a kind of 'surety mandate' (*cautio mandatum*).⁵ Traditionally, surety is a pledge, undertaken through a third party (*Cavent*), by means of which one assures a fellow contractor that he will in fact receive what he is contractually promised. A mandate, on the other hand, is a grant of agency or power to undertake an act on behalf of the grantor. The sovereign, as the representative of the people, may thus be understood as an agent, who, acting in the people's name, coercively guarantees the obedience of each to a contract to which no rational being could otherwise consent. Through his coercive powers the sovereign assures the good faith of all. Kant's understanding of representation sheds light on a question which has puzzled students of Hobbesian representation, namely, how the sovereign can represent (or be the agent of) the people without being answerable to them.⁶ For Kant (as for Hobbes) the sovereign *is* answerable to the people in the only way that he can properly be said to represent them, that is, in his capacity as surety for the social contract. This stipulation is, moreover, self-enforcing; if he cannot guarantee the contract,

3 Ibid.
4 For Achenwall, whose usage Kant noted, a 'representation' was a legative mandate. See GS XIX 430. On notions of representation in revolutionary France and their relation to Kant's thought, see George Gooch *Germany and the French Revolution* and Hasso Hofmann *Repräsentation: Studien zur Wort- und Begriffsgeschichte von der Antike bis ins 19. Jahrhundert* 406. Kant's distinction between active and passive citizenship, his identification of direct democracy with despotism, and his hostility to voting by hereditary order call to mind doctrines of Sieyès and others active in the Constituent Assembly. (See A. Goodwin, ed. *The New Cambridge Modern History* VII (Cambridge, Cambridge University Press 1965) 680–1). (In post-revolutionary France, 'active' voting citizens were required to pay a tax equivalent to ten days' labour.) Kant's moral hopes for the revolution have reminded some of Robespierre (see R.R. Palmer *The Age of the Democratic Revolution: A Political History of Europe and America, 1760–1800* II (Princeton, Princeton University Press 1964) 446–7). For Kant's unpublished observations on contemporary events in France, see GS XIX 603.
5 *Vorarbeiten*, XXIII 350
6 See Hanna Fenichel Pitkin *The Concept of Representation* and Hasso Hofmann *Repräsentation*.

he ceases to rule. The sovereign is the *Cavent* of the social contract.⁷ As the people's universal representative he performs a function analogous to that of money (the universal representative of human labour). The guaranteeing of civil government takes its cue from the enduring forms of commercial exchange.

The surety-mandate of the people can express their agency and intention only by being absolute and irreversible, for only as absolute and irreversible can it assure universal good faith. In the relation of representation, as Kant understands it, the consent of the subject and the irresistibility of the sovereign are inseparable; for only by consenting to such a sovereign can the individual enter civil society at all. The sovereign is that external force through which individuals can bind and be bound by one another in a civil unity. To fulfil his role the sovereign must enjoy actual as well as ideal authority. Civil society necessarily implies an effective highest power.

The regimes of government – autocratic, aristocratic, democratic, or mixed – express the variety of relationships which can obtain between this 'highest power' and the people.⁸ The regime is only the empirical form of the state. As a mere accident of history, it has juridical importance only in so far as it remains subjectively necessary to the maintenance of order. The regimes 'are, as it were, only the letter ... of the original legislation in civil society, and they may therefore continue as long as they are held by ancient long-standing custom ... to be necessary to the machinery of the constitution of the state.'⁹ The rational form of government is not determined by those actually in power. The proper constitution is not for the ruler to choose, but is rather a necessary idea implied by the spirit of the original contract. For Kant (as for Aristotle) the defining element of government is its rational form. For Kant, however, that form is not constituted (as it was for Aristotle) by the regime, but rather by the necessary idea of universal consent, without which civil society would be inconceivable. The regime, as an empirical form, is superseded by the 'constitution' (*Verfassung*), as the form contained in the *a priori* idea of the social contract.¹

The 'spirit' of the original contract obliges those actually in power to bring the empirical form of government into alignment with this idea. The constituted authority ought accordingly 'to change the government gradually and continually, if it cannot be done at one time, so that it will effectively agree with the one and only legitimate constitution, namely that of a pure republic.'

---

7 See DR, VI 284.
8 DR, VI 338 (109)
9 DR, VI 340 (112)
1 Cf. Montesquieu *The Spirit of the Laws* book III, sec. 1.

Coercion ought to be combined with empirical as well as ideal consent. The old, empirical forms of the state, 'which serve only to effect the subjection of the people, must be transmuted into the original (rational) form, which is the only one that makes freedom its principle and ... the condition of every use of coercion.' The ideal constitution ought to be fully actualized so that 'letter' and 'spirit' can become one.[2]

The ideal constitution is one in which the law is self-governing (*selbstherrschend*) and 'not annexed to any particular person.'[3] Ideal government is therefore representative, the people holding effective power through their elected deputies. Under such a system, power, by virtue of its impersonality, belongs to everyone. At the same time, representative rule, unlike direct democracy, maintains that internal tension necessary for true self-government, in which the people not only rule but also obey.[4]

The people cannot directly govern. Once a sovereign exists, there is no reason to return the reins of government to the people, whose absolute will could negate that government and destroy its institutions. Government need not 'return to its foundations' (in the manner of Jefferson) because it carries its foundations with it implicitly. The atemporal ideality of the social contract eliminates the possibility of or the need for a temporal return. Its popular foundation is as implicitly a part of the constitution as is that ideal sovereignty through which the people rule themselves. Representation describes the relation which obtains ideally (even if it does not obtain empirically) between sovereign and people. Individual rights cannot be represented; the people as a whole cannot exist in any other way. Representation is the outer public reflection through which a people comes to be in becoming known to itself. As the highest power of government, the people's representative supplies the guarantee without which private rights would remain provisional and public rights would not exist at all. The sovereign is at once the giver of and the power behind the law.

As the co-determinate powers of government may be regarded as a 'community,' so the sovereign may be regarded as 'substance' (to which the passive citizen relates as an 'Inherence'). The sovereign is the practical representation and reflection through which the united will synthetically constitutes itself and is constituted. Thus the sovereign is to the united will as the theoretical representations of understanding are to self-consciousness. In

---

2 DR, VI 340 (112)

3 Ibid. All goverment, according to Kant, is either republican or despotic. Under despotic government the people are the (private) property of the sovereign. Only republican government is, in the strictest sense, 'public.' See GS XIX 595; DR, VI, 317, 344–5 (82, 117–18).

4 DR, VI 341 (113)

167 *The Doctrine of Right*: A selective commentary

each case representation and synthetic unity go hand in hand. But whereas theoretical representation presupposes a wholly alien and imposing other, practical representation implies an imposition that is self-imposed.

In asserting his rights, a person comes to terms with outer opposition, either by appropriating it (in the case of things) or by consenting to it under a system of mutual compulsion (in the case of other men). Either step requires a united will, secured by a 'representative' and overarching power in which the ideas of reason and the forces of nature (or history) are combined. Through representation the citizen submits to an external force that he has made his own.

The very nature of representation, however, which implies a power *out of* and *against* the people, makes it impossible for the people to install representative government by themselves. Only those in power can change a defective constitution. There can be no legitimate resistance of the people to the legislative chief of state; for juridical status is possible only through subjection to the general legislative will.[5] The people are obliged to obey 'even the most intolerable abuses' of the authorities rather than rebel. It is forbidden to disobey the law which actually holds sway, however much it may deviate from the rational ideal.

There must always be a power over and against the people to execute their sovereign will. Alongside the theoretical sovereignty of the legislator, Kant asserts the effective supremacy of the ruler. Whereas the legislator is 'irreproachable,' the ruler is 'irresistible.'[6] The legislator cannot be blamed; the ruler cannot be opposed. The ruler of the state is he who holds effective power. Although he is empowered only to execute by means of rules and not to legislate, he is the effective judge of whether these rules conform to the law. As there must be a sovereign to 'represent' the people, so must there be an actual power to embody the sovereign, giving it effective as well as ideal force.[7] This power has no coercive duties to the people and is not a party to their contract.

Kant's system of public right is at once radical and conservative, imposing on the moral actor conflicting demands. Like Kant himself, who both applauded and abhorred the French revolution, the citizen longs for perfect justice but obeys the imperfect laws to which history subjects him. The tension between the actual government to which one ought to submit and the ideal which one ought to make one's end is lessened by a spirit of reform supported by a sense of hope. Morality requires and history permits one to

5 DR, VI 320 (86)
6 DR, VI 316 (81)
7 DR, VI 338 (109)

believe that republican government will in the end prevail. It is, however, effective public power which materially supports this thread of progress. Any morally acknowledged breach in the continuity of this thread would call into question the applicability of laws of right to the empirical realm and so would ultimately call into question the moral law itself.[8]

The people are not even permitted to be 'overly curious' about the origins of the power to which they are subject as a matter of fact. The origins of power are 'not open to scrutiny by the people,' who should not be too concerned about these origins, 'as though the right of obedience due it were in doubt.' In order for a people to pretend to judge this supreme power, 'they must already be viewed as united under a general legislative will' which presupposes this power. 'Hence they can and may not judge otherwise than the present chief of state wills ... Whether as a historical fact an actual contract between them originally preceded the submission to authority or whether instead the authority preceded it and the law only came later ... these are pointless questions that threaten the state with danger if asked with too much sophistication by a people who are already subject to the civil law.'[9] In the *Doctrine of Right* and in unpublished notes, Kant suggests that the power of government necessarily precedes its legitimacy. 'In erecting a civil constitution power comes necessarily before legitimacy,'[1] for no one could be obliged to limit his own freedom until assured of the existence of a power that makes others do likewise. The overarching power which public right requires, then, could not have been legitimately established. The 'surety' function of the ruler precludes his initial legitimacy.

It is no wonder that Kant played down the importance of the origins of public authority, fearing a public scrutiny which that authority could not easily endure. The vulnerability of public right lies in its dependence on actual power to enforce the social contract. The fact of force must be accepted as it is 'given'; for without it no juridical condition is possible. The civil constitution is completely dependent on the existence and continuity of power. To doubt or suspend this power even for an instant is to suspend the constitution itself. Kant's distrust of revolution is not simply an antidemocratic impulse, as some have suggested. It is based rather on fear of an anarchy as much metaphysical as political. As an idea of reason, the social contract cannot create power in the world but can only guide it. Since the origin of power cannot be guaranteed

---

8 DR, VI 319 (84): 'A law that is so holy and inviolable that it is a crime even to doubt it or to suspend it for an instant is represented as coming, not from mankind, but from some highest perfect legislator.'

9 DR, VI 318 (84)

1 *Reflexion* #8074; DR, VI 339 (111)

169 *The Doctrine of Right*: A selective commentary

juridically, that origin must be held juridically irrelevant. 'One ought to obey the legislative authority that now exists, regardless of its origin.'[2] Even the constitution cannot provide for an authority in the state to resist the chief magistrate when he violates the law. For such authority would then itself become the chief magistrate. The supreme power to enforce the law cannot be exercised against itself. The identity of the supreme power is ultimately a matter of fact. Right appropriates nature only by to some extent giving it sway.

The rebel who usurps established power disrupts the tenuous synthesis of the ideal and the actual on which juridical community depends. (To be sure, if he succeeds, his power becomes legitimate.) The crime of rebellion, however, pales before that of formally sanctioned regicide, which turns the power of government against itself. Execution of the executive is a kind of 'civic suicide,' dizzying in its logical as well as its moral implications. Such execution is a 'complete subversion of the principles governing the relation between a sovereign and his people,' a subversion which makes 'the people the master over the former, to whose legislation they owe their existence.'[3] Like 'being swallowed up in an abyss [*Abgrund*] from which there is no return,' it entails all the horror of Kantian sublimity without its final triumphant ascent.[4]

'The sovereign in the state has many rights with respect to the subject, but no (coercive) duties ... If the organ of the sovereign, the ruler, proceeds contrary to the laws ... the subject may lodge a complaint, ... but he may not actively resist.'[5] In his lack of (coercive) duties towards the citizen, the sovereign is like God (who has no duties towards the citizen at all).[6] Allowance must be made, however, for the discrepancy between the actual and the ideal. The executive can do wrong.[7] If the sovereign is like God, the executive

---

2 DR, VI 319 (85)

3 DR, VI 322n (88n)

4 Ibid.; cf. CJ, V 264–5 (part i, 115); 'Conjectural Beginning,' VIII 112 (56), CR A/613 = B/641. Kant uses 'abyss' (*Abgrund*) to characterize the unconditioned, the awakening of human foresight, and generally any situation where ground or foundation is lacking. For an account of Kant's own vertiginous experience, see *Anthropology*, VII 169n (46n).

5 DR, VI 319 (85)

6 DR, VI 319 (84). Saner (*Kant's Political Thought* 34) observes that the sovereign is to the community of citizens as God (in Kant's pre-critical thought) is to the community of substances. He goes too far, however, when he adds that 'every right the people may claim to have against this overlord is to Kant presumptuousness and an assault upon justice.' It is precisely such a view that Kant attributes to and condemns in Hobbes. According to Kant, the sovereign (unlike God) has non-coercive duties to the people; see 'Theory and Practice,' VIII 303 (84) and DR, VI 319 (85).

7 See DR, VI 317, 319 (82, 85).

is like nature, to which we resign ourselves grudgingly. The juridical community may indeed be thought of as reconstituting nature, but in such a way as to substantiate rather than threaten humanity. By borrowing nature's power, right is to accomplish externally that ascendence over nature which the moral typic accomplished internally. The doctrine of right lays the foundation for the completion of the human project to transform the world. In such an effort certain inconveniences must – however grudgingly – be borne.

PUBLICITY AND THE SPIRIT OF REFORM

Public law is, by definition, law that must be publicized if it is to bring about a juridical condition. The capacity to be publicized thus may be regarded as a formal criterion of public right. The possibility of publicity is the juridical equivalent of the moral condition of universalizability, providing a test of justice that is both transcendental and easy to apply. We know that a policy is unjust if it cannot be publicized without necessarily frustrating its purpose, that is to say, if it is such that 'a whole people could not *possibly* agree to it.'[8] A policy which cannot be publicized is one to which the people, whatever their situation, could not rationally consent. The consensual form of the social contract supplies a rule to guide the head of state in shaping and executing the law. The constitution does not require the actual political participation of the citizenry. It is enough if policies are ones which all citizens could conceivably endorse.

The doctrine of right is concerned neither with the content of policy nor with its actual genesis but only with its formal universalizability. To be wise and prudent, a ruler needs to know something of the world. To be just he needs only to know and obey the laws of right. The citizen is entitled to the good will of his sovereign, but not to his deference or even to his good judgment. This very disjunction, however, between good judgment and legitimate rule gives the citizen warrant to attempt to correct that judgment publicly when he thinks it errs. Political supremacy does not imply superior knowledge. When it comes to ascertaining the wisest policy, ruler and citizen are, juridically speaking, on an equal footing. The citizen thus has the right to criticize the ruler, so long as he does not actively resist him.[9] Freedom of the press – freedom to *publicize* – constitutes the only legitimate weapon of the people against political abuse.

Publicity furnishes politics with effective as well as formal guidance. The very habit of free speech tends to make unjust policies more difficult to implement. Public disclosure fosters a juridically desirable sense of indepen-

---

8 'Theory and Practice,' VIII 297 (79)
9 Ibid. 304–6 (84–7)

dence, and with it a circumspect regard for one's own rights. Public enlightenment, a process in which ruler and people mutually influence and reform each other, is a vehicle of political change which need never abrogate actual authority.[1]

Public discourse is essentially published discourse. Books, so long as they are freely available (and non-seditious), are juridically desirable, regardless of their actual content.[2] What money does for property, according to Kant, books do for ideas. As 'the greatest means of carrying out the exchange [*Verkehr*] of thought,' books resolve themselves into relations that are purely intellectual and rational.[3] Books are the currency of the rational market-place of ideas. Their circulation, like that of money, not only is empirically expedient but also rationally conforms to the pure concept of right.

Through a formal distinction between public discourse and private speech, Kant determines in principle what sorts of language can and cannot legitimately be forbidden. Kant is willing to grant that private speech (in which category he includes the discourse of the public official!) can be limited where public order so requires. However, the rights of publicity and the *public* domain of knowledge are not to be denied. The truly public life is not that of politics but that of scholarship and the intellect. For Kant, the most important 'public' is the cosmopolitan republic of the mind.

In his essay 'What it is to Orient Oneself in Thinking' Kant elaborates more fully on the nature of this philosophic 'public' and its relation to political emancipation. Just as the free citizen willingly submits to the legislation of the common will (*der allgemeine Wille*), so the free thinker willingly submits to the judgment of sound common reason (*die gemeine gesunde Vernunft*).[4] As the first *Critique* established, thinking for oneself means recognizing that what can be known objectively can in principle be known by, and shared with, others. Like external property, knowledge is an intrinsically exchangeable possession. The logical egoist, who thinks it unnecessary to test his judgments by the understanding of others, is no less presumptuous than the moral egoist, who limits all ends to himself.[5] To make reason the touchstone of one's

---

[1] See 'What is Enlightenment?' VIII 35–42 (3–10)
[2] DR, VI 286, 289; 'What is Enlightenment?' VIII 37 (5). Kant makes an exception in the case of material used without the author's consent. The author, according to Kant, retains personal rights over his work.
[3] DR, VI 286
[4] GS VIII 133–4
[5] *Anthropology*, VII 128–30 (10–12); the opposite of egoism is *pluralism*, or 'the attitude of not being occupied with oneself as the whole world, but regarding and conducting oneself as a citizen of the world.' 'This much,' according to Kant, 'belongs to anthropology.'

opinions is to accept empirical experience as the shared arena of objective knowledge.

However, before reason can come of age, it must come to terms with its need (*Bedürfnis*) or feeling of inadequacy (*Mangel*), a feeling generated by reason's drive for knowledge (*Erkenntnistrieb*). In judging its own powers, reason must avoid the infant's despotic presumption that one's powers and rights are always adequate to one's demands.[6]

Reason's need does, however, authorize it in certain 'rights of use.' For example, although we cannot know that God exists, we are for moral and scientific purposes entitled to assume so. Such rights, unlike the transcendent claims of the sceptic and the dogmatist, acknowledge their subjective source and so do not impinge upon the intellectual rights of others.

The real emancipation of speculative reason thus has immediate political import. Metaphysical no less than political anarchy brings on political repression. When reason oversteps its rights there result political measures hostile to the legitimate exercise of free thought. Kant's essay is itself a response to the public intellectual battles of his contemporaries Mendelssohn and Jacobi, battles of a sort which were soon to succumb, as Kant grimly warned, to tightened censorship.[7] Such censorship, from which Kant himself did not escape, interferes with the invaluable means by which men communicate and so mutually test their knowledge. Moreover, political emancipation is only possible, in the last analysis, through a general intellectual liberation from every belief to which reason cannot 'assent.' Such liberation on any large scale, Kant knew, must be gradual – another explanation for his aversion to precipitate revolutions that leave the inner man unchanged. It was not the overthrow of France's *ancien régime* that he praised, but the moral feelings it evoked in non-participants.

There is, Kant notes elsewhere, a paradoxical tension between the freedom of thought that readies men for self-government and civil freedom, which seems to favour the freedom of mind of the people but which in fact places inescapable limitations upon it. An enlightened and powerful monarch can say what no republic would dare: argue as much as you will, and about what you will; only obey![8] The course of human enlightenment, or 'release from man's self-imposed tutelage,' requires that freedom of thought take precedence over freedom to vote. It is, for purposes of justice, unnecessary that the

---

6 'What it is to Orient Oneself in Thinking,' VIII 139n
7 For an excellent discussion of these controversies see the Commentary by A. Philonenko in Kant *Qu'est-ce que s'orienter dans la pensée* (Paris, Vrin 1972).
8 'What is Englightenment?' VIII 41 (10)

state be a republic, so long as it is governed 'in a republican manner.'[9] If the shadow of Frederick hangs over these lines, it is one that Kant believed to be, in the short run at least, inevitable. Enlightened monarchy seems to be a provisional necessity.

Liberty to publish is the external freedom of the mind. The individual's right to participate in free exchange (be it of goods or of ideas) and thereby 'extend himself to his full capacity,'[1] takes precedence over his right to elect political representatives. By thus heightening the importance of intellectual and economic rights, Kant lessens the significance of the distinction he draws between active and passive citizenship. An empirically republican government is less urgently needful than the formal right to develop fully one's own powers.

THE RIGHT OF NATIONS: STRATEGIES OF PEACE (DR II 2, 3)

The object of all juridical systems is peace. The natural condition of men, however, is antagonism and war. Government releases men from the state of war by enforcing laws to which they have themselves consented. Nations too are naturally in a state of war and are, like individuals, obliged to try to leave this state. The 'right of nations' (*Völkerrecht*) concerns the relations among nations considered as moral persons. The primary object of the law of nations deriving from this right is to secure a firm and lasting peace throughout the world. Such a peace, however, presents difficulties not encountered at the level of civil society. Unlike civil harmony, international peace cannot be secured by an overarching power to which all consent. For nations the social contract exists only as an ideal, without a sovereign to enforce it. In Kant's view a world republic is impossible; such a union would either immediately break apart or collapse into world despotism. Moreover, unlike civil law, the law of nations concerns the relations between citizens of different states. The individual state has a responsibility to its citizens and cannot rightfully be deprived of that sovereignty which they have duly authorized. The 'citizen of the world' never ceases to be also the citizen of a separate state.

Nations are therefore obliged to seek an alliance or confederation which preserves the separate sovereignty of every member. The member-state, unlike the citizen, may withdraw from the union whenever it deems it necessary or just to do so. The right to judge and enforce the law likewise remains

---

9 'An Old Question Raised Again: Is the Human Race Constantly Progressing?' VII 88 (147)
1 'What is Enlightenment?' VIII 41 (10); see also ibid. 40 (8).

with the individual state.² The law of nations does not exclude the right unilaterally to resort to force. The law of nations is thus at least provisionally a law of war. There being no overarching power to secure the rights of all, each is entitled to secure them for itself. This right extends both to the redress of actual injury and to the prevention of potential injury. It does not, however, extend to extermination, subjugation, or punishment.³ As a moral person, the state may be stripped of some of its material support but none of its ideal integrity; as sovereign, it may be taxed and resisted but not subjected to penalties. No nation enjoys a position of moral superiority over any other nation. As in the state of nature generally, resort to force is justified only when necessary to the preservation of property.

Unable to abolish war outright, the law of nations forbids spying, assassination, and other acts of war which in their secretiveness tend to undermine the mutual trust essential to a future peace. Like civil law, international law must be public. The formal vehicle of this publicity is not, however, the constitution but the treaty. In his essay 'Perpetual Peace,' Kant lays down articles, preliminary and definitive, for such a treaty, articles the object of which is to secure a lasting peace in the absence of an overarching power to guarantee it. The preliminary articles lay the foundation for peace by asserting the integrity of each individual nation, by abolishing standing armies and credit-financing for war expenditures, and by forbidding such acts as would, during war, 'make mutual confidence in the subsequent peace impossible.'⁴ These preparatory steps are in time to be superseded by definitive articles, which establish cosmopolitan laws grounded in a federation of free, republican states.⁵

Peace and republicanism finally go hand in hand. War is most deeply abhorrent when it seems to turn men into things to be used and consumed by the state as it will. Monarchs tend to treat their subjects as expendable goods, darkly imagining that they have a right 'to lead [their] subjects into a war as though it were a hunting expedition, and to march them onto a field of battle as though it were a pleasure excursion on the grounds that [their subjects] were a product of [the monarchs'] own activity.'⁶ Monarchs imagine that their subjects may be used, consumed, and destroyed. Men are never the property of their sovereign, however, and can justly be made to go to war only through their own consent. The horror of war, in which men, outdoing the destructive

2 DR, VI 344, 346 (116, 118–19)
3 DR, VI 346–7 (118, 120)
4 'Perpetual Peace,' VIII 346 (89)
5 Ibid. VIII 351 (94–5)
6 DR, VI 345 (118)

fray of nature, literally consume each other, is mitigated only when they enter into war willingly.

The fact of war thus presents most forcefully the case for political representation. The likelihood of war is, however, in turn mitigated by republican government, which places the decision to go to war (at least hypothetically) in the hands of those whose lives are immediately at stake, and which thus gives further encouragement to the spirit of commerce and enlightenment.

The final article of the treaty for perpetual peace limits 'the law of world citizenship [*Weltbürgerrecht*]' to 'conditions of universal hospitality.' By 'hospitality' Kant means 'a right to associate [*Besuchsrecht*] which all men have' by virtue of 'their common possession of the surface of the earth.'[7] This right to associate is, speaking precisely, a right to enter into commerce (*Verkehr*); its typical expression is economic.

The 'community' which all nations originally hold in the earth is one of 'possible physical interaction [*commercium*],' that is to say, a relationship such that 'they can offer to trade with one another.'[8] The right of hospitality implies a right to trade as distinguished from a right to enslave and plunder. Like Locke, Kant emphasizes the pacifying effects of world trade. However, he rejects as moral sophistry the (Lockean) contention that people who refuse to 'do business' may be justly colonized and enslaved.[9] Commerce cannot furnish an excuse to deny the personality which juridically grounds it.

There remains the problem of guaranteeing the peace. Neither individual men nor peoples are obliged to enter into any contract without assurance that the others entering the contract will in fact abide by its terms. For individual men, such assurance is furnished by the power of the sovereign. Since a world treaty cannot be so guaranteed, the duty to enter into or abide by such a treaty can never be absolute and unconditional. Unlike the individual citizen, the state reserves a right to withdraw from its contract whenever it judges that the contract has been or is likely to be violated by others. There must, however, be some guarantee for the articles of peace, lest peace seem impossible and hence seem to be no rational goal at all.

The basis for such a guarantee is history. History emerges in Kant's thought as a substitute on a cosmopolitan scale for that enforcing power which renders feasible the civil state. The essential elements of this philosophy of history are sketched out in Kant's 'Idea for a Universal History from a Cosmopolitan Point of View' and in the First Supplement to 'Perpetual

---

7 'Perpetual Peace,' VII 358 (103)
8 DR, VI 352 (125)
9 DR, VI 353 (126-7)

Peace.' Both essays present the hopeful view that the very antagonisms which divide men assure their eventual conciliation.

Kant attributes this transformation to history, or 'nature's art.' Peace does not depend on human intentions but will occur in spite of them. 'The guarantee of perpetual peace is nothing less than that great artist, nature ... In her mechanical course we see that her aim is to produce a harmony among men, against their will and indeed through their discord.'[1] Nature prepares for such harmony by first enabling and then forcing men to live everywhere, and so drawing them into more or less lawful relations with one another. Initially, war is the vehicle of this dispersion and gradual civilization. 'Even if a people were not forced by internal discord to submit to public laws, war would compel them to do so, for ... nature has placed each people near another which presses upon it, and against this it must form itself [*sich bilden*] into a state in order to defend itself.'[2] Civil government is a reactive construction, formed as a means of defence against alien and imposing powers. Like any other human construction civil society emerges reactively as the response to an external force.

To be secure, civil society need not depend on good intentions. 'The problem, however hard it may seem, of organizing a state can be solved even for a race of devils, if only they are intelligent.' The problem of government is therefore 'to establish the constitution in such a way that, although ... private intentions conflict, they check each other, with the result that their public conduct is the same as if they had no such intentions.'[3] Such a problem must be capable of solution, for it does not require moral improvement, but only knowledge of 'the mechanism of nature' by which private intentions may be so arranged. So to conceive the problem is already to begin to grasp its solution. Acting through human selfishness, nature helps to secure order and peace. Universal understanding of nature's mechanism only furthers its irresistible course.

International order is the best illustration of the beneficent mechanism of enlightened self-interest, a mechanism on which that order so manifestly depends. The very antagonisms which divide nations lead ultimately to an agreement which rests not on individual weakness but on mutual strength. Nature thus prevents a despotic peace and encourages harmony based on 'equilibrium in liveliest competition.' Having divided the states which individuals would merge by force, nature leads them to unite by mutual interest. 'The spirit of commerce, which is incompatible with war, sooner or later gains

---

1 'Perpetual Peace,' VIII 360 (106)
2 Ibid. 365 (111)
3 Ibid. 366 (112)

the upper hand in every state.' Money becomes perhaps the state's most reliable means (*Mittel*) and power (*Macht*).[4] Through money government is forced (*gedrungen*), irrespective of any moral urge, to seek peace and to prevent war.[5] Economics and enlightenment, money and publicity furnish the means by which men unwittingly contrive their collective happiness and freedom.

Within the stream of history, men come to deal lawfully with one another, if not out of moral trust and regard, out of a self-interest which substitutes for that regard. International law may lack direct enforcement; it can, however, fall back on the indirect enforcement provided by a world-wide economy. To be sure, such an economy, based on a monetary system, requires the support of individual governments. Yet money, perhaps the state's most certain power, comes at last to lead the government on which it first depends. Money comes, in a sense, to supersede the state itself. This supremacy is juridically permitted because it in no way threatens the state's legal sovereignty. In submitting to the power of money, the citizens do not bend the knee to any higher will, but rather to the force of history. The progress of man is in this way assured 'without prejudice to his freedom.'[6]

History indicates that peace is possible without morality. In adopting preliminary articles of peace, as in entering the social contract, we need not depend on the good will of others. History 'enforces' in one case what the sovereign enforces in the other. History is a force through which, wittingly or unwittingly, we rule ourselves. The progressive history of Kant points towards the dialectically self-conscious history of Hegel. For Kant, however, history is a willed but largely unwitting product. Unlike the juridical sovereign, it rules through us without representing our united will.

Moral autonomy, the highest stage of reason, is in principle available to any man at any time, and so in the profoundest sense 'unhistorical.' History and morality inhabit different dimensions and develop along separate paths. The Kantian 'cunning of nature' is not yet the Hegelian 'cunning of reason.' The doctrine of right points towards a philosophy of history but does not properly include it. Bound to nature, the guarantees of history lack all theoretical certainty. In the last analysis they do not assure the actualization of a lasting peace, but only a reasonable probability, and with it the rationality of peace as a moral objective.[7]

The human economy is made possible by a juridical usurpation of nature.

---

4 Ibid. 368 (114)
5 Ibid.
6 Ibid. 365 (111)
7 DR, VI 354–5 (127–9). See also 'Perpetual Peace,' VIII 368 (114).

However, in so far as this economy depends on an exchange of things, it also remains part of the economy of nature. Such dependence is compatible with the freedom which prevails in a community of co-dependent and co-determinate beings. All men are free so long as none is juridically preferred; and such preferment nature, with all its power, cannot bestow. History, or nature humanly transformed, proves an appropriate if imperfect guarantor of juridical peace. Kant's historical mechanism makes no heroes and invokes no gods.

Kant's politics, like his metaphysics, finds its only certainty in limitation. The juridical usurpation of nature is incomplete, unleashing a material transformation which may encourage but cannot itself produce the kingdom of ends. The habit of law-abidingness and the discipline of economic rationality Kant believes will foster virtue. He believes that juridical coercion will 'not only [give] a moral veneer ... to the whole' but actually facilitate the development of the 'moral disposition.'[8] Between prudential self-restraint and morality there is, however, a decisive gap which the mechanism of nature cannot span. The absolute demands of inner freedom set a limit to what outer freedom alone can accomplish. Historically as well as morally, juridical community remains a way station between dependency on nature and unconditioned moral freedom.

Right must apply to human activity in space and time without depending on it. The cost of this independence is the tenuousness of the connection, in Kant's thought, between right and human desire. Divorced from nature, right requires us to abstract from our own rational and material needs. The doctrine of right 'naturalizes' our neediness, removing it from the reach of righteous indignation. The inequalities over which legal equality presides men must blame on nature itself, which is as much as to say that they cannot lay blame at all. An argument which began in indignation against nature, which has given us desires we cannot satisfy, ends with the vindication of nature and with the suppression, if not the outright renunciation, of desire. The unhappy must bear their ills without rancour, so long as they enjoy respect. Demands of justice met, our needs might suffer. Kant hoped that legal and material progress would overlap. The rights of man, however, could not be grounded in material progress. In the end, Kant was forced to proclaim, 'fiat justicia, pereat mundus' – let justice prevail though the world perish.[9]

It seems in retrospect a strange slogan for the author of 'Perpetual Peace,'

---

8 'Perpetual Peace,' VIII 375n (123n)
9 Kant quotes the original Latin, rendering it in translation as: 'Let justice prevail though all the scoundrels in the world perish.'

itself a model for the League of Nations and other expressions of cosmopolitan optimism. Those who treat Kant's work as a recipe for peace ignore both the irony of its title – an irony Kant thought he had made obvious – and its more serious intention. Peace is a practical, not a theoretical, necessity. History provides moral hope, not objective assurance. Even as a ground of hope Kant ultimately preferred to the contingencies of history the *a priori* (if undemonstrable) certainty of God and an afterlife.[1] His cosmopolitan history arises less out of the necessities of criticism than out of a subjectively irrepressible demand for justice on earth. The tension throughout Kant's thought between desire and renunciation, satisfaction and right, is also evident in his teachings concerning the practicality and probability of world order. He hoped that the dissemination of his vision of the future would itself have a pacifying as well as a consoling effect. This hope rested, however, on an uncertain identification of peace and commerce, an identification which, in our own age, should be even more difficult to accept.

Both Kant's metaphysics and his jurisprudence are theories of property. Both knowing and having are ways of appropriating or securing a right to the use of a thing, be it a concept or an object in the world. In renouncing our demand for satisfaction, rational and material, we acquire the means to labour to attain it.[2] Reason, able to claim each of a totality of representations as its own, is matched by the acting person, able to appropriate for his own use anything on earth. The possessions of the thinking self secure its coherent identity; those of the acting person establish his participation in a substantial community. In both theory and practice, man is 'the proprietor of the world.'[3]

For Kant, however, ownership implies only a will to benefit, not the actual ability to do so. As he rejected the classical association of knowledge with happiness, so he rejects the classical association of title to a thing with the ability to use it well. The rights of man do not include the right to happiness. Modern men who complacently join in the Kantian project should find in the melancholy indignation at its heart a reason for concern.[4]

1 Cf. *Religion*, VI 50, 66, 75–6 (46, 62, 70).
2 On philosophy as labour (*Arbeit*), see Kant's essay *Von einem neuerdings erhobenen vornehmen Ton in der Philosophie* (1796), VIII 387–406; see also his introduction to a work by Jachman (1800), GS VIII 341–2. Kant takes issue with the neo-Platonists and Jacobi. According to Kant, philosophy is only a 'commodity' unless it concerns itself with the (practical) end of humanity.
3 *Opus post.*, XXI 45
4 On melancholy and indignation, see Kant *Observations on the Feeling of the Beautiful and Sublime*, II 219, 221 (63, 66). Also see *Bemerkungen*, XX 62–4: 'The melancholy [person] is righteous and embittered by injustice.' On Kantian *melancholia*, see Christian Ritter *Der Rechtsgedanke Kants* 216–17; Ernst Cassirer *Rousseau, Kant and Goethe* 12.

Conclusion

This book has interpreted the rights of reason in both a revolutionary and a conservative sense – revolutionary because the rights pertain to ground Kant thought newly won, and conservative because of the continuing effort he thought necessary to retain this ground. The revolution was Copernican. Reversing man's accustomed notion of his relation to nature and its objects, it was to unleash further revolts, philosophic and political, which its author did not anticipate and could not have condoned. For Kant the one ongoing revolt by which man establishes over things his ideal but ambiguous ascendency was enough, our other energies to be employed conservatively in a partial holding action.

The struggle for ascendency begins for Kant with the perception of nature as an opposer of human aims and an encumbrance on the human spirit. This book has examined the role of opposition in Kant's thought. Beginning with his early treatment of natural opposition, we have moved through subsequent stages of his thought, in which the object (*Gegenstand*), that which stands against us, is progressively re-examined until it is at last understood as a necessary if impenetrable correlate of our own self-identity and awareness. Permanence, limitation, and objectivity, all of which seem to hinder the free movement of the mind, also give it purchase against the otherwise amorphous flow of time and happening. The pre-revolutionary mind is, to Kant, like a dove that, cleaving the air in her free flight, fails to recognize that the resistance of the air against which she struggles is the necessary condition of her own upward motion.

The mind's acceptance of and reconciliation with limitation, an effort which constitutes the core of the *Critique of Pure Reason*, is as ubiquitous for Kant as it is difficult. Almost from the moment of birth we meet with opposition which, inhibiting our will, also prompts our mental and moral development. Conceptualization and assertion, the German 'grasping' or *Begriff* and an appropriating apprehension, enjoy here a unity which for Kant is never entirely severed. Pressure, impact, and resistance, which constitute our primary experience of the natural world, help to construct our moral world as well. The infant's ready indignation towards all opposition is the first expression of its 'freedom.' It competes with objects for space, as it will soon learn to compete with other wills.

With indignation comes a capacity to resist the forces of nature, a capacity that is essential to the development of reason. The human ability to abstract or turn away from what 'imposes itself on man through his senses,' for example, is bound up with our experience of power and impotence. Even the famous informing capacity of the mind takes its first cue from touch, the organ most sensitive to repulsion. Sight and attraction, which played such an important role in classical theories of mind, are for Kant upstaged by touch in the awakening of reason to its powers.

Touch and feel also play an essential role in Kant's moral theory. Subjectively, the moral law cannot be 'seen' but only 'felt' as inner opposition, a moral counterpart to the resistance of the external world. In typifying the law, or rendering it 'visible' to intuition, Kant uses elements of construction analogous to the *schemata* and *Bilder* of theoretical understanding. The concept of right lends itself especially well to such construction, the physical relations between mechanical bodies standing in for the juridical relations between wills. If there is an essential difference between the two systems of reciprocal restraint, it lies in the inwardness of the latter, involving as it does recognition and acceptance, in place of the purely external forces of mechanics. Juridical constraint internally mirrors mechanical opposition, the mutual cancellation of opposing wills evincing a freedom to which Kant compares the dynamics of physics.

Kant's model of the mind's primal encounter with resistance mediates between his mechanical and juridical systems. Between our experience of external and internal opposition, right is the revolutionary pivot. To the indignant and quarrelsome infant Kant attributes a primitive concept of right as corollary to its freedom. But the indignation cannot be properly righteous until the anger vented outwards by the child is turned inwards. The desires whose frustration was initially the cause of the vexation, along with the rational capacity to foresee the inevitability of such frustration, must themselves become objects of this anger.

This inward revolution is profoundly anti-erotic, sacrificing to righteous self-assertion men's natural relation to desire. That this relation is a 'submissive' one only underscores the tension in Kant's thought between desire and freedom. The price of righteous indignation is, paradoxically, the relinquishment of our claim to happiness. The moral autonomy that permits us to transcend nature ideally requires a recognition that as material creatures we remain beings of need. For the happiness we cannot legitimately demand we can at most express a pious hope, and that in the name of a virtue we cannot properly assume.

There is of course an important place in Kant's thought for the pragmatic pursuit of pleasure. Duty permitting, the rational individual will strive to maximize his satisfaction, though his calculus will remain indeterminate, lacking as it does a standard, other than formal self-consistency, by which to choose among competing impulses. There are for Kant no higher or lower impulses, only ones more or less consistent with the satisfaction of the rest. Perhaps inspired by, but certainly at odds with, the classical analogy between the city and the soul, Kant expostulated a pragmatic psychology akin to his politics. The business of reason, like that of government, is not to define happiness but rather to arbitrate fairly among its satisfaction-seeking constituents. In forsaking the classical ideal of the wise ruler, whose just title derives from rational desire for and pursuit of the (common) good, Kant also abandoned the standard of rational desire itself.

Kant's classical predecessors could speak of rational desire as the ruling principle of the soul. For Kant, however, desirous reason is reason in a pathological and potentially dangerous state against which it must protect itself through hard-won powers of self-discipline. The highest achievement of reason, classically identified with *eros*, is identified by Kant with the negation of *eros*. For Kant, the passionate vehicle of reason is not desire but indignation. *Eros* is the wayward steed of Kant's chariot.

For the traditional – and to his mind futile – philosophic goal of satisfaction Kant substituted the principle of self-consistency. Against the world's flux, the mind secures its own identity as it secures its relation to things. For Kant, this activity typically takes the form of 'possessing' or 'having,' property being understood as that over the use of which one may legitimately claim a right.

As a student of the 'economy of nature,' the young Kant called man a 'stranger on earth, who owns no property.' As an aged philosopher, compiling notes towards what he hoped would be his crowning work, he declared himself 'proprietor of the world.' Kant's philosophic development, and his critical thought in particular, can be understood as an explanation and defence of man's appropriation of the world. In both the *Critique of Pure Reason* and the *Doctrine of Right* Kant presents his most crucial arguments as 'deductions,' by which he means justifications of a claim to property. Both deductions would establish how it is possible to possess or have something as one's own. The Transcendental Deduction would establish the 'rights of reason' to its use of concepts of objects; the juridical deduction would establish the rights of rational beings to their use of objects in the natural world. The central problem uniting Kant's speculative philosophy and his politics is his perception of the human subject as a 'stranger' who must appropriate and so transform the world if it is to be his own.

Like right itself, consciousness for Kant is fundamentally proprietary. The mind establishes its identity through a transcendental synthesis by means of which it lays claim to all that it can call its own. By an equally proprietary synthesis, humanity at large lays claim to all that it can freely use. The transcendental ego of the mind parallels the united will of the juridical community.

The unity of mind has to do with what is 'mine'; juridical unity has to do with what is either 'mine' or 'yours.' The proper role of government, according to Kant, is to protect the rights of men through the protection of their private property. The formal equality of man thereby secured, material inequality is relegated to the realm of nature or chance. Like illness, poverty is a misfortune which one may bemoan but may not rightfully protest.

Even unjust (as opposed to merely unpleasant) laws must be obeyed. So tenuous is the connection between the ideal and material bases of the state that to disobey a single law, however ill-conceived, is to call into question the possibility of political legitimacy. It is to throw into doubt the presumed unity of force and right on which all governments depend, a presumption which, like the emperor's clothes, cannot bear too close a public scrutiny. This presumption can also be shaken by the presence of multiple sovereignties, which tends to undermine the sovereignty of each, as it undermines the peace for the sake of which government exists. The anarchy Kant fears is as much logical as political; for Kant, to question the authority of any state is to question the authority of them all.

Given these strains in the juridical synthesis, it is no wonder that Kant comes to depend more and more on the invisible (and extra-political) hands of commerce and enlightenment to guarantee the peace and to install materially the republican government whose form all states ideally presume. Asserting a duty to obey the powers that be, Kant softens the rigours of that command with the hope of political improvement brought on by intellectual and economic progress, that is, the so-called spirit of enlightenment and commerce. Money and thought for Kant almost supplant politics as the means by which men are to secure justice. As universal medium of human exchange, money is the man-made, material expression of an *a priori* rational form. Likening it to books (which similarly facilitate the circulation of ideas), Kant describes money as matter – mined from the earth – to which man himself gives form. Money mediates between juridical and natural substance (the earth itself) and thereby imitates unwittingly the appropriating unity of will and nature implicit in the state. As the product of both nature and universal human consent, money is a prototype of and partial substitute for the world government which would, if only it could be achieved, embody the general will on earth.

Nature, according to Kant, can be appropriated but not cancelled (*aufgehoben*). Property is made possible by our capacity to think (but never know) the object both as external, that is, as separate from ourselves, and as our own. To deduce one's claims to property is, for Kant, to discover the limits of one's claims. There is no getting around these limits. Theoretical possession entails the concept of a transcendental ego inaccessible to consciousness; practical possession entails the concept of an ideal community unattainable through politics. In justifying our claims we necessarily run up against the limits of our powers.

In a sense, the poor cosmopolite universalized his own situation. For Kant, poverty is man's natural condition. Man is a 'being of needs' which are not met by nature as his due but only through his own strenuous and imperfect efforts. The cosmos in which he is a stranger is an 'economy' in which he does not reckon. Long before Marx spoke of the alienating effects of capital, Kant recognized a disjunction between property and human happiness. For Kant, however, property was not the cause of unhappiness but the best response humanly possible to natural dissatisfaction. If our possessions, material and mental, fail to satisfy, the nature of things is at fault, not property as an institution.

Like liberal political economists before and after him, Kant was convinced of the necessity of private property but lacked their sanguine belief in its happy consequences. The justification of property for Kant lies not in its utility but in its logical necessity, as a condition of rational thought and action. Later thinkers as diverse as Stirner and Marx would come to treat ownership as the quintessential human capacity. Kant was too committed to reason with all its human limitations to accept such a reduction of human personality. For him it was enough to demonstrate the inadequacy of Lockean and Humean empiricism – for political economy as well as epistemology – and show that our relation to things – our property – can only be secured through the acknowledgment and acceptance of our own necessities.

Property is the mind's ballast and hedge against the metaphysical insecurity – the dizzying *Abgrund* – towards which desire impels it. Confronted with both opposition and abyss, reason learns to take comfort in the lesser evil. Rationally defining our relation to opposition, property is the ideal embodiment of material control. Through its property, the mind extends its authority over the earth, securing a human economy in which men's own aims reckon. But the conquest remains incomplete. Desire can be held down in the service of legitimacy but cannot entirely be suppressed.

Kant's is a philosophy of poverty for an age of plenty. However much he aided and applauded the intellectual and political revolutions of his day, an awareness of the fundamental insubstantiality of human things always tempered his zeal. That this awareness and the righteous response which for Kant it provoked help to define the substance of his thought has been the ongoing argument of this book. That this awareness may also help to define the problems of our own age, in which the management of desire and the appropriation of nature have proceeded so far, is a thesis which may provoke further argument.

In a context and age different from our own, Kant struggled with problems that continue to haunt liberal thought. His most important contributions to the liberal tradition stem from his denial of the right to happiness and simultaneous endorsement of the infinite conquest of nature in the service of a freedom without natural limits. From Kant liberalism receives a metaphysical basis for respect for the individual, and with it a moral depth and power previously lacking. At the same time, Kantian liberalism moves away from the sentiment and compassion of the British Moralists and Rousseau, affording the harshness of the free market a moral sanction previously lacking. Long before Social Darwinism and similar movements of the nineteenth century gave to inequality a new kind of natural sanction alien to the 'natural aristocracies' of Locke, Rousseau, and Jefferson, Kant argued that our very moral equality entails a natural inequality that is beyond just reproach. However much Kant insisted on it, this connection between moral equality and material inequality is disputable and was disputed. Prior even to the publication of Kant's *Rechtslehre* Fichte advanced a jurisprudence based on allegedly Kantian principles in which the achievement of material equality and satisfaction was explicitly set forth as a jurisprudential goal. Today as well, socialists and liberals of the left, claiming to be heirs of Kant, set forth egalitarian aims which he would not have endorsed.

Kant's doctrine of obedience to the powers that be is even more disputable. Kantian principles and youthful fervour led Fichte to champion the very right to revolution that Kant rejected. Kant himself had difficulty reconciling his doctrine of obedience with his approval of the accomplishments of the French revolution, though the difficulty never led him to abandon the doctrine; Kant's doctrine does seem unduly cautious and severe, even when allowance is made for (passive) resistance to manifestly unjust laws. In his defence it may be said that for Kant, unlike later proponents of the absolute state, the ground and touchstone of obedience remained individual consent.

Here, as elsewhere, Kant's caution and severity are an indication of his sensitivity to and grasp of problems that lesser thinkers have underestimated or ignored. His doctrine of obedience underscores the threat of the gap he perceived between the ideal and the real, a gap between pragmatic goals and moralizing mission, between the 'free market' and the 'free world' that liberal statesmanship has not yet closed. Likewise, his distinction between rights and satisfaction draws attention to problems of value and distribution with which social theorists are still grappling. And his arguments for the absolute responsibility of the individual, for all their punitive harshness, provide his theory of right with a morally compelling foundation that more easy-going theories have sought in vain. Kant's critical affirmation of the rights of reason provides the liberal republic of the mind with a philosophic and moral foundation that is uniquely powerful. If Kant is guilty of any intrinsic partisanship, it lies in his attachment to freedom and concomitant distrust of all that man cannot accomplish for himself. Given the prevailing view of nature as an alien territory for unlimited human conquest, Kant's theory of right, whatever its shortcomings, can provide much-needed support for a humane science and a moderate, morally self-confident politics.

Bibliography

CITED TRANSLATIONS OF KANT'S WORKS

'An Old Question Raised Again: Is the Human Race Constantly Progressing?' ('Erneuerte Frage: Ob das menschliche Geschlecht im beständigen Fortschreiten zum Besseren sei,' *Der Streit der Facultäten* part 2)

Anthropology from a Pragmatic Point of View (*Anthropologie in pragmatischer Hinsicht*) trans. with an Introduction and Notes by Mary J. Gregor. The Hague, Martinus Nijhoff 1974

'Conjectural Beginning of Human History' (Mutmasslicher Anfang der Menschengeschichte) trans. by Emil L. Fackenheim in *On History* ed. with an Introduction by Lewis White Beck. Indianapolis, Bobbs-Merrill 1963

The Critique of Judgement (*Kritik der Urteilskraft*) trans. with Analytical Indexes by James Creed Meredith. Oxford, Clarendon Press 1952

Critique of Practical Reason trans. with an Introduction by Lewis White Beck. Indianapolis, Bobbs-Merrill 1956

Critique of Pure Reason (*Kritik der reinen Vernunft*) trans. by Norman Kemp Smith, 2nd impression with corrections. London, Macmillan 1933; repr. 1950

Dissertation on the Form and Principles of the Sensible and Intelligible World (*De mundi sensibilis atque intelligibilis forma et principiis*) trans. by John Handyside in *Kant's Inaugural Dissertation and Early Writings on Space*. Chicago and London, Open Court 1929

The Doctrine of Right (*Metaphysische Anfangsgründe der Rechtslehre, Die Metaphysik der Sitten* part 1) trans. as *The Metaphysical Elements of Justice* by John Ladd. Indianapolis, Bobbs-Merrill 1968; the translation is incomplete.

The Doctrine of Virtue (*Metaphysische Anfangsgründe der Tugendlehre, Die Metaphysik der Sitten* part 2) trans. with an Introduction and Notes by Mary J. Gregor. New York, Harper and Row 1964

192 Bibliography

Dreams of a Spirit-Seer (*Träume eines Geistersehers, erläutert durch Träume der Metaphysik*) trans. by E.F. Goerwitz. London, Swann Sonnenschein 1900

Groundwork of the Metaphysic of Morals (*Grundlegung zur Metaphysik der Sitten*) trans. and analyzed by H.J. Paton. New York, Harper & Row 1964

'Idea for a Universal History from a Cosmopolitan Point of View' (Idee zu einer allgemeinen Geschichte in weltbürgerlicher Absicht) trans. by Lewis White Beck in *On History* ed. with an Introduction by Lewis White Beck. Indianapolis, Bobbs-Merrill 1963'

Lectures on Ethics trans. by Louis Infield, with a Foreword by Louis White Beck. New York, Harper & Row 1963

Logic trans. by Robert Hartman and Wolfgang Schwarz. Indianapolis, Bobbs-Merrill 1974

The Metaphysical Elements of Justice (referred to above as *The Doctrine of Right*)

Metaphysical Foundations of Natural Science (*Metaphysische Anfangsgründe der Naturwissenschaften*) trans with an Introduction and Essay by James Ellington. Indianapolis, Bobbs-Merrill 1970

Observations on the Feeling of the Beautiful and Sublime (*Beobachtungen über das Gefühl des Schönen und Erhabenen*) trans. by John T. Goldthwait. Berkeley and Los Angeles, University of California Press 1960

'On the Common Saying: "This May be True in Theory, but it Does not Apply in Practice"' (Über den Gemeinspruch: Das mag in der Theorie richtig sein, taugt aber nicht für die Praxis) trans. by H.B. Nisbet in *Kant's Political Writings* ed. with an Introduction and Notes by Hans Reiss. Cambridge, Cambridge University Press 1970.

'On the Failure of All Attempted Philosophical Theodicies' (Über das Misslingen aller philosophischen Versuche in der Theodicee) trans. by Michel Despland in his *Kant on History and Religion*. Montreal and London, McGill-Queen's University Press 1973

'Perpetual Peace' (Zum ewigen Frieden) trans. by Lewis White Beck in *On History* ed. with an Introduction by Lewis White Beck. Indianapolis, Bobbs-Merrill 1963

Philosophical Correspondence 1759–99 ed. and trans. by Arnulf Zweig. Chicago, University of Chicago Press 1967

Prolegomena to Any Future Metaphysics (*Prolegomena zu einer jeden künftigen Metaphysik*) trans. with an introduction by Lewis White Beck. Indianapolis, Bobbs-Merrill 1950

Religion within the Limits of Reason Alone (*Religion innerhalb der Grenzen*

der blossen Vernunft) trans. with an Introduction and Notes by T.M. Greene and Hoyt H. Hudson, 2nd ed. New York, Harper Brothers 1960
Universal Natural History and Theory of the Heavens (Allgemeine Naturgeschichte und Theorie des Himmels) trans. by W. Hastie in *Kant's Cosmology* (Glasgow 1900). Repr. Ann Arbor, University of Michigan Press 1969; the translation is incomplete.
'What is Enlightenment?' (Beantwortung der Frage: Was ist Aufklärung?) trans. by Lewis White Beck in *On History* ed. with an Introduction by Lewis White Beck. Indianapolis, Bobbs-Merrill 1963

SELECTED SECONDARY SOURCES

Arendt, Hannah *Thinking* New York and London, Harcourt Brace Jovanovich 1971, 1977, 1978
Aris, Reinhold *History of Political Thought in Germany from 1790 to 1815* London, G. Allen and Unwin, 1936
Batscha, Zwi *Materialien zu Kants Rechtsphilosophie* Frankfurt am Main, Suhrkamp Verlag 1976
Beck, Lewis White *A Commentary on Kant's Critique of Practical Reason* Chicago, University of Chicago Press 1960
– 'Les deux concepts kantiens du vouloir dans leur contexte politique' *Annales de philosophie politique* 4 (1962): 119–38
– *Studies in the Philosophy of Kant* Indianapolis, Bobbs-Merrill 1965
– *Essays on Kant and Hume* New Haven and London, Yale University Press 1978
Borowski, L.E. *Darstellung des Lebens und Charakters Immanuel Kant's* Königsberg, F. Nicolovius 1804
Borries, Kurt *Kant als Politiker* Leipzig, F. Meiner 1928
Caird, Edward *A Critical Account of the Philosophy of Kant* Glasgow, Maclehose 1877
Cassirer, Ernst *Kants Leben und Lehre* Berlin, B. Cassirer 1921
– *Rousseau, Kant, and Goethe* New York, Harper & Row 1962
Cohn, Leonard *Das objective Richtige (Kantstudien* Ergänzungshefte no. 46) Berlin, Reuther & Reichard 1919
Composto, Renato *La Quarta Critica Kantiana* Palermo, Palumbo 1954
Delbos, Victor *La Philosophie pratique de Kant* Paris, Alcan 1903
– 'Rousseau et Kant' *Revue de métaphysique et de morale* 20 (1912): 429–39
Despland, Michel *Kant on History and Religion* Montreal and London, McGill-Queen's University Press 1973
De Vleeschauwer, Herman-J. *The Development of Kantian Thought* trans. by A.R.C. Duncan. London, New York, T. Nelson 1962

Dietrichson, Paul 'Kant's Criteria of Universalizability' in *Kant: Foundations of the Metaphysics of Morals, Texts and Critical Essays* ed. by Robert Paul Wolff. Indianapolis and New York, Bobbs-Merrill 1969, 163–207

Ebbinghaus, Julius 'Interpretation and Misinterpretation of the Categorical Imperative' in *Kant: Foundations of the Metaphysics of Morals* ed. by Robert Paul Wolff. Indianapolis and New York, Bobbs-Merrill 1969, 97–116

Fackenheim, Emil L. 'Kant and Radical Evil' *University of Toronto Quarterly* 23 (1954): 339–53

- 'Kant's Concept of History' *Kant-Studien* 48 (1957): 381–98

Friedrich, C.J. 'L'essai sur la paix: Sa position centrale dans la philosophie morale de Kant' *Annales de philosophie politique* 4 (1962): 139–62

Galston, William A. *Kant and the Problem of History* Chicago and London, University of Chicago Press 1975

Goedeckemeyer, Albert *Kants Lebensanschauung in ihren Grundzügen* (*Kantstudien* Ergänzungshefte no. 54) Berlin, Reuther & Reichard 1921

Goldmann, Lucien *Immanuel Kant* trans. by Robert Black. London, NLB 1971

Gooch, George *Germany and the French Revolution* London, Longmans 1920

Gregor, Mary J. *Laws of Freedom: A Study of Kant's Method of Applying the Categorical Imperative in the 'Metaphysik der Sitten'* New York, Barnes & Noble 1963

Gueroult, Martial 'Nature humaine et état de nature chez Rousseau, Kant et Fichte' *Revue philosophique de la France et de l'Etranger* 31 (1941): 379–97

Habermas, Jürgen *Knowledge and Human Interest* trans. by Jeremy J. Shapiro. Boston, Beacon Press 1968

Haensel, Werner *Kants Lehre vom Widerstandsrecht* (*Kantstudien* Ergänzungshefte no. 60) Berlin, Pan-Verlag Rolf Heise 1926

Hassner, Pierre 'Situation de la philosophie politique chez Kant' *Annales de philosophie politique* 4 (1962): 77–103

- 'Les concepts de guerre et de paix chez Kant' *Revue française de science politique* 11 (1969): 642–70

- 'Immanuel Kant' *History of Political Philosophy* 2nd ed. Ed. by Leo Strauss and Joseph Cropsey. Chicago, Rand McNally 1972, 554–93

Hegel, G.W.F. *Encyclopedia of the Philosophical Sciences* part 3: Philosophy of Mind, trans. by William Wallace and A.V. Miller. Oxford, Oxford University Press 1971

- *The Philosophy of Right* trans. by T.M. Knox. London, Oxford University Press 1952
Hegler, Alfred *Die Psychologie in Kants Ethik* Freiburg, J.C.B. Mohr (P. Siebeck) 1891
Heidegger, Martin *Kant and the Problem of Metaphysics* trans. with an introduction by James S. Churchill. Bloomington, Ind., Indiana University Press 1962
- *What is a Thing?* trans. by W.B. Barton, Jr. and Vera Deutsch with Analysis by Eugene T. Gendlin. Chicago, Henry Regnery Co. 1967
Heimsoeth, Heinz 'Metaphysical Motives in the Development of Critical Idealism' in *Kant: Disputed Questions* ed. by Moltke S. Gram. Chicago, Quadrangle Books 1967
Henrich, Dieter 'Hutcheson und Kant' *Kant-Studien* 49 (1957–8): 49–69
- 'Über Kants Früheste Ethik' *Kant-Studien* 54 (1963): 404–31
Hofmann, Hasso *Repräsentation: Studien zur Wort- und Begriffsgeschichte von der Antike bis ins 19. Jahrhundert* Berlin, Duncker & Humblot 1974
Hutchings, P.A.E. *Kant on Absolute Value* London, George Allen & Unwin 1972
Jaspers, Karl *Kant* ed. by H. Arendt. New York, Harcourt, Brace & World 1962
Kelly, George Armstrong *Idealism, Politics, and History: Sources of Hegelian Thought* Cambridge, Cambridge University Press 1969
Kojève, Alexandre *Kant* Paris, Gallimard 1973
Kroner, Richard *Kant's Weltanschauung* trans. by John E. Smith. Chicago, University of Chicago Press 1956
Krüger, Gerhard *Philosophie und Moral in der Kantischen Kritik* Tübingen, Paul Siebeck 1931
Lisser, Kurt *Der Begriff des Rechts bei Kant* (*Kantstudien* Ergänzungshefte no. 58) Berlin, Reuther & Reichard 1922
Martin, Gottfried *Kant's Metaphysics and Theory of Science* trans. by P.G. Lucas. Manchester, Manchester University Press 1955
Marty, Fr. 'La typique du jugement pratique pur: la morale kantienne et son application aux cas particuliers' *Archives de philosophie* 1 (1935): 56–87
McFarland, John *Kant's Concept of Teleology* Edinburgh, Edinburgh University Press 1970
Menzer, Paul 'Der Entwicklungsgang der Kantischen Ethik in den Jahren 1760–1785' *Kant-Studien* 2 (1897): 290–322; 3 (1898): 40–104
Metzger, Wilhelm *Gesellschaft, Recht und Staat in der Ethik des deutschen Idealismus* Heidelberg, C. Winter 1917

Murphy, Jeffrie G. *Kant: The Philosophy of Right* London, Macmillan 1970
Nicholas, Barry *An Introduction to Roman Law* Oxford, Clarendon Press 1962
Oberer, Hariolf 'Zur Frügeschichte der Kantischen Rechtslehre' in *Kant-Studien* 64 (1973); 88-102
Paton, H.J. *The Categorical Imperative: A Study in Kant's Moral Philosophy* Philadelphia, University of Pennsylvania Press 1971
Pitkin, Hanna Fenichel *The Concept of Representation* Berkeley, University of California Press 1967
Polonoff, Irving I. *Force, Cosmos, Monads and Other Themes of Kant's Early Thought* (*Kantstudien* Ergänzungshefte no. 107). Bonn, Bouvier Verlag Herbert Grundmann 1973
Rawls, John *A Theory of Justice* Cambridge, Mass., Harvard University Press, Belknap Press 1971
Riedel, Manfred 'Die Aporie von Herrschaft und Vereinbarung in Kants Idee des Sozialvertrags' in *Kant: Zur Deutung seiner Theorie von Erkennen und Handeln* ed. by Gerold Prauss. Köln, Kiepenheuer & Witsch 1973, 337-49
Riley, Patrick 'Kant on Will, "Moral Causality," and the Social Contract' *The Modern Schoolman* 51 (1977): 107-22
Ritter, Christian *Der Rechtsgedanke Kants nach den frühen Quellen* Frankfurt/M., Klosterman 1971
Saner, Hans *Kant's Political Thought: Its Origins and Development* trans. by E.B. Ashton. Chicago, University of Chicago Press 1973
Schilpp, Paul Arthur *Kant's Pre-Critical Ethics* Evanston, Northwestern University Press 1938
Shklar, Judith N. *Men and Citizens* Cambridge, Cambridge University Press 1969
Silber, John 'Kant's Conception of the Highest Good as Immanent and Transcendent' *Philosophical Review* 68 (October 1959): 469-92
- 'The Copernican Revolution in Ethics: The Good Re-examined' *Kant-Studien* 51 (1959-60): 85-101
Simmel, Georg 'How is Society Possible?' trans. by Kurt H. Wolff in *On Individuality and Social Forms: Selected Writings* ed. by Donald N. Levine. Chicago, University of Chicago Press 1971
- *Kant, Sechzehn Vorlesungen gehalten an der Berliner Universität* Leipzig, Duncker & Humblot 1904
Smith, Norman Kemp *A Commentary to Kant's 'Critique of Pure Reason'* 2nd ed. New York, Humanities Press 1962
Starobinski, Jean *Jean-Jacques Rousseau: La transparence et l'obstacle* Paris, Librarie Plon 1957

Strauss, Leo *Natural Right and History* Chicago and London, University of Chicago Press 1953
Van de Pitte, Frederick P. *Kant as Philosophical Anthropologist* The Hague, Martinus Nijhoff 1971
Vlachos, Georges *La Pensée politique de Kant: Métaphysique de l'ordre et dialectique du progrès* Paris, Presses Universitaires de France 1962
Vuillemin, Jules *L'héritage kantien et la révolution copernicienne* Paris, Presses Universitaires de France 1954
Ward, Keith *The Development of Kant's View of Ethics* Oxford, Blackwell 1972
Weil, Eric 'Kant et le problème de la politique' *Annales de philosophie politique* 4 (1962): 1-32
- *Problèmes kantiens* Paris, J. Vrin 1963
Williams, Howard 'Kant's Concept of Property' *Philosophic Quarterly* 27 (1977) 32-40
Wolff, Robert Paul *Kant's Theory of Mental Activity: A Commentary on the Transcendental Analytic of the 'Critique of Pure Reason'* Cambridge, Mass., Harvard University Press 1963
- *The Autonomy of Reason* New York, Harper & Row 1973

Index

abstraction 115n, 118–20, 183
abyss 44, 56n, 58–9, 116n, 169, 187
Achenwall, Gottfried 164n
activity and passivity 35–7, 39–41, 47
afterlife 16–17, 19, 42, 60–1, 94–5, 101, 179
agreeableness 76, 78–80
anger 3–4, 25–6, 102–5, 109–10, 122, 155, 160, 162; and infant 29–30, 112–17, 125, 183–4; justification of 116–17
An Old Question Raised Again: Is the Human Race Constantly Progressing? 172–3
anthropology 5–6, 46n, 60, 81, 100n, 154–5, 171n; of reason 46, 48, 51, 53–8
Anthropology from a Pragmatic Point of View 5–6, 22n, 28–30, 48n, 74n, 76n, 101–2, 112–22, 149n, 154–5, 161, 169n, 171
antinomy 32, 46, 49, 97; and conflict between science and morality 42–6; practical 94–5, 97; juridical 130
anxiety 74–5, 103, 119n
archetype and ectype 36, 83–88, 105
Arendt, Hannah 18n, 40n, 56n
Aristotle 3, 15–16n, 114, 154, 158, 165
autonomy 68, 73, 76, 109, 120, 140–1; as ideal of reason 83, 86, 90n, 91; and citizenship 156

Bacon, Francis 3
beauty 14, 100n, 101, 116n, 119n
Beccaria, Marquis di 161–2
Beck, Lewis White 29n, 47n, 65n, 73n, 81n, 89–90n, 100–1n, 122n
belief 95–6, 98, 99. *See also* God, belief in
Bemerkungen (on *Observations on the Feeling of the Beautiful and the Sublime*) 21–8, 60, 109, 111n, 125n, 179n
benevolence 90–91, 92
Bennett, Jonathan 41n
Blake, Ralph Mason 76n
blame 54, 99–105, 123–4, 178
body 127–8, 141
books 171
Borowski, L.E. 18n, 21
British moralists 28, 188
Buchanan, J.M. 79n

Caird, Edward 40n
care *see* anxiety
Cassirer, Ernst 179n
categorical imperative 69, 70, 73–4, 102n, 155; and formula of the law of nature 88–91; and juridical postulate 117, 152. *See also* moral law
causality: concept of 88, 142; moral 71–2; juridical 145
Cavent see surety
Christianity 12n, 18, 93

citizenship 173; criteria of 156–60; active and passive 164n, 166, 173
Cohen, Hermann 41n
commerce 136, 175–9, 186. *See also* right, reciprocity of
community 72n, 136, 142, 150–2; moral 30–1, 71, 81, 88, 104; juridical 118, 123–4, 131, 135–6, 140–1, 153, 169–70, 178, 185; original in the soil 135–6, 139, 175; domestic 150–2; and powers of government 162–4, 166
Conjectural Beginning of Human History 57–60, 74, 78, 100–5, 109, 116, 119n, 131, 169n
consciousness: and will 115n; proprietary aspects of 133–5, 179, 185–6
consent 117, 123–6, 129, 140–1, 150–1, 163, 166, 188
constitution 165–6
contemplation 14–17, 19–20, 21, 60, 67
contract 99, 135, 145–7, 151–3, 175; social 164–8, 173
Copernican hypothesis 38–9, 41, 45–6, 47, 60
Copernicus 3
cosmology 12–13, 18–19, 53
cosmopolitanism 171, 173–79, 187
critical philosophy 37, 56–7, 65, 109; development of 31–2, 43n, 46, 60–1; juridical character of 48–52, 61, 132–5, 185–7
Critique of Judgment 13, 50, 51, 71n, 76–7n, 79, 86–7n, 116n, 129n
Critique of Practical Reason 5, 7n, 20, 57, 92–4, 99–105, 149n; and moral experience 65–9; and the moral law 70–4, 81–91; and happiness 74–81, 93–4; and highest good 93–9
Critique of Pure Reason 3n, 5, 65–6, 83–7, 95–9, 155, 183–7; and resolution of antinomies 31–2, 42–6, 96–7; and conditions of knowledge 35–42, 60, 78, 111–12, 119n, 132–42; and anthropology of reason 46–60, 61

Day, J.P. 161n
deduction 49, 185; transcendental 53, 111, 132–5; of pure practical principles 86; juridical 130–41, 185
Delbos, Victor 11n, 22n
desert 94
desire 4, 6, 50, 77, 109, 147, 184, 187–8; psychological concept of 6n; for knowledge 24; and development of reason 29, 58–9; suppression and renunciation of 29, 32, 101, 152, 178–9; of reason 44, 48, 50–1, 57, 61, 70–4, 185; limitlessness of 56n, 58–9, 74–5; contingent satisfaction of 93–4; formal 118–22, 148–9; natural relation to 118–20; sexual 119n, 151–2
De Vleeschauwer, Herman-J. 11n, 43n
Dietrichson, Paul 90n
discipline 29, 50, 56, 60, 185
Doctrine of Right 5, 49, 80, 109–10, 185–9; introduction to 111–27; and external private right 127–52; and juridical deduction 130–41, 185; and public right 152–79; and right of nations 173–9. *See also* right
Doctrine of Virtue 53, 81n, 113n, 121, 124n, 162
Downs, A. 79n
Dreams of a Spirit-Seer 30–2, 86–7n
dualism 3–4, 37–8, 89–91, 111–12; of man 3–4, 7, 31, 73–4, 77–8, 110, 141
duty 67–8, 92, 124, 154; perfect and imperfect 124; of sovereign 167, 169–70

Ebbinghaus, Julius 90n
egoism 81, 90–1n, 92–3, 121, 155, 176–8; logical 171–2
enlightenment 170–3, 175–7, 186
Epicurus 12n
equality 22–4, 116–17, 150–2, 156–60, 178, 186–8; and retribution 160–2
Essay to Introduce into Philosophy the Concept of Negative Quantity 77n

esteem 17, 68, 80–1, 82, 93, 100–1
evil 93, 118, 121, 149n

Fackenheim, Emil 58n
faith *see* belief
feeling 92, 94; distinguished from sensation 77–8; of reason 172
Fichte, Johann Gottlieb 37n, 40, 53, 188
Fontan, Pierre 18n
freedom 42–3, 61, 73, 114–15, 119–21, 177, 188–9; Kant's early treatment of 22, 26–7; lawless 25, 103–5, 120–2; external 26, 27n, 105, 120, 122–6, 153, 178; emergence of 57–60, 102–5, 109–10, 112–13, 116n; interim 59; positive and negative 73; civic 156, 172–3, 178
French revolution 21, 23–4, 164, 167, 172, 188
Fried, Charles 149n
fungible 148, 151–2, 174–5

Galston, William A. 5n, 58n, 100–1n, 122n
general will 31, 131. *See also* united will
Gewirth, Allan 71–2n
God 12–19, 42, 140n, 179; in Kant's early thought 12–19, 85, 169n; belief in 95–6, 99–100, 172; and creation 129, 139–40; and sovereign 169–70
Goldmann, Lucien 52n, 95
good will 66–9, 94, 99
government: co-ordinate powers of 163, 166–70; legitimacy of 168–9; role of 186
Gregor, Mary J. 124n, 128n
Groundwork of the Metaphysic of Morals 50, 65–9, 72–3, 76–7n, 80–85, 89–93, 103–3, 116n, 117, 124, 149n

Habermas, Jürgen 97n
happiness 4, 99n, 123n, 178–9, 184, 187–8; and self-sufficiency 15, 19, 75–6; problem of 30, 67, 74–81, 90n, 109; and worthiness 75–6, 93–6, 101; as incentive 92–5; distinguished from speculative satisfaction 93–4; desire for as historical force 120–1; as natural end 159–160
Hare, H.M. 71–2n
Hassner, Pierre 5n
Hegel, Georg Wilhelm Friedrich von 4, 40, 53, 57, 97, 130, 133, 137, 177
Heidegger, Martin 37n, 46n
Henrich, Dieter 21n, 132n
Heraclitus 138
Herder, Johann Gottfried 21
highest good 93–6, 99
history 57–8, 100–01, 109–10, 120–1, 131n, 155, 167–8; philosophy of 59–60, 94; as guarantor 175–9
History of the 1755 Earthquake 12, 16–17
Hobbes, Thomas 51, 74, 80n, 119n, 153–6, 160–1, 164, 169n
Hofmann, Hasso 164n
hope 4n, 94–9, 102, 153, 167, 179, 184
Hume, David 32n, 44, 128–9n, 187

idea 50, 53–5, 71; metaphysical 42, 60–1; source of 47, 101; and ideal 83–5, 86–7n
Idea for a Universal History from a Cosmopolitan Point of View 115, 121
illusion 22–3, 48n, 96n; dialectical 45–8, 53–7, 95; and evil 118, 121
imagination 74–5, 77–8, 82, 86–8, 116n, 118–19
immortality *see* afterlife
Inaugural Dissertation 35–7, 61
incentive 30–1, 92–9, 123
injury 28, 112, 129–30, 161, 173–4
intuition 36–40, 46–7, 50, 60, 82, 87–8; divine 85–6

Jacobi, Friedrich Heinrich 172, 179n
Jaspers, Karl 5n

Jefferson, Thomas 188
Jones, Hardy E. 81n
justice *see* right; theodicy

Kelly, George Armstrong 42n, 111
Kemp Smith, Norman 41n, 47n, 85n
kingdom of ends 88, 117, 123, 178
Körner, S. 37n
Krüger, Gerhard 42n, 46n, 87n

Laberge, Pierre 16n
labour 56n, 121, 139–40; necessity of 30, 109, 114; and philosophy 56, 179n; exchange of 80, 147–9, 152; and property 128–9n, 143–4; and citizenship 157–60
Lambert, Johann Heinrich 35
law: Roman 128, 139, 144, 147, 150, 164; feudal 139; Anglo-Saxon 145; Greek 145. *See also* moral law
Leibniz, Gottfried Wilhelm 11, 17–18, 37, 136
liberalism 4, 187–9
Locke, John 128–9n, 129, 135, 139n, 140n, 143–4, 153, 162, 175, 187–8
logic 96–9
Logic 73, 95–9
Lucretius 13n, 112

man: duality of 3–4, 7, 31, 73–4, 77–8, 89–91, 110, 111–12, 141; neediness of 15, 17, 24–5, 90n, 92–3, 102, 122–3, 156, 178, 187; purposiveness of 67; sociability of 100–2, 114–17, 119n; as end in himself 81, 117, 120–2, 126n, 131, 152, 161; security of 129–30, 137–9
Mansfield, Harvey C., Jr. 44n
marriage 150–2
Martin, Gottfried 41n
Marx, Karl 4, 80–1, 135, 149, 158, 187
matter 15, 17, 29, 111, 113–14, 136–8
maxim 71, 90, 102, 119

means 73, 116–17, 131, 146–7, 152; (and power) in general; 72n, 117–23, 149, 153; and ends 89–90
Mendelssohn, Moses 172
Menzer, Paul 11n
Metaphysical Foundations of Natural Science 113–14
Milton, John 18
money 79–81, 146–9, 171, 177, 186
Montesquieu, Charles-Louise Secondat de 162n, 165n
Moore, James 128–9n
moral feeling 93–5
morality 11, 30–2, 42–3, 57, 94–5; *a priori* character of 6n, 69, 81–2; primacy of 20–5, 60–1, 98–9, 109; ordinary understanding of 65–9; development of 100–5, 109–10, 116–22, 183–4
moral judgment 104
moral law 83, 92–3, 99–100, 147, 154; application of 6n, 81–92. *See also* categorical imperative
moral philosophy 66, 69
moral responsibility 31–2, 43n, 70, 161
Murphy, Jeffrie G. 5n, 81n, 159n, 161n

nature 3–4, 11–20, 30–2, 138, 148–9, 178, 183, 186–9; and freedom 7, 42–6, 58–60, 151; dependence on 12–13, 24–6, 28–9, 77–8, 93–4, 136, 178; economy of 12–13, 16–17, 20, 68, 93, 152, 178, 185; lawfulness of 12n, 40, 89; juridical emptiness of 16–17, 131–2, 143–5; purpose in 16n, 17n, 89–91; stint of 24–8, 57; necessity in 38, 128; supersensuous 86; revolt against 101–5, 109–10, 116; appropriation of 110–11, 126; usurpation and transformation of 130–1, 155, 169–70, 177–9; cunning of 176–7
Nell, Onora 71–2n, 90–1n
Neo-Platonists 18, 37, 179n

Newton, Isaac 11-12, 15, 19, 24, 27-28, 114
Nietzsche, Friedrich 122
noumena 37, 41, 66n. *See also* thing in itself

object 48, 53, 134, 136-7, 141-3; of reason 48, 50; of will 70-4, 127-32, 141-5; transcendental 72, 97n; determination of 83-4
objective knowledge 35-41, 60, 104n, 171-2
objectivity, theoretical and practical 70-4, 78, 104
Observations on the Feeling of the Beautiful and Sublime 179n
Only Conceivable Proof of the Existence of God 17n
On the Common Saying: 'This May be True in Theory, but it Does not Apply in Practice' 123, 156-60, 169n, 170
On the Failure of All Attempted Philosophical Theodicies 4n, 28
opposition 25-6, 53, 100, 109, 155, 183-4, 187; material 15-17, 29-30, 35, 60, 111-17; wilful 25-7, 28-9, 101, 110-16, 120, 126, 158, 160; inner 31, 65-9, 82-3, 100-1, 110n, 116n; outer 65, 122-3, 138, 176; acceptance of 123, 126, 167; cancellation of 125-6, 131, 155
optimism: of Hegel and Marx 4; of Kant 4, 17n, 18
Optimism, Essay on 17n, 18
Opus postumum 4, 46, 114n, 139n, 155

pain 74, 76-7n
Pascal, Blaise 95
passion 118-22
Paton, H.J. 89-90n, 90-1n, 92n
peace 160, 173-9
Pedagogy 29, 118, 121
Perpetual Peace 149n, 174-8

personality 20, 73-4, 126n, 138-9, 141, 157
pessimism 11n, 76-7n
phenomena 37, 41
Philonenko, A. 172n
Pitkin, Hanna 164n
Plato 3, 4, 50, 52, 70-1, 84-5, 113
pleasure 6n, 71n, 76-9, 119n, 184-5
Pope, Alexander 14, 18-19, 27
possession: physical and ideal 130, 144-5; as having 141-2, 144
poverty 159, 186-7
practical reason 48, 50, 56, 61, 139, 141-2; principles of 70, 104; postulates of 94; object of 96
price 80, 147
pride 93, 100
progress 110, 153, 168, 178
Prolegomena 32n, 41, 51, 53
property 16, 126, 127-52, 155, 174, 179, 185-7; internal 127; labour theory of 128-9n, 143-4; movable and immovable 139; exchange of 140, 142, 145-9, 151-2, 157-60, 175; and having 141-2, 144; division of 142-52; and original acquisition 142-5; protection of 153
psychology 100, 113n
publicity: as criterion of justice 153; right of 170-2
punishment 152, 160-2, 173-4

Rawls, John 79n
reason 15, 17, 37, 47-59, 61, 65, 70, 109, 139; limits of 14-15, 17, 23, 35, 48, 50, 52-3, 71-5, 98; development of 29, 58-9, 115n, 118-20, 183-4; demand of 36, 47-8, 50-1, 54-5, 99; and satisfaction 44, 48-52, 55-6, 61, 98; task-setting nature of 45, 56-7, 61, 72-3, 95, 98, 119-20, 158; interest of 48-9, 57, 65, 72-3, 96-7, 109; architectonic character of 50, 54-7; independence of 52, 55-6; and infant

52, 61; and judgment 61; purposiveness of 72–3, 89–91, 96; as object of blame 103; juridical aspects of 120, 141–2; need of 172. *See also* anthropology, of reason; desire, of reason; practical reason; right, of reason; understanding, distinguished from reason
rebellion 167–70, 172, 188
Reboul, Olivier 18n, 77n
reform 167–8, 170–2
religion, philosophy of 94
Religion within the Limits of Reason Alone 83, 116n, 118n, 179
representation, civic 157, 164–7, 175, 177
republicanism 163–7, 172–3, 174
resistance 52, 72, 183; formal 160. *See also* opposition
respect *see* esteem
revenge 16, 115, 121–2, 162
Ricardo, David 158
Riedel, Manfred 158n
right 3–4, 5–7, 20–30, 60, 99, 109–10 186; and merit 4n; primitive notion of 29–30, 112–16; of reason 48–52, 61, 91, 172, 183; and compulsion 105, 124–6, 178; and system of mechanics 112–17, 124–6, 150, 184; reciprocity of 116–18, 123, 125–6, 136, 140, 150–2, 184; moral aspects of 123n, 124, 139, 152–5, 177–8; private (innate and acquired) 127–52; and relation between ideal and real 141, 155–7; and modes of acquisition 142–52; public 152–79; of nations 173–9; and need 178–9
Riley, Patrick 5n
Ritter, Christian 5n, 21n, 80n, 179n
Robespierre, Maximilien 164n
Rousseau, Jean-Jacques 19n, 20–30, 42n, 58, 93, 100–1, 121, 153, 162, 188
Russell, Bertrand 18n
Ruyssen, Théodore 11n

Saner, Hans 5n, 139n, 169n
Schilpp, Paul Arthur 11n
science 3, 54–5; conflict of with morality 11–20, 42–6, 94–5; as model for metaphysics 38, 60
self-consistency 43–5, 49, 52, 96–7, 109, 120–1, 185; Kant's early treatment of 28–9, 32
self-determination 71–2, 74, 138–41. *See also* autonomy
shame 100
Shklar, Judith N. 30n
Sieyès, Emmanuel-Joseph 164n
Simmel, Georg 141
Singer, M.T. 71–2n, 90–1n
Smith, Adam 80, 102, 147
sovereign 146, 149, 162–70, 173, 177; as guarantor of social contract 155–6, 175; and people 163–4, 166–8; duty of 167, 169–70; and ruler 167, 169, 174
Starobinski, Jean 119n
state 158–61; power of 141, 156, 164–5, 177; and international relations 173–7
state of nature 51, 153–4, 173
Stirner, Max 187
Strauss, Leo 119n
Strawson, P.F. 39–40n, 41n
sublimity 68, 116, 119n, 169
substance 129, 133n, 136–9; moral and juridical 4, 139–41, 156, 162, 186; material 113–14, 136–8, 140–1; and exchange of ideas 133n; and money 133n, 147, 186; and soil 133n, 139–40, 143, 186; and sovereign 166–7, 169n
suicide 76–7n, 121, 169
surety 146, 164–5

teleology 12, 16n, 17n, 48n, 51, 53–8, 89–91, 92n
theodicy 11–20, 24–5, 27–8, 59, 94, 179
theory and practice, relation between 61, 65, 82–5, 89, 97–9, 104, 109–10, 111, 142, 179, 185–6

Index

thing in itself 35–7, 41–2, 51–3, 60–1, 111, 136–7; and intelligent beings 72
touch and sight 82–3, 91, 113–14, 183–4
Transcendental Idealism 41–2
transcendental unity of apperception 73–4, 132–5, 185
Tullock, Gordon 79n
Turgot, Anne Robert Jacques 79n
typic 81–91, 99, 102, 111, 184

unconditioned 32, 43–5, 50–3, 61, 95–6, 169n; and metaphysical ideas 42, 54–5; moral notion of 42, 66–9; regress to 47–50
understanding 37, 39–40, 46–7, 53, 87–9; distinguished from reason 46–9, 54–5; and conceptualization 87, 183
united will 130–6, 139–40, 149, 155, 166–7, 171, 177; and appropriation 142, 144–6 185; determination of 157n; and legislation 163
universalization 71–2n, 101–5, 122, 162, 170
Universal Natural History and Theory of the Heavens 11–20, 31, 35, 60

value: relative 68, 79–81, 147; confusion over 149n. *See also* worth
virtue 123n, 124, 139, 153
Vlachos, Georges 5n, 24n, 43n, 115n

Ward, Keith 21n
Weldon, T.D. 41n, 45n
What is Enlightenment? 170–3
What it is to Orient Oneself in Thinking 171–3
will 66–7, 83, 92, 102–3, 116–26, 127; object of 70–4, 98, 127–32, 141–5; purposiveness of 89–91; as *Wille* and as *Willkür* 93, 118, 122–3; distinguished from thing 126, 131; possession of 145–6. *See also* general will; good will; united will
Williams, T.C. 90–1n
Wolff, Christian 11, 15, 28
Wolff, Robert Paul 39–40n, 41n, 53n, 89–90n, 92n
work *see* labour
worth 4, 11, 20, 66–7, 75–6, 80–1, 121–2, 126n, 151; and sacrifice 67–8, 116n; and worthiness 79–81, 94–5; of life 101n

www.ingramcontent.com/pod-product-compliance
Lightning Source LLC
Chambersburg PA
CBHW020409080526
44584CB00014B/1237